The Green Reader

THE GREEN READER

edited by
ANDREW DOBSON

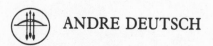

ANDRE DEUTSCH

First published 1991 by
Andre Deutsch Limited
76 Dean Street, London W1V 5HA

Second paperback impression 1994
Third paperback impression 1998

British Library Cataloguing in Publication Data
The Green reader,
   I. Environment. Conservation
   I. Dobson, Andrew
   333-72

   ISBN 0-233-98652-9
   ISBN 0-233-98653-7 pbk

Phototypeset by Input Typesetting Ltd., London
Printed in Great Britain by
WBC Bridgend

Contents

GREEN ECONOMICS

GREEN POLITICAL STRATEGIES

Ecology

Oxford English Dictionary (2nd edn)
(Oxford: Clarendon Press, 1989) Vol. 5, p. 58.
ecology(i:'kɑləd31). Also œcology. [mod. f. Gr. οικ-ος house,
dwelling + −(o)LOGY: after *œconomy*.]
   1. The science of the economy of animals and plants; that branch
of biology which deals with the relations of living organisms to their
surroundings, their habits and modes of life, etc.
   A supposed use of *ecology* in Thoreau's letters represents a mis-
reading of *geology*: see *science* 1965) 13 Aug. 707 and *Bull. Thoreau
Soc.* (1973) No. 123.6.
   1873 tr. *Haeckel's Hist. Creat.* Pref., The great series of phenomena of comparative anatomy and ontogeny . . . chronology and
œcology. 1879 tr. *Haeckel's Evol. Man* I. 114 All the various
relations of animals and plants to one another and to the outer
world, with which the Oekology of organisms has to do . . . admit
of simple and natural explanation only on the Doctrine of Adaptation and Heredity. 1893 *Brit. Med. Jrnl.* 16 Sept. 613/1 Œcology,
which uses all the knowledge it can obtain from the other two
[physiology and morphology], but chiefly rests on the exploration
of the endless varied phenomenons of animal and plant life as they
manifest themselves under natural conditions. 1894 *Proc. Madison
Bot. Congr.* 36 The separation of . . . vegetable physiology into two
departments: physiology proper and ecology. 1896 *Pop. Sci. Monthly* Dec. 185 Botany. . . especially with reference to the physiology
and ecology of plants. 1902 *Nature* 17 Apr. 574/1 The ecology of a
glacial lake. 1904 C. L. LAURIE *Flowering Plants* 6 The study of
plants that grow together, forming plant associations, in some
respects the most interesting part of Ecology. 1916 F. E. CLEMENTS
Plant Succession 73 It is one of the most important tasks of ecology
to determine the root and shoot relations of communal plants. 1928
R. S. TROUP *Silveicultural Syst.* xix. 183 The development of ecology as a science has given a special impetus to the study of the
physical and physiological conditions bearing on natural regeneration. 1931 H. G. WELLS *Work, Wealth & Happiness of Mankind*

(1932) i. 29 Economics . . . is spoken of in the *Science of Life* as a branch of ecology; it is the ecology of the human species. 1933 – *Shape of Things to Come* I. §12. III Of human ecology he betrays no knowledge. 1935 *Nature* 2 Feb. 168/1 The study of such interactions under the given conditions of habitat is the most important part of what is called plant ecology. 1941 AUDEN *New Year Letter* 1. 23 And grasped in its complexity The Catholic ecology. 1967 *Listener* 6 Apr. 459/3 In different ecologies territorial systems will vary or even be absent altogether.

  2. Used *attrib.* (and *absol.*) with reference to ecological issues such as industrial pollution considered in a political context; *spec.* applied to various political movements (esp. in western Europe) which represent the environmental or 'green' interest.

  [1963 A. HUXLEY (*title*) The politics of ecology.] 1970 *Environmental Quality Mag.* I. 1. 30/2 Write to Granny . . . and tell her about your ecology activities and ideas . . . Wear your ecology symbol [*sc.* a pin] to promote a better environment. 1973 *Antioch Rev.* XXXII. 111. 449 Ecologists as scientists may or may not share the perspectives of the ecology movement. 1974 RATHER & GATES *Palace Guard* i. 6 Some of the leaders wound up in jail. . . still others, buckling under pressure, turned their attention to less threatening issues, like ecology. 1979 Ecology-conscious [see GREEN *sb.* 17]. 1980 J. F. PILAT *Ecological Politics* 73 The United Kingdom has no significant ecological parties; the Ecological party recently had only 600 members. 1985 *Observer* 22 Sept. 2/8 The Ecology Party changed its name to the Green Party at its annual conference in Dover. 1986 *New Socialist* Sept. 36/1 The strongest organized hesitation before socialism is perhaps the diverse movement variously identified as 'ecology' or the 'the greens'.

  Hence ecol'logical, eco'logic *a.*, pertaining to ecology; eco'logically *adv.*, e'cologist.

  1893 J. S. BURDON-SANDERSON in *Nature* 14 Sept. 465/1 Whether with the œcologist we regard the organism in relation to the world, or with the physiologist as a wonderful complex of vital energies, the two branches have this in common. 1896 *Pop. Sci. Monthly* May 72 These ecologic color adaptations. 1899 *Natural Sci.* July 11 One of the most important oecological studies which has yet appeared in the United States. 1904 C. L. LAURIE *Flowering Plants* 8 Ecological classification of plants. 1909 WEBSTER Ecologically. 1909 E. WARMING *Oecol. Plants* p. v, I have given my views on oecological classification in a more comprehensive and detailed manner. 1926 *Spectator* 25 Sept. 492/1 Part of the distinctively modern progress in palaeontology has just been this ecological outlook. 1930 C. ELRON *Anim. Ecol. & Evolution* 7 Evolution . . . is not at all a popular subject among animal ecologists to-day. 1935 *Times* 6 Mar. 10/3 We know that in some cases ecologically related trees can well gain the freedom of another country. 1936 H. G. WELLS *Anat. Frustration* ix. 86. I assume the world community . . . subject to general ecological laws. 1955 M. GLUCKMAN *Custom & Conflict in Africa* i. 7 The ecological needs for this friendship and peace lessen as the distance grows greater. 1959 A. HARDY *Fish & Fisheries* xvi. 302 The work of the marine ecologists is only in its infancy.

Introduction

Despite the giant strides made by the Green movement throughout the world in recent years, there are still many people (probably a majority) who think that Green politics is nothing more than a grand form of nature conservation.

It is true, of course, that Greens will always be found at the heart of campaigns against seal culling and in favour of new national parks, but it would be wrong to think that Green politics begins and ends there. The big difference between single-issue environmental campaigns and Green politics proper is that the former treats symptoms while the latter deals with causes. Single-issue environmentalists rarely make a wide-ranging political analysis of the reasons for the problems they confront, while Green political activists most certainly do.

Environmentalists, for example, may campaign against inorganic fertilizers, and in favour of organic farming, but they will do so without considering the political, economic and social factors which have led to industrialized farming. Greens, on the other hand, will see industrialized farming as just another blighted example of a way of life which has produced a long series of environmental single issues, such as acid rain, global warming and holes in the ozone layer. None of these issues, they say, can be treated either in isolation from each other, or from the political and economic system which has given rise to them. Throughout the rest of this book I shall use 'green' (lower case 'g') to refer to those who think that environmental problems can be solved within the present political and economic system, and 'Green' (capital 'G') for those who think sustainability depends upon the system being fundamentally changed.

So, on the one hand, Greens base their analysis of environmental problems on a critique of present politics and economics and, on the other, they supply us with a series of suggestions for political and economic change. This wide-ranging project is what the present anthology represents.

The most basic criticism Greens make of our current way of life is that we aspire to infinite growth on a planet which is finite in size and capacity. This observation has implications for every single feature of our social and economic life and not only for those most obviously related to the environment.

Resources are finite, say the Greens, yet we extract and use them as if they were limitless. We make little effort to control population growth, despite the finite amount of land on which to put people and from which to feed them. We pour our waste and pollution into the land and sea as though they could absorb it for ever. All this, for Greens, means that we are living 'unsustainably'. We need to understand that just because something is good does not mean to say that more of the same will be better.

Greens argue that in the context of a finite planet the only viable society is a 'sustainable' society, and they suggest that none of the societies we have at present is sustainable beyond the next few decades. A sustainable society would find ways of minimizing the extraction of resources and the production and consumption of goods, rather than maximizing them as we do now. Such an approach would deal with the environmental problems caused by the politics and economics of growth in a more fundamental way than single-issue environmentalism – for all its importance – can ever do.

Green politics, then, is more than nature conservation. It begins with environmental problems but it does not end with them. It seeks the reasons for environmental degradation and finds them in the politics and economics of growth – precisely the politics and economics pursued by virtually every society on the planet. In arguing for their version of sustainability Greens oppose many of the assumptions of late-twentieth century society, and find new reasons for supporting those with which they do agree.

The Green sustainable society is a Utopian society, properly speaking, but it differs from many others in being designed to cope with our weaknesses rather than celebrate our strengths. In this sense Green politics is a politics for an age of uncertainty. Future historians may characterize the latter decades of the twentieth century as ones of growing timidity; decades in which each moment of extravagant optimism has been followed by the fear, and sometimes the experience, of failure.

Splitting the atom was to bring us cheap and virtually unlimited energy, but it has brought us the arms race, Chernobyl and thousands of years worth of contaminated waste. Biotechnology promised food for all, but our television screens annually remain filled with bloated bellies and dark staring eyes. The United Nations presaged planetary peace, but there have been more war deaths around the world since 1945 than during the whole of the Second World War. Space travel promised . . . well, what *did* it promise?

For better or worse, things used to be very different. Parallels recently have been drawn between the French Revolution of 1789 and the events in Eastern Europe of 1989, but the sense of these phenomena is as different as the dates are accidental. Compare the revolutions of 1789 and 1989, and consider how a present-day Delacroix – he who painted 'Liberty guiding the People' to celebrate the French Revolution – might represent the events in Eastern Europe.

In Delacroix's 1831 painting, 'Liberty' holds a standard in her right hand and a rifle in her left; she glances backwards at those who follow her, and her stride is confident as it takes her forward out of the painting. She is doing what no politics dares do as the twenty-first century approaches: she is leading her people to a place they, and no one else, has ever been before. This place was to be so different from anything that had ever existed that it was literally indescribable. When, some time later, Karl Marx was asked to say what communist society would look like, he replied that he could not write recipes for the cookshops of the future.

So each step of Delacroix's 'Liberty' forges the contours of a previously unimagined future. This is not a gathering up and a putting together of the jigsaw scraps of past political experiments, but a leap into the unknown. These are steps into uncharted territory, but there is no fear here, no uncertainty – only a sense of buoyant anticipation. Ever since, though, a long line of disasters running from Robespierre's 'Terror' to Stalin's 'Gulags' and beyond has deflated this buccaneering spirit, and particularly on the left.

It is hard to imagine anything like Delacroix's 'Liberty' emerging from Eastern Europe in 1989. The characters are the same, indeed; these revolutions were fought in the name of freedom – but they were fearful revolutions, content to copy rather than create. The Eastern European aspiration is not to make a new future, but to look like Western Europe. Delacroix might paint a 'Liberty', but she would be crabbing sideways rather than striding forwards, with the rifle in her left hand replaced by a credit card.

The French Revolution of 1789 pointed to liberty and justice for all, while the Industrial Revolution which followed it in Britain promised standards of material well-being hitherto undreamed of. They both produced blood, filth and immense suffering, of course, but the voices of the Romantics who called for a wholesale abandonment of the project were relatively few and far between. Progress was uncomplicated and every setback was seen as a necessary stage on the way to a gilded age. Friedrich Engels was horrified by the poverty and squalor of mid-century Manchester, yet the answer to such misery was not to be found in a return to the past but in a beckoning and unvisited future.

Now, though, the gilded age has turned into a gilded cage. Politics and technology and the politics of technology have become arenas of conflict rather than consensus. In among all this a principal role of Green politics has been to point out to us that every silver lining has a cloud, and that the clouds are gathering. Long ago (in 1798), Thomas Malthus warned that the population was growing so fast that it would eventually outstrip food supply. On that occasion (but after Malthus himself was dead) technology rescued us, in the form of refrigeration and fertilizers. Now Malthusian voices are raised again, as the planet's population pushes towards six billion, with about four billion more expected by 2030.

But this time, our faith in technology to get us out of the fix has been shaken. The vaunted 'Green Revolution' which was to have fed the Indian subcontinent turned, instead, into a nightmare of sick plants with poor resistance to pests, of water contaminated by pesticides and inorganic fertilizers, and of salinization, desertification and erosion. Within a few weeks of each other, in 1986, the Chernobyl nuclear power plant in the Soviet Union and the American space shuttle, Challenger, both exploded. Despite mutterings on both sides which sought to place the blame for these accidents on the inefficiencies of bureaucratic centralism and disorganized capitalism respectively, many were left with the sneaking suspicion that no political system can contain the folly of our Promethean aspirations. Prometheus stole fire from the gods and gave it to human beings. He was punished by Zeus by being chained to a rock and having his liver chewed by a vulture every day for thirty years. Prometheus was rescued by Heracles – we might not be so lucky.

So the push towards an undiscovered future appears to be at an end, for the moment at least. There used to be space into which to move, and further frontiers to overcome, but now few remain. Where they do exist, as in Antarctica and the deepest reaches of the rainforest, our growing sense is to leave them alone. We have tramped all over the planet, and the geographical exhaustion of space seems to parallel the exhaustion of our political imagination.

Delacroix's 'Liberty' has nowhere to go, other than sideways or backwards. Intellectual trends and political projects point towards a marking of time, and this is why Green politics so suits a tenor of our age. It tracks our uncertainty. It speaks to many constituencies, and manages to combine a search for stability with genuine radicalism. Green politics seeks to transcend fear by feeding off it. It holds before us the spectre of a planet held together with sticking plaster: bursting at the seams with people who are surrounded by barren and sterile landscapes, and drowning in a stinking soup of chemical cocktails. It holds this spectre before us and it says: the roundabout has been going for too long; it is time to get off and walk away.

These are vague generalizations, and it might seem inappropriate to make them about a politics of which it has been said that there are as many versions as there are supporters. But while differences of interpretation remain, there will always be a carefully nurtured flame at the centre of Green doctrine where all its disciples can warm their hands. In a secular age of shallow and homogeneous cultures the search for belonging is on. The present rise of nationalism illustrates the potent need to associate with a project bigger than the individual human being. In these restless and rootless days, the project must provide for security, and that is why the fearless and open-ended schemes of the eighteenth and nineteenth centuries hold little attraction. We want to live according to universal laws rather than try to redesign them.

Green politics settles human beings by humbling them first. The science of ecology teaches us that we are part of a system which stretches back into an unfathomable past and reaches forward into an incalculable future, and that the whole planetary community is bound by ties of interdependence which makes a mockery of mastery. There is no room for Prometheus here. The talk around the tables in vegetarian restaurants is of limits: not only limits to industrial and population growth, but of the limits to human knowledge that produce the dark side of ingenuity. We take refuge in our ignorance, relieved at last of the awful responsibility of choosing a new future from a limitless number of designs. There is solace to be had once we realize that the wisdom of God passeth all understanding. Green politics responds to an age of uncertainty by teaching us to know our place.

Greens are also lucky in having at their disposal the most persuasive idiom of the modern age – science. Like the nineteenth-century Romantics they do have recourse to poetry to celebrate the natural world, but they also have a wealth of computer predictions to help them along. The limits to growth thesis, the Gaia hypothesis, and articles on the dangers of pesticides and insecticides (each represented in the extracts which follow) have all appeared in scientific journals over the years. Greens cannot be accused of a blind mysticism, and the combination of secular science and verdant spirituality is a powerful one – especially when the aim is to make us feel at home both in the remains of an age that is gone and the dangers of one that is yet to come.

The conclusion should not be drawn from all this that Green politics is a doctrine of despair. After all, why exhort us to political action if such action is pointless? It is within the wit of humanity to rescue itself from the abyss towards which it is plunging, but the general direction of rescue lies in the adoption of humility rather than the acceleration of hubris. This sense comes through strongly in the majority of the extracts which follow. They have all been chosen to illustrate what I take to be the various informing principles of Green politics. None of them is about environmental problems as such, so readers will find nothing explaining the phenomenon of global warming, or the causes and effects of acid rain. They do contain, however, a full and clear indication of what it is about our societies that causes these problems, as well as speculations as to what changes need to take place for us to deal with them. There is little or no history in the pieces I have chosen, either, and this too is intentional. The guiding idea has been to select texts which tell us what Greens are thinking today, not what their historical antecedents have been. Likewise, I have wanted to give each extract a fair exposure and have therefore erred on the side of fullness rather than brevity. There seems little point in choosing an extract for its importance and then converting it into an enigma.

Finally, the short introductions to each piece are intended to constitute an informal story by indicating the importance of each extract to Green politics as a whole. I have put an asterisk (*) after the name of words, people or ideas which receive fuller treatment elsewhere in the collection. In the end, though, the value of the passages is intrinsic, and they speak eloquently for themselves.

Andrew Dobson
Keele University
1991

THE GREEN CRITIQUE

The Limits to Growth

In the summer of 1970 an international group of scientists, researchers and industrialists came together to discuss the future of the planet and its inhabitants. This group, which came to be known as The Club of Rome, produced a report, entitled *The Limits to Growth* which has provided a constant source of inspiration and information for the environmental movement ever since its publication in 1972. Its basic message – that infinite growth in a finite system is impossible – is the foundation-stone of Green political thinking. Greens will admit that the report's estimates as to the likely life expectancy of various resources were over-pessimistic and they will agree that the Club of Rome's world computer models were crude, but they still subscribe to the report's conclusion that the days of uncontrolled growth (of the five elements mentioned in extract 2) are numbered.

The first extract briefly presents the group's conclusions, while the second explains the nature of the exponential growth of the five variables under consideration. The third focuses specifically on the issue of resource consumption as an example of the adverse effects of attempts at infinite growth in a finite system, and shows how growth in the use of resources in turn leads to increases in pollution. This introduces the notion of *interdependence* – centrally important in the Green lexicon – and illustrates how a systems view (see Capra*) highlights the inadvisability of dealing with problems as though they were isolated from one another. From a Green perspective, the inter-related nature of environmental problems is one reason why sticking-plaster solutions will not suffice: root-and-branch change is required (see holism*).

Greens will argue that attending to consequences will only buy (ever-decreasing amounts of) time; what is required is an attack on the causes, and *The Limits to Growth* report shows us that the fundamental cause of our problems is the attempt to grow beyond the limits imposed by the earth itself.

From D. Meadows *et al*, *The Limits to Growth* (London: Pan Books, 1983) pp. 23–4, 25–9, 66–9.

The following conclusions have emerged from our work so far. We are by no means the first group to have stated them. For the past several decades, people who have looked at the world with a global, long-term perspective have reached similar conclusions. Nevertheless, the vast majority of policy-makers seem to be actively pursuing goals that are inconsistent with these results.

Our conclusions are:

1. If the present growth trends in world population, industrialization, pollution, food production, and resource depletion continue unchanged, the limits to growth on this planet will be reached sometime within the next one hundred years. The most probable result will be a rather sudden and uncontrollable decline in both population and industrial capacity.

2. It is possible to alter these growth trends and to establish a condition of ecological and economic stability that is sustainable far into the future. The state of global equilibrium could be designed so that the basic material needs of each person on earth are satisfied and each person has an equal opportunity to realize his individual human potential.

3. If the world's people decide to strive for this second outcome rather than the first, the sooner they begin working to attain it, the greater will be their chances of success.

These conclusions are so far-reaching and raise so many questions for further study that we are quite frankly overwhelmed by the enormity of the job that must be done. We hope that this book will serve to interest other people, in many fields of study and in many countries of the world, to raise the space and time horizons of their concerns and join us in understanding and preparing for a period of great transition – the transition from growth to global equilibrium. . . .

All five elements basic to the study reported here – population, food production, industrialization, pollution, and consumption of non-renewable natural resources are increasing. The amount of their increase each year follows a pattern that mathematicians call exponential growth. . . .

Most people are accustomed to thinking of growth as a *linear* process. A quantity is growing linearly when it increases by a constant amount in a constant time period. For example, a child who becomes one inch taller each year is growing linearly. If a miser hides $10 each year under his mattress, his horde of money is also increasing in a linear way. The amount of increase each year is obviously not affected by the size of the child nor the amount of money already under the mattress.

A quantity exhibits *exponential* growth when it increases by a constant percentage of the whole in a constant time period. A colony of yeast cells in which each cell divides into two cells every ten minutes is growing exponentially. For each single cell, after ten minutes there will be two cells, an increase of 100 per cent. After the next ten minutes there will be four cells, then eight, then sixteen. If a miser takes $100 from his mattress and invests it at 7 per cent (so that the total amount accumulated increases by 7 per cent each year), the invested money will grow much faster than the linearly increasing stock under the mattress. The amount added each year to a bank account or each ten minutes to a yeast colony is not constant. It continually increases, as the total accumulated amount increases. Such exponential growth is a common process in biological, financial, and many other systems of the world.

Common as it is, exponential growth can yield surprising results – results that have fascinated mankind for centuries. There is an old Persian legend about a clever courtier who presented a beautiful chessboard to his king and requested that the king give him in return one grain of rice for the first square on the board, two grains for the second square, four grains for the third, and so forth. The king readily agreed and ordered rice to be brought from his stores. The fourth square of the chessboard required eight grains, the tenth square took 512 grains, the fifteenth required 16,384, and the twenty-first square gave the courtier more than a million grains of rice. By the fortieth square a million million rice grains had to be brought from the storerooms. The king's entire rice supply was exhausted long before he reached the sixty-fourth square. Exponential increase is deceptive because it generates immense numbers very quickly.

A French riddle for children illustrates another aspect of exponential growth – the apparent suddenness with which it approaches a fixed limit. Suppose you own a pond on which a water lily is growing. The lily plant doubles in size each day. If the lily were allowed to grow unchecked, it would completely cover the pond in thirty days, choking off the other forms of life in the water. For a long time the lily plant seems small, and so you decide not to worry about cutting it back until it covers half the pond. On what day will that be? On the twenty-ninth day, of course. You have one day to save your pond. . . .

The earth's crust contains vast amounts of those raw materials which man has learned to mine and to transform into useful things. However vast those amounts may be, they are not infinite. Now that we have seen how suddenly an exponentially growing quantity approaches a fixed upper limit, the following statement should not come as a surprise. *Given present resource consumption rates and the projected increase in these rates, the great majority of the currently impor-tant non-renewable resources will be extremely costly a hundred years from now.* The above statement remains true regardless of the most optimistic assumptions about undiscovered reserves, technological advances, substitution, or recycling, as long as the demand for resources continues to grow exponentially. The prices of those resources with the shortest static reserve indices have already begun to increase. The price of mercury, for example, has gone up 500 per cent in the last twenty years; the price of lead has increased 300 per cent in the last thirty years. . . .

Are there enough resources to allow the economic development of the seven billion people expected by the year 2000 to a reasonably high standard of living? Once again the answer must be a conditional one. It depends on how the major resource-consuming societies handle some important decisions ahead. They might continue to increase resource consumption according to the present pattern. They might learn to reclaim and recycle discarded materials. They might develop new designs to increase the durability of products made from scarce resources. They might encourage social and eco-nomic patterns that would satisfy the need of a person while minimi-zing, rather than maximizing, the irreplaceable substances he pos-sesses and disperses.

All of these possible courses involve trade-offs. The trade-offs are particularly difficult in this case because they involve choosing between present benefits and future benefits. In order to guarantee the availability of adequate resources in the future, policies must be adopted that will decrease resource use in the present. Most of these policies operate by raising resource costs. Recycling and better product design are expensive; in most parts of the world today they are considered 'uneconomic'. Even if they were effectively instituted, however, as long as the driving feedback loops of population and industrial growth continue to generate more people and a higher resource demand per capita, the system is being pushed toward its limit – the depletion of the earth's non-renewable resources.

What happens to the metals and fuels extracted from the earth after they have been used and discarded? In one sense they are never lost. Their constituent atoms are rearranged and eventually dispersed in a diluted and unusable form into the air, the soil, and the waters of our planet. The natural ecological systems can absorb many of the effluents of human activity and reprocess them into substances that are usable by, or at least harmless to, other forms of life. When any effluent is released on a large enough scale, however, the natural absorptive mechanisms can become saturated. The wastes of human civilization can build up in the environment until they become visible, annoying, and even harmful. Mercury in ocean fish, lead particles in city air, mountains of urban trash, oil slicks on beaches – these are the results of the increasing flow of resources into man's hands. It is little wonder, then, that another exponentially increasing quantity in the world system is pollution.

The Science of Ecology

In 1985 the British Ecology Party changed its name to the Green Party, partly to fall into line with other Green parties around the world, and partly for fear that 'ecology' was too technical and difficult a word for political marketing purposes. But what the party gained in marketability it lost in clarity, for 'ecology' tells us much more about the movement's *raison d'être* than 'green' does. Green politics is a politics born of a science, and in the extracts below, chosen from a classic study, Denis Owen explains what the science of ecology is and shows how easily and obviously it can become a politics. The central observation is that 'man [*sic*] is a part of nature' – an observation to which Green politics is a very lengthy footnote.

From Denis Owen, *What is Ecology?* (Oxford: Oxford University Press, 1980) pp. 1–4, 22–3, 26–7, 194–5.

Ecology is concerned with the relationships between plants and animals and the environment in which they live. This simple explanation is the kind of answer a school child would offer if asked 'What is ecology?' But the explanation, although apparently neat and simple, does not specify what is meant by relationships and what is meant by environment. These two words occur throughout this book and we shall therefore begin by considering what they mean.

There are many possible kinds of relationships between organisms (plants, animals, and other living things like viruses) and that part of the non-living world in which they occur. An extremely important one is who eats whom, and another, perhaps equally important, is who breeds with whom.

The concept of the environment covers just about everything associated with organisms, and includes other organisms and the non-living part of the world in which life occurs. The weather, the physical and chemical composition of the soil, and seasonal changes in the length of daylight, are all parts of an organism's environment, and the word therefore has about the same meaning as surroundings.

No organism exists without an environment; organisms and the environments in which they live constitute an extremely thin layer on the surface of the earth, often called the biosphere, in which the very complexity of ecological relationships tends to frustrate scientific analysis. Nevertheless careful consideration reveals some order in the biosphere which can be understood and defined, although it must be admitted that we are still a long way from formulating general theories of the kind familiar to students of chemistry, physics, and mathematics.

The essential feature of living organisms as opposed to non-living objects is that they reproduce and replicate themselves. Organisms are associated with land or with water; many kinds spend the greater part of their life in the air, but none exists entirely in the air. The most familiar organisms, trees and plants, and the animals that feed on them, are obviously associated with the ground, but everyone knows that both fresh and salt water support a variety of plant and animal life.

The Greeks used the word *oikos* to describe a home, a place to which you could return and where you understood and were familiar with the local environment. From this word we have derived the terms ecology and economics to describe the subjects concerned with aspects of home life. Ecology began as descriptive natural history but nowadays scientists study and describe ecological phenomena in quantitative terms, often to such an extent that scientific magazines devoted to ecology publish articles that look more like pages from textbooks in mathematics. Much the same applies to the scientific study of economics. But economics and ecology are subjects in which intuition also plays an important role, and although both subjects have received rigorous mathematical treatment it could be doubted if this has told us a great deal that we did not know already.

In recent years ecology has become a household word. It has begun to enter into discussions about economic development, industrial growth, and standards of living, but there is often confusion. Many people think ecology is another word for pollution or the conservation of rare animals: others see it as something of a political plot against economic growth. Only now have a substantial number of people become concerned about trends in the growth of the human population and the consumption of natural resources, and with this concern fears for the future are increasingly expressed.

What exactly has generated this interest, and why has ecology, until recently a rather obscure subject, come to the forefront?

In industrial countries the most important single event has been the realization and demonstration that pollution resulting from industry and agriculture is harmful to people and to the surroundings in which people live. Industrial pollution comes from waste products of the manufacturing and service industries, and these products are difficult, or at least expensive, to dispose of, while agricultural pollution results from the accumulation of toxic chemicals derived from pesticides and fertilizers. But although the present awareness of ecology may have been stimulated by the apparent dangers of pollution, this is not primarily what ecology is about. It is a much bigger and more complex subject than this, and to understand ecology we must move away from this restricted though common viewpoint. Ecology is not even primarily about man; indeed it covers all living organisms, and although most people will undoubtedly be interested in the implications of ecology for human life and welfare, to understand the subject it is necessary to abandon an entirely man-oriented approach and to consider instead the interrelationship of all life and the environment. Hopefully this will lead to a better understanding and more respect for plant and animal life and perhaps help to explain how the present lack of balance between man and the environment has come about.

Evidently, then, there are two faces to our subject. One is mainly but not entirely disinterested scientific inquiry, the other more diffuse and concerned with political and economic problems of over-population, the consumption of resources, pollution, conservation, and the plight of under-developed countries. Ecology as a science involves detailed and painstaking measurements of population sizes of plants and animals, birth and death rates, the supply and utilization of energy and nutrients in the environment, and related subjects. It is really a sophisticated and academic form of natural history. The other facet is more concerned with man's place in nature and threats to the quality of life. The two facets are compatible although curiously enough people active and vocal in one are rarely active and vocal in the other. Most scientific ecologists take no public stand on the wider, less clearly defined issues that afflict mankind, but apart from journalists and writers there are few professional 'political' ecologists.

One way to begin an understanding of a new subject is to inquire into the activities of those who practise it, and this is what we shall now attempt. . . .

The importance of ecology

Most relationships between plants and animals and their environment are baffling in their complexity and it is virtually impossible to make assumptions about the outcome of a deliberate change in or interference with the natural environment. This is because ecological relationships tend to be more than the sum of the component parts. You can take a machine to pieces and gain a fair idea of how it works from the constituent parts and their arrangement relative to each other, and you can with some confidence re-assemble the parts and end up with what you started with, but such an approach would be impossible with an assemblage of plants and animals that constitutes a natural environment. As each new component (an individual or a species) is added to the assemblage, new properties and new attributes are developed from the new relationships that arise. Many complex natural environments such as tropical forest are largely self-regulating as long as they are not tampered with; thus an alteration in one part of the system generates compensation in another part, a balancing process known as homeostasis.

There are probably no areas in the world however high, deep, cold, or barren, that are entirely free from the influence of man. It is therefore self-consciously academic to consider ecology as something apart from man and then assess man's impact on the 'natural' world. Rather, man's activities from building and operating nuclear power stations to factory farming should be considered as an integral part of the complexity of the living world and are just as 'ecological' as a fen or a forest. Ecology has grown from being a minor branch of biology to an interdisciplinary study which, as the American ecologist E. P. Odum suggests, 'links the natural and the social sciences'. Hence the special role of the ecologist may well be to take an all-inclusive approach to the world's problems in contrast to the approaches taken by economists and politicians and, it may be added, many scientists. . . .

⁞⁞⁞⁞⁞

Many human activities produce changes in the environment, frequently of a disrupting nature, but similar events occur in the natural world where man's impact is negligible. Natural environments have a remarkable capacity to resist change, but the trouble with human activities is that they are on such a massive scale.

Leaving aside for the moment the effects of man, it appears

that natural environments persist for long periods more or less unchanged. Various species of plants and animals occur year after year, interacting with each other in a highly intricate way, yet despite the enormous potential of all species for increase in numbers, most species remain relatively rare for most of the time. A professional ecologist is interested in finding out how this balance of nature is achieved and his findings are likely to be of significance to us all because they will help to suggest the consequences of upsetting the balance.

It might be argued that lawns are not especially important, but at the same time maintaining a lawn is an example of upsetting the balance of nature because a lawn would not persist unless constantly attended by man. Cutting down a vast area of tropical rainforest, the most complex environment in the world, is an ecological event of enormous magnitude, the consequences of which are poorly understood, although the result is often an impoverished environment in which few crops can be grown. There is really much in common between maintaining a lawn and cutting down tropical forest, except that the effect of one seems small while the effect of the other may be disastrous to human welfare.

A world dominated by people who are systematically destroying natural environments that have taken millions of years to develop seems to be an inescapable legacy of the agricultural and industrial evolutions. Let us hope that there will be another revolution in which attempts will be made to reduce exploitation and to conserve environments, although it must be admitted that the prospects of such a revolution seem slender at the present time. Demands for space, food, and resources are now so intense that possibilities for conservation are becoming more and more remote, but we should at least be aware of what we are doing.

From what has been said so far it will be evident that ecology is not a discrete subject and that it can be approached at several levels. In the remainder of this book we shall examine some of the more important ecological properties of living organisms and their environments, and when this has been complete we shall try and place man in an ecological framework. It is possible that some of the lessons of ecology can offer scope for planning more intelligently the kind of world that will be inherited by our children. . . .

Thinking ecologically

The first important lesson to learn is that man is part of nature and that the rest of nature was not put there for man to exploit, the claims of business, political, and religious leaders notwithstanding. In 1894 T. H. Huxley wrote an essay called 'Man's place in nature', and others have since argued that as we are a product of evolution it is legitimate to consider ourselves in the context of the rest of the living world, no matter what special properties, spiritual or otherwise, we may attribute to ourselves. If, then, we acknowledge our evolutionary origin, we can rather more easily try and put ourselves into ecological perspective; and in attempting this we shall draw on the principles discussed in the preceding chapters.

It is an axiom of ecological theory that all organisms modify to some extent the ecosystems in which they live. Organisms are of course part of ecosystems, and the presence of this or that individual or species is bound to affect the way in which an ecosystem works. The spectrum of species in an ecosystem depends on a variety of factors, including climate, the amount of light, and the availability of inorganic materials (in both soil and water) which determine the productivity and diversity of photosynthetic plants. The plants and the animals that feed on them are capable of rapid population growth, but this tends to occur only when there is a breakdown of the natural balance of the ecosystem. It is, as we have seen, more likely to occur in 'simple' ecosystems, such as those at high latitudes or in environments unfavourable to all but a few species. Evidently complexity (in terms of species diversity) is correlated with stability. All tendencies for growth in numbers or consumption are necessarily temporary and sooner or later they are halted and stabilized by pressures exerted by the environment.

There is no reason to suppose that man's present rapid rates of population growth and consumption will remain immune from regulation, and unless there is a man-induced catastrophe like a nuclear war there is every reason to suppose that stability will be brought about in a density-dependent manner in the not too distant future. The question, of course, is how exactly this will occur, and when. It is particularly clear that our present consumption of oil will have to come to an end soon, as at the present rate there will be none left worth exploiting in the very near future. The price of petrol may soon become so prohibitive that the ordinary motorist will be unable to afford to run a car, although it must be admitted that the substantial increases in price since 1973 have not resulted in less petrol being used. Man's use of metals, at present an extremely wasteful process, could be reorganized in such a way that a substantial amount of material now thrown away is recycled in much the same way as materials are cycled in natural ecosystems.

Attempts to increase agricultural productivity to provide food for an expanding population merely postpone what is inevitable, as there is ultimately a limit to what can be produced that is suitable for human consumption. Indeed one could argue that the more food produced the worse the long-term prospects for mankind: the bigger the population the more dramatic its crash. We should therefore be on the look-out for events likely to control human population growth.

Silent Spring

Many people have come to date the rise of the modern environmental movement at 1962, the year of the first publication of Rachel Carson's book *Silent Spring*. There can be no doubt that this book has exerted a powerful influence on the nature and development of Green politics. It tells of the indiscriminate use of modern chemical pesticides, fungicides and herbicides on the land and warns of the ensuing environmental damage. Beyond the obvious relationship between this topic and the concerns of the Green movement, *Silent Spring* also sets the tone for much subsequent Green political activity with its potent mixture of restrained emotion and thorough scientific research: organizations such as Friends of the Earth owe much of their success to the kinds of campaigning writing techniques so ably demonstrated by Rachel Carson. The first of the following extracts appeals to our lyrical sensibility with its evocation of a silent spring in a middle-American town, while the second presents a general factual picture of the use of synthetic pesticides and insecticides.

From Rachel Carson, *Silent Spring* (Harmondsworth: Penguin, 1965) pp. 21–2; pp. 31–2.

There was once a town in the heart of America where all life seemed to live in harmony with its surroundings. The town lay in the midst of a checkerboard of prosperous farms, with fields of grain and hillsides of orchards where, in spring, white clouds of bloom drifted above the green fields. In autumn, oak and maple and birch set up a blaze of colour that flamed and flickered across a backdrop of pines. Then foxes barked in the hills and deer silently crossed the fields, half hidden in the mists of the autumn mornings.

Along the roads, laurel, viburnun and alder, great ferns and wildflowers delighted the traveller's eye through much of the year. Even in winter the roadsides were places of beauty, where countless birds came to feed on the berries and on the seed heads of the dried

weeds rising above the snow. The countryside was, in fact, famous
for the abundance and variety of its bird life, and when the flood
of migrants was pouring through in spring and autumn people
travelled from great distances to observe them. Others came to fish
the streams, which flowed clear and cold out of the hills and con-
tained shady pools where trout lay. So it had been from the days
many years ago when the first settlers raised their houses, sank their
wells, and built their barns.

Then a strange blight crept over the area and everything began
to change. Some evil spell had settled on the community: mysterious
maladies swept the flocks of chickens; the cattle and sheep sickened
and died. Everywhere was a shadow of death. The farmers spoke
of much illness among their families. In the town the doctors had
become more and more puzzled by new kinds of sickness appearing
among their patients. There had been several sudden and unex-
plained deaths, not only among adults but even among children,
who would be stricken suddenly while at play and die within a few
hours.

There was a strange stillness. The birds, for example – where
had they gone? Many people spoke of them, puzzled and disturbed.
The feeding stations in the backyards were deserted. The few birds
seen anywhere were moribund; they trembled violently and could
not fly. It was a spring without voices. On the mornings that had
once throbbed with the dawn chorus of robins, catbirds, doves,
jays, wrens, and scores of other bird voices there was now no sound;
only silence lay over the fields and woods and marsh.

On the farms the hens brooded, but no chicks hatched. The
farmers complained that they were unable to raise any pigs – the
litters were small and the young survived only a few days. The
apple trees were coming into bloom but no bees droned among the
blossoms, so there was no pollination and there would be no fruit.

The roadsides, once so attractive, were now lined with browned
and withered vegetation as though swept by fire. These, too, were
silent, deserted by all living things. Even the streams were now
lifeless. Anglers no longer visited them, for all the fish had died.

In the gutters under the eaves and between the shingles of the
roofs, a white granular powder still showed a few patches; some
weeks before it had fallen like snow upon the roofs and the lawns,
the fields and streams.

No witchcraft, no enemy action had silenced the rebirth of new
life in this stricken world. The people had done it themselves.

This town does not actually exist, but it might easily have a thousand counterparts in America or elsewhere in the world. I know of no community that has experienced all the misfortunes I describe. Yet every one of these disasters has actually happened somewhere, and many real communities have already suffered a substantial number of them. A grim spectre has crept upon us almost unnoticed, and this imagined tragedy may easily become a stark reality we all shall know.

What has already silenced the voices of spring in countless towns in America? This book is an attempt to explain. . . .

For the first time in the history of the world, every human being is now subjected to contact with dangerous chemicals, from the moment of conception until death. In the less than two decades of their use, the synthetic pesticides have been so thoroughly distributed throughout the animate and inanimate world that they occur virtually everywhere. They have been recovered from most of the major river systems and even from streams of ground-water flowing unseen through the earth. Residues of these chemicals linger in soil to which they may have been applied a dozen years before. They have entered and lodged in the bodies of fish, birds, reptiles, and domestic and wild animals so universally that scientists carrying on animal experiments find it almost impossible to locate subjects free from such contamination. They have been found in fish in remote mountain lakes, in earthworms burrowing in soil, in the eggs of birds – and in man himself. For these chemicals are now stored in the bodies of the vast majority of human beings, regardless of age. They occur in the mother's milk, and probably in the tissues of the unborn child.

All this has come about because of the sudden rise and prodigious growth of an industry for the production of man-made or synthetic chemicals with insecticidal properties. This industry is a child of the Second World War. In the course of developing agents of chemical warfare, some of the chemicals created in the laboratory were found to be lethal to insects. The discovery did not come by chance: insects were widely used to test chemicals as agents of death for man.

The result has been a seemingly endless stream of synthetic insecticides. In being man-made – by ingenious laboratory manipulation of the molecules, substituting atoms, altering their arrangement – they differ sharply from the simpler inorganic insecticides of prewar days. These were derived from naturally occurring minerals and plant products – compounds of arsenic, copper, lead, manganese, zinc, and other minerals, pyrethrum from the dried flowers of chrysanthemums, nicotine sulphate from some of the relatives of tobacco, and rotenone from leguminous plants of the East Indies.

What sets the new synthetic insecticides apart is their enormous biological potency. They have immense power not merely to poison but to enter into the most vital processes of the body and change them in sinister and often deadly ways. Thus, as we shall see, they destroy the very enzymes whose function is to protect the body from harm, they block the oxidation processes from which the body receives its energy, they prevent the normal functioning of various organs, and they may initiate in certain cells the slow and irreversible change that leads to malignancy.

The Problem of Production

German-born Dr Fritz Schumacher has long been recognized as one of the gurus of the Green movement – on the face of it an unlikely accolade for someone who was economic adviser to the British National Coal Board from 1950 to 1970. The message of *Small is Beautiful* resounded around the alternative political world in the mid-1970s, and the phrase has since passed into our everyday language. But in some respects the striking title of Schumacher's book has helped to obscure some of its other merits, among which is the opening chapter, entitled 'The Problem of Production', part of which is reproduced below. Here Schumacher states a basic Green principle: that it is the illusion of the modern age that the problem of production has been solved; i.e. that we can continue to produce and consume at ever-increasing rates, virtually for evermore. This illusion, he says, is based on our unwillingness to recognize that the finite planet is our capital and so capital is not something we create but something off which we live. In the extract below he then goes on to suggest that blind productivism threatens two other aspects of our 'capital,' too: the tolerance margins of nature and the non-material needs of human beings.

From E. F. Schumacher, *Small is Beautiful* (London: Abacus, 1974) pp. 10–16.

One of the most fateful errors of our age is the belief that 'the problem of production' has been solved. Not only is this belief firmly held by people remote from production and therefore professionally unacquainted with the facts – it is held by virtually all the experts, the captains of industry, the economic managers in the governments of the world, the academic and not-so-academic economists, not to mention the economic journalists. They may disagree on many things but they all agree that the problem of production has been solved: that mankind has at last come of age. For the rich countries, they say, the most important task now is 'education for leisure' and, for the poor countries, the 'transfer of technology'.

That things are not going as well as they ought to be going must be due to human wickedness. We must therefore construct a political system so perfect that human wickedness disappears and everybody behaves well, no matter how much wickedness there may be in him or her. In fact, it is widely held that everybody is born good; if one turns into a criminal or an exploiter, this is the fault of 'the system'. No doubt 'the system' is in many ways bad and must be changed. One of the main reasons why it is bad and why it can still survive in spite of its badness, is this erroneous view that the 'problem of production' has been solved. As this error pervades all present-day systems there is at present not much to choose between them.

The arising of this error, so egregious and so firmly rooted, is closely connected with the philosophical, not to say religious, changes during the last three or four centuries in man's attitude to nature. I should perhaps say: *western* man's attitude to nature, but since the whole world is now in a process of westernization, the more generalized statement appears to be justified. Modern man does not experience himself as a part of nature but as an outside force destined to dominate and conquer it. He even talks of a battle with nature, forgetting that, if he won the battle, he would find himself on the losing side. Until quite recently, the battle seemed to go well enough to give him the illusion of unlimited powers, but not so well as to bring the possibility of total victory into view. This has now come into view, and many people, albeit only a minority, are beginning to realize what this means for the continued existence of humanity.

The illusion of unlimited powers, nourished by astonishing scientific and technological achievements, has produced the concurrent illusion of having solved the problem of production. The latter illusion is based on the failure to distinguish between income and capital where this distinction matters most. Every economist and businessman is familiar with the distinction, and applies it conscientiously and with considerable subtlety to all economic affairs – except where it really matters: namely, the irreplaceable capital which man has not made, but simply found, and without which he can do nothing.

A businessman would not consider a firm to have solved its problems of production and to have achieved viability if he saw that it was rapidly consuming its capital. How, then, could we overlook this vital fact when it comes to that very big firm, the economy of Spaceship Earth and, in particular, the economies of its rich passengers?

One reason for overlooking this vital fact is that we are estranged from reality and inclined to treat as valueless everything that we have not made ourselves. Even the great Dr Marx fell into this devastating error when he formulated the so-called 'labour theory of value'. Now, we have indeed laboured to make some of the capital which today helps us to produce – a large fund of scientific, technological, and other knowledge; an elaborate physical infrastructure; innumerable types of sophisticated capital equipment, etc. – but all this is but a small part of the total capital we are using. Far larger is the capital provided by nature and not by man – and we do not even recognize it as such. This larger part is now being used up at an alarming rate, and that is why it is an absurd and suicidal error to believe, and act on the belief, that the problem of production has been solved.

Let us take a closer look at this 'natural capital'. First of all, and most obviously, there are the fossil fuels. No one, I am sure, will deny that we are treating them as income items although they are undeniably capital items. If we treated them as capital items, we should be concerned with conservation; we should do everything in our power to try and minimize their current rate of use; we might be saying, for instance, that the money obtained from the realization of these assets – these irreplaceable assets – must be placed into a special fund to be devoted exclusively to the evolution of production methods and patterns of living which do *not* depend on fossil fuels at all or depend on them only to a very slight extent. These and many other things we should be doing if we treated fossil fuels as capital and not as income. And we do not do any of them, but the exact contrary of every one of them: we are not in the least concerned with conservation; we are maximizing, instead of minimizing, the current rates of use; and, far from being interested in studying the possibilities of alternative methods of production and patterns of living – so as to get off the collision course on which we are moving with ever-increasing speed – we happily talk of unlimited progress along the beaten track, of 'education for leisure' in the rich countries, and of 'the transfer of technology' to the poor countries.

The liquidation of these capital assets is proceeding so rapidly that even in the allegedly richest country in the world, the United States of America, there were many worried men, right up to the White House, calling for the massive conversion of coal into oil and gas, demanding ever more gigantic efforts to search for and exploit the remaining treasures of the earth . . .

The explanation is not difficult to find. As with fossil fuels, we have indeed been living on the capital of living nature for some time, but at a fairly modest rate. It is only since the end of World War II that we have succeeded in increasing this rate to alarming proportions. In comparison with what is going on now and what has been going on, progressively, during the last quarter of a century, all the industrial activities of mankind up to, and including, World War II are as nothing. The next four or five years are likely to see more industrial production, taking the world as a whole, than all of mankind accomplished up to 1945. In other words, quite recently – so recently that most of us have hardly yet become conscious of it – there has been a unique quantitative jump in industrial production.

Partly as a cause and also as an effect, there has also been a unique qualitative jump. Our scientists and technologists have learned to compound substances unknown to nature. Against many of them, nature is virtually defenceless. There are no natural agents to attack and break them down. It is as if aborigines were suddenly attacked with machine-gun fire: their bows and arrows are of no avail. These substances, unknown to nature, owe their almost magical effectiveness precisely to nature's defencelessness – and that accounts also for their dangerous ecological impact. It is only in the last twenty years or so that they have made their appearance *in bulk*. Because they have no natural enemies, they tend to accumulate, and the long-term consequences of this accumulation are in many cases known to be extremely dangerous, and in other cases totally unpredictable.

In other words, the changes of the last twenty-five years, both in the quantity and in the quality of man's industrial processes, have produced an entirely new situation – a situation resulting not from our failures but from what we thought were our greatest successes. And this has come so suddenly that we hardly noticed the fact that we were very rapidly using up a certain kind of irreplaceable capital asset, namely the *tolerance margins* which benign nature always provides. . . .

And this takes us to the third category of 'natural capital' which we are recklessly squandering because we treat it as if it were income: as if it were something we had made ourselves and could easily replace out of our much-vaunted and rapidly rising productivity.

Is it not evident that our current methods of production are already eating into the very substance of industrial man? To many people this is not at all evident. Now that we have solved the problem of production, they say, have we ever had it so good? Are we not better fed, better clothed, and better housed than ever before – and better educated? Of course we are: most, but by no means all, of us: in the rich countries. But this is not what I mean by 'substance'. The substance of man cannot be measured by Gross National Product. Perhaps it cannot be measured at all, except for certain symptoms of loss. However, this is not the place to go into the statistics of these symptoms, such as crime, drug addiction, vandalism, mental breakdown, rebellion, and so forth. Statistics never prove anything.

I started by saying that one of the most fateful errors of our age is the belief that the problem of production has been solved. This illusion, I suggested, is mainly due to our inability to recognize that the modern industrial system, with all its intellectual sophistication, consumes the very basis on which it has been erected. To use the language of the economist, it lives on irreplaceable capital which it cheerfully treats as income. I specified three categories of such capital: fossil fuels, the tolerance margins of nature, and the human substance. Even if some readers should refuse to accept all three parts of my argument, I suggest that any one of them suffices to make my case.

Industrialism

Most Greens are keen to stress that they are not particularly interested in the battles which have traditionally raged along the left-right political spectrum. They see their target as a much more basic one than either capitalism or socialism, because they believe both of these to be parts of a larger world-view which Jonathon Porritt, below, calls 'industrialism'. According to Greens, both capitalists and socialists (as proponents of industrialism) reckon that the best way to increase human welfare is to increase economic growth, whereas from a Green point of view the challenge of the modern age is to increase human welfare while calling economic growth into question. In fact it is simply not possible for Greens to transcend the left-right spectrum, as they would wish, because they hold left or right positions on all the age-old political values such as liberty, equality and community. Nevertheless, Porritt's concentration on the similarities between capitalism and socialism rather than the differences helps to situate Green politics as a challenge to the one consensus which has dominated our lives since the Industrial Revolution: that expanding production is a good thing. Jonathon Porritt is probably the best-known Green spokesperson in Great Britain and is cutting an ever larger figure on the world environmental stage. Until recently he was Director of Friends of the Earth (Britain).

From Jonathon Porritt, *Seeing Green: the politics of ecology explained* (Oxford: Blackwell, 1984) pp. 43–4.

The claim made by Green politics that it's 'neither right, nor left, nor in the centre' has understandably caused a lot of confusion! For people who are accustomed to thinking of politics exclusively in terms of the left-right polarity, Green politics has to fit in somewhere. And if it doesn't, then it must be made to.

But it's really not that difficult. We profoundly disagree with the politics of the right and its underlying ideology of capitalism; we profoundly disagree with the politics of the left and its adherence, in varying degrees, to the ideology of communism. That leaves us little choice but to disagree, perhaps less profoundly, with the politics of the centre and its ideological pot-pourri of socialized capitalism. The politics of the Industrial Age, left, right and centre, is like a three-lane motorway, with different vehicles in different lanes, but *all* heading in the same direction. Greens feel it is the very direction that is wrong, rather than the choice of any one lane in preference to the others. It is our perception that the motorway of industrialism inevitably leads to the abyss – hence our decision to get off it, and seek an entirely different direction.

Yet it's built into our understanding of politics today that capitalism and communism represent the two extremes of a political spectrum. The two poles are apparently separated by such irreconcilable differences that there is no chance of them ever coming together. According to such a view, the history of the world from now on (however long or short a time-span that may be) is predicated upon the separateness of these two ideologies.

There are, indeed, many differences; in social and political organization; in democratic or totalitarian responses; in economic theory and practice. But for the moment, let's not dwell on these. Let us consider the *similarities* rather than the differences. Both are dedicated to industrial growth, to the expansion of the means of production, to a materialist ethic as the best means of meeting people's needs, and to unimpeded technological development. Both rely on increasing centralization and large-scale bureaucratic control and co-ordination. From a viewpoint of narrow scientific rationalism, both insist that the planet is there to be conquered, that big is self-evidently beautiful, and that what cannot be measured is of no importance. Economics dominates; art, morals and social values are all relegated to a dependent status.

I shall be arguing two things in this chapter: first, that the similarities between these two dominant ideologies are of greater significance than their differences, and that the dialectic between them is therefore largely superficial. If this is the case, it may be claimed that they are united in one, all-embracing 'super-ideology', which, for the sake of convenience, I intend to call industrialism. Second, that this super-ideology, in that it is conditioned to thrive on the ruthless exploitation of both people and planet, is *itself* the greatest threat we face. As Roszak puts it: 'The two ideological camps of the world go at one another; but, like antagonists in a nightmare, their embattled forms fuse into one monstrous shape, a single force of destruction threatening every assertion of personal rights that falls across the path of their struggle.'

If that is so, there must be something with which we can replace it; not another super-ideology (for ideologies are themselves part of the problem), *but a different world view*. That is the not unambitious role that Green politics is in the process of carving out for itself.

The Tragedy of the Commons

If it is rational for us to maximize our own gain from common-ly-held land, sea and air, and if we are free to do so, then what do we get? Garrett Hardin's famous answer is: tragedy – the 'tragedy of the commons'. When populations were low, he writes, the commons were effectively limitless and little damage could be done to them. As populations grow, pressure on the commons increases to the point where rational maximization by each results in devastation for all. Hardin prescribes different solutions to the tragedy for different cases – private property, pollution taxes and (notoriously) curbs on population growth and immigration. What each of these has in common is, as he writes below, an 'infringement of somebody's personal liberty'; but, he argues, we must learn that freedom is the recognition of necessity and accept the need for coercion.

From Garrett Hardin, 'The Tragedy of the Commons' in Garrett Hardin and John Baden (eds.), *Managing the Commons* (San Francisco: W H Freeman and Co., 1977) pp. 20, 28–9 (first published in *Bioscience*, **162**, 1968).

The tragedy of the commons develops in this way. Picture a pasture open to all. It is to be expected that each herdsman will try to keep as many cattle as possible on the commons. Such an arrangement may work reasonably satisfactorily for centuries because tribal wars, poaching, and disease keep the numbers of both man and beast well below the carrying capacity of the land. Finally, however, comes the day of reckoning, that is, the day when the long-desired goal of social stability becomes a reality. At this point, the inherent logic of the commons remorselessly generates tragedy.

As a rational being, each herdsman seeks to maximize his gain. Explicitly or implicitly, more or less consciously, he asks, 'What is the utility *to me* of adding one more animal to my herd?' This utility has one negative and one positive component.

1. The positive component is a function of the increment of one animal. Since the herdsman receives all the proceeds from the sale of the additional animal, the positive utility is nearly +1.

2. The negative component is a function of the additional overgrazing created by one more animal. Since, however, the effects of overgrazing are shared by all the herdsmen, the negative utility for any particular decision-making herdsman is only a fraction of −1.

Adding together the component partial utilities, the rational herdsman concludes that the only sensible course for him to pursue is to add another animal to his herd. And another.

But this is the conclusion reached by each and every rational herdsman sharing a commons. Therein is the tragedy. Each man is locked into a system that compels him to increase his herd without limit – in a world that is limited. Ruin is the destination toward which all men rush, each pursuing his own best interest in a society that believes in the freedom of the commons. Freedom in a commons brings ruin to all.

Some would say that this is a platitude. Would that it were! In a sense, it was learned thousands of years ago, but natural selection favours the forces of psychological denial. The individual benefits as an individual from his ability to deny the truth even though society as a whole, of which he is a part, suffers. Education can counteract the natural tendency to do the wrong thing, but the inexorable succession of generations requires that the basis for this knowledge be constantly refreshed.

▓▓▓▓

Recognition of necessity

Perhaps the simplest summary of this analysis of man's population problems is this: the commons, if justifiable at all is justifiable only under conditions of low-population density. As the human population has increased, the commons has had to be abandoned in one aspect after another.

First we abandoned the commons in food gathering, enclosing farm land and restricting pastures and hunting and fishing areas. These restrictions are still not complete throughout the world.

Somewhat later we saw that the commons as a place for waste

disposal would also have to be abandoned. Restrictions on the disposal of domestic sewage are widely accepted in the western world; we are still struggling to close the commons to pollution by automobiles, factories, insecticide sprayers, fertilizing operations, and atomic energy installations. . . .

Every new enclosure of the commons involves the infringement of somebody's personal liberty. Infringements made in the distant past are accepted because no contemporary complains of a loss. It is the newly proposed infringements that we vigorously oppose; cries of 'rights' and 'freedom' fill the air. But what does 'freedom' mean? When men mutually agreed to pass laws against robbing, mankind became more free, not less so. Individuals locked into the logic of the commons are free only to bring on universal ruin; once they see the necessity of mutual coercion, they become free to pursue other goals. I believe it was Hegel who said, 'Freedom is the recognition of necessity.'

The most important aspect of necessity that we must now recognize, is the necessity of abandoning the commons in breeding. No technical solution can rescue us from the misery of overpopulation. Freedom to breed will bring ruin to all. At the moment, to avoid hard decisions many of us are tempted to propagandize for conscience and responsible parenthood. The temptation must be resisted, because an appeal to independently-acting consciences selects for the disappearance of all conscience in the long run, and an increase in anxiety in the short.

The only way we can preserve and nurture other and more precious freedoms is by relinquishing the freedom to breed, and that very soon. 'Freedom is the recognition of necessity' – and it is the role of education to reveal to all the necessity of abandoning the freedom to breed. Only so, can we put an end to this aspect of the tragedy of the commons.

The Turning Point

Greens will locate the source of our malaise at any one, or more than one, of a number of points. But the most general analysis has it that our problems have their root in the bankruptcy of a dominant 'way of thinking' – a way of thinking usually linked to the rise of mechanistic science in Europe during the sixteenth century. A very popular source of evidence for this thesis is the work of American physicist Fritjof Capra. He has argued in *The Tao of Physics* and *The Turning Point* that mechanistic science had, and has, the effect of destroying the benign projects typical of the organic world view of medieval European society, and replacing them with manipulative and domineering ones. As a result, our relationship with the natural world changed from one of contemplation to one of control, and in our insistence that the natural world was just another machine we lost sight of the complex interactions of which it is constituted. Capra (and others) argue that this is the root of our environmental insensitivity today, typified in projects such as industrial agriculture and genetic engineering. But, says Capra, the wheel has turned full circle. If Newton and Descartes took the world to pieces, then quantum physics has put it back together again (extract 2). The mechanistic paradigm must give way to the systems paradigm, and on this latter we can re-found a humbler and more sensitive relationship with the natural world.

From Fritjof Capra, *The Turning Point* (London: Fontana Flamingo series, 1983) pp. 37–41, 66–70.

The world view and value system that lie at the basis of our culture and that have to be carefully re-examined were formulated in their essential outlines in the sixteenth and seventeenth centuries. Between 1500 and 1700 there was a dramatic shift in the way people pictured the world and in their whole way of thinking. The new mentality and the new perception of the cosmos gave our western civilization the features that are characteristic of the modern era. They became the basis of the paradigm that dominated our culture for the past three hundred years and is now about to change.

Before 1500 the dominant world view in Europe, as well as in most other civilizations, was organic. People lived in small, cohesive communities and experienced nature in terms of organic relationships, characterized by the interdependence of spiritual and material phenomena and the subordination of individual needs to those of the community. The scientific framework of this organic world view rested on two authorities – Aristotle and the Church. In the thirteenth century Thomas Aquinas combined Aristotle's comprehensive system of nature with Christian theology and ethics and, in doing so, established the conceptual framework that remained unquestioned throughout the Middle Ages. The nature of medical science was very different from that of contemporary science. It was based on both reason and faith and its main goal was to understand the meaning and significance of things, rather than prediction and control. Medieval scientists, looking for the purposes underlying various natural phenomena, considered questions relating to God, the human soul, and ethics to be of the highest significance.

The medieval outlook changed radically in the sixteenth and seventeenth centuries. The notion of an organic, living, and spiritual universe was replaced by that of the world as a machine, and the world-machine became the dominant metaphor of the modern era. This development was brought about by revolutionary changes in physics and astronomy, culminating in the achievements of Copernicus, Galileo, and Newton. The science of the seventeenth century was based on a new method of inquiry, advocated forcefully by Francis Bacon, which involved the mathematical description of nature and the analytic method of reasoning conceived by the genius of Descartes. Acknowledging the crucial role of science in bringing about these far-reaching changes, historians have called the sixteenth and seventeenth centuries the Age of the Scientific Revolution . . .

While Galileo devised ingenious experiments in Italy, Francis Bacon set forth the empirical method of science explicitly in England. Bacon was the first to formulate a clear theory of the inductive procedure – to make experiments and to draw general conclusions from them, to be tested in further experiments – and he became extremely influential by vigorously advocating the new methods. He boldly attacked traditional schools of thought and developed a veritable passion for scientific experimentation.

The 'Baconian spirit' profoundly changed the nature and purpose of the scientific quest. From the time of the ancients the goals of science had been wisdom, understanding the natural order and living in harmony with it. Science was pursued 'for the glory of God', or, as the Chinese put it, to 'follow the natural order' and 'flow in the current of the Tao'. These were yin, or integrative, purposes; the basic attitude of scientists was ecological, as we would say in today's language. In the seventeenth century this attitude changed into its polar opposite; from yin to yang, from integration to self-assertion. Since Bacon, the goal of science has been knowledge that can be used to dominate and control nature, and today both science and technology are used predominantly for purposes that are profoundly antiecological.

The terms in which Bacon advocated his new empirical method of investigation were not only passionate but often outright vicious. Nature, in his view, had to be 'hounded in her wanderings', 'bound into service', and made a 'slave'. She was to be 'put in constraint', and the aim of the scientist was to 'torture nature's secrets from her'. Much of this violent imagery seems to have been inspired by the witch trials that were held frequently in Bacon's time. As attorney general for King James VI and I, Bacon was intimately familiar with such prosecutions, and because nature was commonly seen as female, it is not surprising that he should carry over the metaphors used in the courtroom into his scientific writings. Indeed, his view of nature as a female whose secrets have to be tortured from her with the help of mechanical devices is strongly suggestive of the widespread torture of women in the witch trials of the early seventeenth century. Bacon's work thus represents an outstanding example of the influence of patriarchal attitudes on scientific thought.

The ancient concept of the earth as nurturing mother was radically transformed in Bacon's writings, and it disappeared completely as the scientific revolution proceeded to replace the organic view of nature with the metaphor of the world as a machine. This shift, which was to become of overwhelming importance for the further development of western civilization, was initiated and completed by two towering figures of the seventeenth century, Descartes and Newton. . . .

⁞⁞⁞⁞⁞⁞⁞

In contrast to the mechanistic Cartesian view of the would, the world view emerging from modern physics can be characterized by words like organic, holistic, and ecological. It might also be called a systems view, in the sense of general systems theory. The universe is no longer seen as a machine, made up of a multitude of objects, but has to be pictured as one indivisible, dynamic whole whose parts are essentially interrelated and can be understood only as patterns of a cosmic process. . . .

The experimental investigation of atoms at the beginning of the century yielded sensational and totally unexpected results. Far from being the hard, solid particles of time-honoured theory, atoms turned out to consist of vast regions of space in which extremely small particles – the electrons – moved around the nucleus. A few years later quantum theory made it clear that even the subatomic particles – the electrons and the protons and neutrons in the nucleus – were nothing like the solid objects of classical physics. These subatomic units of matter are very abstract entities which have a dual aspect. Depending on how we look at them, they appear sometimes as particles, sometimes as waves; and this dual nature is also exhibited by light, which can take the form of electromagnetic waves or particles. The particles of light were first called 'quanta' by Einstein – hence the origin of the term 'quantum theory' – and are now known as photons. . . .

The discovery of the dual aspect of matter and of the fundamental role of probability has demolished the classical notion of solid objects. At the subatomic level, the solid material objects of classical physics dissolve into wave-like patterns of probabilities. These patterns, furthermore, do not represent probabilities of things, but rather probabilities of interconnections. A careful analysis of the process of observation in atomic physics shows that the subatomic particles have no meaning as isolated entities but can be understood only as interconnections, or correlations, between various processes of observation and measurement. As Niels Bohr wrote, 'Isolated material particles are abstractions, their properties being definable and observable only through their interaction with other systems.'

Subatomic particles, then, are not 'things' but are interconnections between 'things', and these 'things', in turn, are interconnections between other 'things', and so on. In quantum theory you never end up with 'things'; you always deal with interconnections.

This is how modern physics reveals the basic oneness of the universe. It shows that we cannot decompose the world into independently existing smallest units. As we penetrate into matter, nature does not show us any isolated basic building blocks, but rather appears as a complicated web of relations between the various parts of a unified whole. As Heisenberg expresses it, 'The world thus appears as a complicated tissue of events, in which connections of different kinds alternate or overlap or combine and thereby determine the texture of the whole.'

The universe, then, is a unified whole that can to some extent be divided into separate parts, into objects made of molecules and atoms, themselves made of particles. But here, at the level of particles, the notion of separate parts breaks down. The subatomic particles – and therefore, ultimately, all parts of the universe – cannot be understood as isolated entities but must be defined through their interrelations. Henry Stapp, of the University of California, writes, 'An elementary particle is not an independently existing unanalysable entity. It is, in essence, a set of relationships that reach outward to other things.'

This shift from objects to relationships has far-reaching implications for science as a whole. Gregory Bateson even argued that relationships should be used as a basis for *all* definitions, and that this should be taught to our children in elementary school. Any thing, he believed, should be defined not by what it is in itself, but by its relations to other things.

The Arrogance of Humanism

Greens think that many of our problems stem from having too inflated an idea of the scope of our capacity to reason. We think, they say, that our rational faculty not only separates us from other animals, but also that we can use it to 'rearrange both the world of Nature and the affairs of men and women so that human life will prosper' (see below). This is dangerous folly. In the passage below, David Ehrenfeld suggests that we should call into question the power of reason and the faith in science and technology which goes with it, and he wants to rebuild the bridges between humanity and nature which humanism has helped bring down. Reading this extract together with those of Capra, Plant, Naess, Shiva, Schwarz and Smuts puts into perspective the Green call for a new consciousness – one that makes humanity a part of the natural world rather than apart from it.

From David Ehrenfeld, *The Arrogance of Humanism* (New York: Oxford University Press, 1978) pp. 5–6, 9–12.

Setting aside the notion of human worth and dignity, which is part of many religions, we come at once to the core of the religion of humanism: a supreme faith in human reason – its ability to confront and solve the many problems that humans face, its ability to rearrange both the world of Nature and the affairs of men and women so that human life will prosper. Accordingly, as humanism is committed to an unquestioning faith in the power of reason, so it rejects other assertions of power, including the power of God, the power of supernatural forces, and even the undirected power of nature in league with blind chance. The first two don't exist, according to humanism; the last can, with effort, be mastered. Because human intelligence is the key to human success, the main task of the humanists is to assert its power and protect its prerogatives wherever they are questioned or challenged.

Among the correlates of humanism is the belief that humankind should live for itself, because we have the power to do so, the capacity to enjoy such a life, and nothing else to live for. Another correlate is the faith in the children of pure reason: science and technology. Although shaken in recent years and the source of much confusion among humanists, this faith continues to permeate our existence and influence our behaviour, like the universal assumptions that day will always follow night and water will always flow downhill. There is also a strong anti-Nature (at least raw Nature) element in humanism, although it is not always expressed and is sometimes denied. . . .

Having no desire to discard the wheat with the chaff, I must admit that humanism includes several quite different although subtly related ideas. Absolute faith in our ability to control our own destiny is a dangerous fallacy, as I will try to show. But belief in the nobility and value of humankind and a reasonable respect for our achievements and competences are also in humanism, and only a misanthrope would reject this aspect of it. Misanthropy will also be discussed later.

To some, humanism serves to protect us from the darker side of nature, a side that all but the most hopelessly naive and sheltered of urban pastoralists know well. Anyone who copes regularly with nature has met the winds, frosts, droughts, floods, heat waves, pests, infertile soils, venoms, diseases, accidents, and general uncertainty that it offers in succession or simultaneously. The primitive way to confront this darker side is with toil, and the human faculty of invention has ever worked to lessen that toil. Small wonder that humanism, which elevates our inventiveness to divine levels and celebrates it as infallible, has been embraced by many of those who believe they have been released from toil.

Setting aside for the moment the question of the side-effects and durability of the release, what are the implications of this way of thinking about humanity and Nature? At the outset it is clear that a dichotomy has been created: people vs. Nature. . . .

The dichotomy between humanity and Nature is not the only one that has been imposed or supported by a humanistic way of thought. There is also the logic vs. emotion dichotomy, which although founded in fact has been exaggerated and distorted by humanism. Both will be dealt with later.

The arrogance of the humanist faith in our abilities was nurtured by the late Renaissance triumphs of science and technology working in tandem. These triumphs were seen or discussed everywhere; they ranged from a profusion of new techniques for modifying landscapes to a flood of information about the natural world. Perhaps this alone would have been sufficient to swell the collected heads of humanity, but another factor helped enormously. Until the middle of the eighteenth century, hardly anyone seems to have suspected that there might be absolute limits to the environment-controlling powers of human beings. By then it was too late for most societies to change. Attitudes were set, and were further hardened by the accelerating impulse of the scientific revolution, which continues, unabated, today. Now, when the suspicion of limits has become certainty, the great bulk of educated people still believe that there is no trap we cannot puzzle our way out of as surely and noisily as we blundered into it. Visions of Utopia still jostle one another in the tainted air, and every fresh disaster is met with fresh plans of power and still more power.

Problems with the Enlightenment

We have already seen the physicist Fritjof Capra* laying the
blame for our insensitive relationship with the natural world at
the door of mechanistic science. Ecofeminists* have applied
similar analyses to a man's domination of woman. They point
out that women and nature have traditionally been closely
associated and so the intellectual structures which have made
destruction of the environment fair game are easily transferred
to help legitimize the oppression of women (see Merchant*).
More far-reaching still, though, than this critique of mechanistic science is the contemporary critique of the wider intellectual framework that helped produce it – the Enlightenment.
Critics have seen the Enlightenment as at least as much an
aggressive as a benign phenomenon, and from this point of
view any scheme written in the Enlightenment's political language (e.g. liberty, equality, progress) will have a dark as well
as a bright side to it. In the following extract Vandana Shiva,
who lives in the foothills of the Himalayas, weaves together a
critique of mechanistic science and the Enlightenment's theory
of progress, showing how they simultaneously lead to the
despoilation of nature, the oppression of women, and the practice of inappropriate and destructive development projects in
the Third World.

From Vandana Shiva, *Staying Alive* (London: Zed Books, 1988)
pp. xiv-xviii.

The Age of Enlightenment, and the theory of progress to which it
gave rise, was centred on the sacredness of two categories: modern
scientific knowledge and economic development. Somewhere along
the way, the unbridled pursuit of progress, guided by science and
development, began to destroy life without any assessment of how
fast and how much of the diversity of life on this planet is disappear-
ing. The act of living and of celebrating and conserving life in all
its diversity – in people and in nature – seems to have been sacrificed

to progress, and the sanctity of life been substituted by the sanctity of science and development.

Throughout the world, a new questioning is growing, rooted in the experience of those for whom the spread of what was called 'Enlightenment' has been the spread of darkness, of the extinction of life and life-enhancing processes. A new awareness is growing that is questioning the sanctity of science and development and revealing that these are not universal categories of progress, but the special projects of modern western patriarchy. This book has grown out of my involvement with women's struggles for survival in India over the last decade. It is informed both by the suffering and insights of those who struggle to sustain and conserve life, and whose struggles question the meaning of a progress, a science, a development which destroys life and threatens survival.

The death of nature is central to this threat to survival. The earth is rapidly dying: her forests are dying, her soils are dying, her waters are dying, her air is dying. Tropical forests, the creators of the world's climate, the cradle of the world's vegetational wealth, are being bull-dozed, burnt, ruined or submerged. . . .

With the destruction of forests, water and land, we are losing our life-support systems. This destruction is taking place in the name of 'development' and progress, but there must be something seriously wrong with a concept of progress that threatens survival itself. The violence to nature, which seems intrinsic to the dominant development model, is also associated with violence to women who depend on nature for drawing sustenance for themselves, their families, their societies. This violence against nature and women is built into the very mode of perceiving both, and forms the basis of the current development paradigm. This book is an attempt to articulate how rural Indian woman, who are still embedded in nature, experience and perceive ecological destruction and its causes, and how they have conceived and initiated processes to arrest the destruction of nature and begin its regeneration. From the diverse and specific grounds of the experience of ecological destruction arises a common identification of its causes in the development process and the view of nature with which it is legitimized. This book focuses on science and development as patriarchal projects not as a denial of other sources of patriarchy, such as religion, but because they are thought to be class, culture and gender neutral.

Seen from the experiences of Third World women, the modes of thinking and action that pass for science and development, respectively, are not universal and humanly inclusive, as they are made out to be; modern science and development are projects of male, western origin, both historically and ideologically. They are the latest and most brutal expression of a patriarchal ideology which is threatening to annihilate nature and the entire human species. The rise of a patriarchal science of nature took place in Europe during the fifteenth and seventeenth centuries as the scientific revolution. During the same period, the closely-related industrial revolution laid the foundations of a patriarchal mode of economic development in industrial capitalism. Contemporary science and development conserve the ideological root and biases of the scientific and industrial revolutions even as they unfold into new areas of activity and new domains of subjugation.

The scientific revolution in Europe transformed nature from *terra mater* into a machine and a source of raw material; with this transformation it removed all ethical and cognitive constraints against its violation and exploitation. The industrial revolution converted economics from the prudent management of resources for sustenance and basic needs satisfaction into a process of commodity production for profit maximization. Industrialism created a limitless appetite for resource exploitation, and modern science provided the ethical and cognitive licence to make such exploitation possible, acceptable – and desirable. The new relationship of man's domination and mastery over nature was thus also associated with new patterns of domination and mastery over women, and their exclusion from participation *as partners* in both science and development.

Contemporary development activity in the Third World superimposes the scientific and economic paradigms created by western, gender-based ideology on communities in other cultures. Ecological destruction and the marginalization of women, we know now, have been the inevitable results of most development programmes and projects based on such paradigms; they violate the integrity of one and destroy the productivity of the other. Women, as victims of the violence of patriarchal forms of development, have risen against it to protect nature and preserve their survival and sustenance. Indian women have been in the forefront of ecological struggles to conserve forests, land and water. They have challenged the western concept of nature as an object of exploitation and have protected her as Prakriti, the living force that supports life. They have challenged the western concept of economics as production of profits and capital accumulation with their own concept of economics as production of sustenance and needs satisfaction. A science that does not respect nature's needs and a development that does not respect people's needs inevitably threaten survival. In their fight to survive the onslaughts of both, women have begun a struggle that challenges the most fundamental categories of western patriarchy – its concepts of nature and women, and of science and development. Their ecological struggle in India is aimed simultaneously at liberating nature from ceaseless exploitation and themselves from limitless marginalization. They are creating a feminist ideology that transcends gender, and a political practice that is humanly inclusive; they are challenging patriarchy's ideological claim to universalism not with another universalizing tendency, but with diversity; and they are challenging the dominant concept of power as violence with the alternative concept of non-violence as power.

The everyday struggles of women for the protection of nature take place in the cognitive and ethical context of the categories of the ancient Indian world view in which nature is Prakriti, a living and creative process, the feminine principle from which all life arises. Women's ecology movements, as the preservation and recovery of the feminine principle, arise from a non-gender based ideology of liberation, different both from the gender-based ideology of patriarchy which underlies the process of ecological destruction and women's subjugation, and the gender-based responses which have, until recently, been characteristic of the west.

Inspired by women's struggles for the protection of nature as a condition for human survival, this book goes beyond a statement of women as special victims of the environmental crisis. It attempts to capture and reconstruct those insights and visions that Indian women provide in their struggles for survival, which perceive development and science from outside the categories of modern western patriarchy. These oppositional categories are simultaneously ecological and feminist: they allow the possibility of survival by exposing the parochial basis of science and development and by showing how ecological destruction and the marginalization of women are not inevitable, economically or scientifically.

The Real and Surrogate Worlds

Green theorists are relentless in their reminding us that the things human beings do to reproduce their lives – eat, build shelters, create artefacts – would not be possible without the earth and the resources with which it provides us. At times the aim of this reminder is simply to ensure that we take better care of that – the environment – on which we depend for our welfare. At other times, though, Greens give the impression that that world on which we depend is more authentic and altogether more worthy of awe than the world we create from it. This is the root both of the pervasive notion that what is 'natural' is 'good', and of the Green demand that human beings swallow their hubris and recognize that they are partners in, rather the lords of, creation. Here Edward Goldsmith, founder and publisher of *The Ecologist* magazine, refers to these two worlds as the 'real' and the 'surrogate' worlds and argues that production of the second results necessarily in the deterioration of the first. Hence it is incumbent upon us to do as little surrogate world-building as possible.

From Edward Goldsmith, 'De-industrializing society' (first published 1977) in *The Great U-Turn: De-industrializing Society* (Bideford: Green Books, 1988) pp. 185–7.

Let us look a little more closely at this process of 'development', or more precisely 'industrialization' – its latest phase. First, it is not autonomous. It does not occur in a vacuum as is implied by modern economics. If the world were a lifeless waste, as is the moon, there could be no industrialization. If it has occurred at all, it is that over the last few thousand million years the primaeval dust has slowly been organized into an increasingly complex organization of matter – the biosphere, or world of living things – or the 'real world' as we might refer to it – which provides the resources entering into this process. Industrialization is something which is happening to the biosphere. *It is the biosphere, in fact – the real world –* that is being industrialized.

In this way, a new organization of matter is building up: the technosphere or world of material goods and technological devices: or the *surrogate world*.

This brings us to the second important feature of industrialization: the surrogate world it gives rise to is in direct competition with the real world, since it can only be built up by making use of resources extracted from the latter, and by consigning to it the waste products this process must inevitably generate.

Let us see why this must be so. The actual building up of the surrogate world occurs in three steps: *First*, resources are extracted from the real world, which can only lead to its contraction and deterioration. Thus, to obtain timber, forests must be felled, causing soil erosion, a fall in the water table, the drying up of streams and increasing the incidence and severity of droughts and floods. To obtain other building materials such as stones, or clay for brick making, still more areas must be deprived of their trees and topsoil.

Second, so as to build up the surrogate world of cities, factories, motorways and airports, these materials must be organized differently *elsewhere*. Hence, the land must also be deprived of its trees and its topsoil before being covered with materials such as cement and asphalt which are random to the processes of the real world.

Third, this process, like all others, must give rise to waste products. These become increasingly toxic as industrialization proceeds (as synthetics take over from naturally-occurring materials). Unfortunately the processes of the surrogate world, being far more rudimentary than those of the real world, give rise to correspondingly more wastes, and as they are neither arranged in such a way, nor are they of the right sort to serve as the necessary raw materials for the further development of the surrogate world *let alone for the restoration of the real one*, they simply tend to accumulate as 'randomness' *vis-à-vis* both of these rival organizations of matter.

To illustrate this point, consider a modern city of a million inhabitants. Wolman has likened it to some vast beast with a very specific metabolism. Every day it must take in some 9,500 tons of fossil fuels, 2,000 tons of food, 625,000 tons of water, 31,500 tons of oxygen plus unknown quantities of various minerals while it must also emit, during the same period, some 28,500 tons of CO_2, 12,000 tons of H_2O (produced in the combustion of fossil fuels), 150 tons of particles, 500,000 tons of sewage, together with vast quantities of refuse, sulphur and nitrogen oxides and various other heterogeneous materials.

If the beast is to keep alive, its metabolism cannot be stopped any more than can that of any other beast. This means that the resources must be extracted from somewhere, the wastes released somewhere else. The latter . . . cannot simply be made to vanish. Pollution-control simply consists in diverting them to where they are likely to do the least harm or to dilute them in the atmosphere or in the seas. (The loss during the recycling process, in the case of most materials, is so great that this does not provide any long-term solution). Pollution-control, in fact, is only possible when there are few such beasts around, impossible when there are a large number – for then pollution becomes global rather than local, there is nowhere to divert it to, and nothing left to dilute it in.

It must follow that all three steps involved in the process of building up the surrogate world give rise to a corresponding contraction and deterioration of the real one. Economic growth, in terms of which the former process is measured, is thereby biological and social contraction and deterioration. *They are just different sides of the same coin.*

Unfortunately, we are part of the real world not the surrogate one. In fact, we have been designed phylogenetically (and at one time culturally, too) to fulfil within it specific differentiated functions. It would be very naive to suppose that its systematic destruction would not affect us in some way. To understand exactly how, we must consider the basic features of the real world. Unfortunately, these tend to be disregarded by most of today's scientists, who are more concerned with accumulating trivia than in understanding basic principles.

Population Explosion

While most of us might accept that there is a limit to the amount of oil and platinum that can be extracted from a finite earth, it seems to be harder for us to go along with the idea that there is a limit to the human population that can be sustained on it. However regularly we are bombarded with the figures, we cling to the belief that fairer distribution of food, improved technology or greater wealth will see us through the crisis. But it is a fundamental – and highly sensitive – Green political belief that population growth needs to be stabilized as soon as possible, both to improve the life expectancy of those who are born, and to secure the long-term sustainability of the planet as a whole. The arguments in favour of population control and some suggestions as to how to bring it about are put below by Sandy Irvine and Alec Ponton, of the British Green Party. It is easy to see why the issue is such a delicate one, particularly when viewed in terms of a restriction of free- dom of choice, but note that in among the sticks and carrots lies the assertion that 'there is a happy correlation between women's liberation and population control'. While patriarchal societies might presently find this hard to swallow, there may be more long-term political acceptability in it than handing out transistor radios to sterilization 'volunteers'.

From Sandy Irvine and Alec Ponton, *A Green Manifesto* (London: Macdonald Optima, 1988) pp. 17–18, 22–3.

The explosion in human numbers is the greatest long-term threat to the future of human and non-human inhabitants of the earth. While nuclear arsenals present grave potential dangers, the predomi- nant crisis of overpopulation is with us today.

When faced with this fact most people bury their heads in the sand. Major political parties and pressure groups in such fields as world poverty share this blinkered approach. Often, books and articles on environmental destruction either simply fail to mention population growth, or go out of their way to deny its dangers. Those who have drawn attention to the problem, like American scientists Paul Ehrlich and Garrett Hardin*, have been subject to abuse from across the political spectrum. Robert (sic) Malthus, who at the end of the eighteenth century warned of the inherent dangers of rising human numbers, is regularly disinterred for ritual retrial and execution. Could it be that essentially he was right after all, but that too many people have a vested ideological interest in denying the truth?

Human numbers have now passed the five billion mark. They are doubling in shorter and shorter timespans. If trends continue (it is the number of young people in the world that propels the momentum) there will be almost two billion more people within just twenty years. These additional numbers are greater than the total world population of the 1930s. In the time it takes to read this page, about 250 babies will be born. The planet, however, does not grow any bigger.

Some people recognize the danger but hope it will go away by itself, or believe it can be defused by technology, better planning and management or greater affluence. Underlying such optimism is a range of taboos, instincts and values, from religious convictions through concepts of individual rights to plain male machismo. Humans readily apply population control to other species by means of pesticides and herbicides, culling and habitat destruction. We claim it is for their own good as we thin out animals and plants in the name of the environment's capacity to support them. The simple fact is that we humans are no more exempt from biological laws than any other species.

Overpopulation problems in the rest of nature have ways of resolving themselves. Populations which have overshot their environmental limits come crashing down. This would be our eventual fate, though we may try to escape it by directing more of the planet's biological production to our needs. Paul and Anne Ehrlich estimate that 'our one species has co-opted or destroyed some 40 per cent of potential terrestrial productivity'. In so doing, we not only rob other species of their means of life, but we also damage the planet's life-support systems, thus robbing our descendants as well. Nature would eventually solve the problem of human numbers, but in ways unacceptable to civilized thinking. The only alternative, therefore, is human self-restraint. . . .

Overpopulation – everybody's baby

Population pressure is not only a Third World problem. As Paul and Anne Ehrlich say, 'the entire planet is overpopulated'. Countries like Britain and the Netherlands already have too many people. Yet government projections forecast that Britain's population will have grown nearly 4 per cent by the year 2001. Such numbers are a problem in their own right, and are compounding others. How many of these – urban sprawl, unemployment, traffic congestion, homelessness, pressure on welfare services, rural land use conflicts, resource depletion, pollution, destruction of wildlife – would be so severe if there were fewer people?

Garrett Hardin goes to the heart of this issue: 'There is a cliché that says that 'freedom is indivisible'. Properly interpreted, this saying has some wisdom in it, but there is also a sense in which it is false. Freedom is divisible – and we must find how to divide it if we are to survive in dignity. There are many identifiable freedoms, among which are freedom of speech, freedom of assembly, freedom of association, freedom in the choice of residence, freedom in work, and freedom to travel.

'You can make the list as long as you like. After you have finished, ask yourself this question. Is there one freedom on the list that would increase if our population became twice as great as it is now? Freedom is divisible. If we want to keep the rest of our freedoms, we must restrict the freedom to breed. How we can accomplish this is not at this moment clear; but it is surely subject to rational study. We had better begin our investigations now. We have not long to find acceptable answers.'

In places where growth in human numbers has stabilized, it has done so at levels which are not only overtaxing the environment, but which also make these countries vulnerable to any resurgence. For example, reputable estimates have put Britain's optimum carrying capacity at about thirty million, nearly half its present level of population. In view of this, the urgency of Hardin's message must be emphasized.

Confronting the issue

There is more to population policy than just birth control. It involves putting together a comprehensive package of technical, economic and social changes to reverse the widespread discrimination in favour of childbearing. The foundation of a population policy must be education. From an early age, children should be taught the constraints placed upon us by the limits of the planet, and their own resulting responsibilities.

In more direct measures a stick and carrot approach is needed, both nationally and internationally. There could be payments for periods of non-pregnancy and non-birth (a kind of no claims bonus); tax benefits for families with fewer than two children; sterilization bonuses; withdrawal of maternity and similar benefits after a second child; larger pensions for people with fewer than two children; free, easily available family planning; more funds for research into means of contraception, especially for men; an end to infertility research and treatment; a more realistic approach to abortion; the banning of surrogate motherhood and similar practices; and the promotion of equal opportunities for woman in all areas of life.

Many such measures are already successfully employed in the few places that have confronted the problem of overpopulation. As with other Green policies, they lose their value if pursued in isolation. In such a programme redistribution of wealth, desirable on many other grounds, becomes even more necessary to ensure that parenting does not become a privilege of the rich.

In terms of foreign aid, the cruel truth is that help given to regimes opposed to population policies is counter-productive and should cease. They are the true enemies of life and do not merit support. So too are those religions which do not actively support birth control. Green governments would reluctantly have to challenge head-on such damaging beliefs. To do otherwise would merely exacerbate the problem.

Some measures may seem Draconian. But they are mild compared to what will be required if active steps are not taken now. Moreover, nothing could be more Draconian than that major cultural source of overpopulation, male dominance over women. There is a happy correlation between women's liberation and population control. Doubtless, as ecologist Kenneth Watt says, 'all our problems would be easier to solve if there were fewer people'. Yet this is only one part of a total equation to harmonize the needs of both people and planet.

Social Ecology

Most Green politics focuses on the relationship between human beings and their 'natural' environment, and suggests that the root cause of our environmental problems is the exploitative relationship of the former towards the latter. Many Greens will also claim that our exploitation of the environment is the most fundamental form of exploitation there is, and that we shall not be able to stop exploiting people until we learn to respect the earth. The most extreme version of this point of view is called 'deep ecology'* (see Arne Naess p. 242). While deep ecology has taken root in Europe and been picked up in the United States, the American anarchist writer Murray Bookchin has developed an alternative view of things in the form of what he calls 'social ecology', which is described in the extract below. For Bookchin, the most fundamental form of exploitation is not that of the environment by human beings, but of human beings by human beings. As long as hierarchy in human society exists, he writes, so 'the project of dominating nature will continue'. Bookchin's point of view has proved to be a useful antidote to claims that Greens are more interested in porpoises than people. The extract also introduces us to the tension in Green politics between those who believe that salvation lies in improving ecological technologies (the 'technotwits'), and those – like Bookchin himself – who argue for 'changing the basic structure of our anti-ecological society'. Environmentalism has been taken up as an issue by powerful forces (political parties, the market), but has it been swallowed up? he asks.

From Murray Bookchin, 'Open Letter to the Ecology Movement' in *Toward an Ecological Society* (Montreal: Black Rose Books, 1980) pp. 76–8, 82–3.

Ecology, in my view, has always meant social ecology: the conviction that the very concept of dominating nature stems from the domination of human by human, indeed, of women by men, of the young by their elders, of one ethnic group by another, of society by the state, of the individual by bureaucracy, as well as of one economic class by another or a colonized people by a colonial power. To my thinking, social ecology has to begin its quest for freedom not only in the factory but also in the family, not only in the economy but also in the psyche, not only in the material conditions of life but also in the spiritual ones. Without changing the most molecular relationships in society – notably, those between men and women, adults and children, whites and other ethnic groups, heterosexuals and gays (the list, in fact, is considerable) – society will be riddled by domination even in a socialistic 'classless' and 'non-exploitative' form. It would be infused by hierarchy even as it celebrated the dubious virtues of 'people's democracies', 'socialism' and the 'public ownership' of 'natural resources'. And as long as hierarchy persists, as long as domination organizes humanity around a system of élites, the project of dominating nature will continue to exist and inevitably lead our planet to ecological extinction.

The emergence of the women's movement, even more so than the counterculture, the 'appropriate' technology crusade and the anti-nuke alliances (I will omit the clean-up escapades of 'Earth Day'), points to the very heart of the hierarchical domination that underpins our ecological crisis. Only insofar as a counterculture, an alternate technology or anti-nuke movement rests on the non-hierarchical sensibilities and structures that are most evident in the truly radical tendencies in feminism can the ecology movement realize its rich potential for basic changes in our prevailing anti-ecological society and its values. Only insofar as the ecology movement consciously cultivates an anti-hierarchical and a non-domineering sensibility, structure, and strategy for social change can it retain its very identity as the voice for a new balance between humanity and nature and its goal for a truly ecological society.

This identity and this goal is now faced with serious erosion. Ecology is now fashionable, indeed, faddish – and with this sleazy popularity has merged a new type of environmentalist hype. From an outlook and movement that at least held the promise of challenging hierarchy and domination have emerged a form of *environmentalism* that is based more on tinkering with existing institutions, social relations, technologies, and values than on changing them. I use the word 'environmentalism' to contrast it with ecology, specifically with social ecology. Where social ecology, in my view, seeks to eliminate the concept of the domination of nature by humanity by eliminating the domination of human by human, environmentalism reflects an 'instrumentalist' or technical sensibility in which nature is viewed merely as a passive habitat, an agglomeration of external objects and forces, that must be made more 'serviceable' for human use, irrespective of what these uses may be. Environmentalism, in fact, is merely environmental engineering. It does not bring into question the underlying notions of the present society, notably that man must dominate nature. On the contrary, it seeks to facilitate that domination by developing techniques for diminishing the hazards caused by domination. The very notions of hierarchy and domination are obscured by a technical emphasis on 'alternative' power sources, structural designs for 'conserving' energy, 'simple' lifestyles in the name of 'limits to growth' that now represent an enormous growth industry in its own right – and, of course, a mushrooming of 'ecology'-oriented candidates for political office and 'ecology'-oriented parties that are designed not only to engineer nature but also public opinion into an accommodating relationship with the prevailing society.

Nathan Glazer's 'ecological' twenty-four square-mile solar satellite, O'Neil's 'ecological' spaceships, and the DOE's giant 'ecological' windmills, to cite the more blatant examples of this environmentalistic mentality, are no more 'ecological' than nuclear power plants or agribusiness. If anything, their 'ecological' pretensions are all the more dangerous because they are more deceptive and disorienting to the general public. The hoopla about a new 'Earth Day' or future 'Sun Days' or 'Wind Days', like the pious rhetoric of fast-talking solar contractors and patent–hungry 'ecological' inventors, conceal the all-important fact that solar energy, wind power, organic agriculture, holistic health, and 'voluntary simplicity' will alter very little in our grotesque imbalance with nature if they leave the patriarchal family, the multinational corporation, the bureaucratic and centralized political structure, the property system, and the prevailing technocratic rationality untouched. Solar power, wind power, methane, and geothermal power are merely *power* insofar as the devices for using them are needlessly complex, bureaucratically controlled, corporately owned or institutionally centralized. Admittedly, they are less dangerous to the physical health of human beings than power derived from nuclear and fossil fuels, but they are clearly dangerous to the spiritual, moral and social health of humanity if they are treated merely as *techniques* that do not involve new relations between people and nature and within society itself. The designer, the bureaucrat, the corporate executive, and the political careerist do not introduce anything new or ecological in society or in our sensibilities toward nature and people because they adopt 'soft energy paths', like all 'technotwits' (to use Amory Lovins'* description of himself in a personal conversation with me), they merely cushion or conceal the dangers to the biosphere and to human life by placing ecological technologies in a straitjacket of hierarchical values rather than by challenging the values and the institutions they represent. . . .

Ecology is being used against an ecological sensibility, ecological forms of organization, and ecological practices to 'win' large constituencies, *not to educate them*. The fear of 'isolation', of 'futility', of 'ineffectiveness' yields a new kind of isolation, futility and ineffectiveness, namely, a complete surrender of one's most basic ideals and goals. 'Power' is gained at the cost of losing the only power we really have that can change this insane society – our moral integrity, our ideals, and our principles. This may be a festive occasion for careerists who have used the ecology issue to advance their stardom and personal fortunes; it would become the obituary of a movement that has, latent within itself, the ideals of a new world in which masses become individuals and natural resources become nature, both to be respected for their uniqueness and spirituality.

An ecologically-oriented feminist movement is now emerging and the contours of the libertarian anti-nuke alliance still exist. The fusing of the two together with new movements that are likely to emerge from the varied crises of our times may open one of the most exciting and liberating decades of our century. Neither sexism, ageism, ethnic oppression, the 'energy crisis', corporate power, conventional medicine, bureaucratic manipulation, conscription, militarism, urban devastation or political centralism can be separated from the ecological issue. All of these issues turn around hierarchy and domination, the root conceptions of a radical social ecology.

It is necessary, I believe, for everyone in the ecology movement to make a crucial decision: will the 1980s retain the visionary concept of an ecological future based on a libertarian commitment to decentralization, alternative technology, and a libertarian practice based on affinity groups, direct democracy, and direct action? Or will the decade be marked by a dismal retreat into ideological obscurantism and a 'mainstream politics' that acquires 'power' and 'effectiveness' by following the very 'stream' it should seek to divert? Will it pursue fictitious 'mass constituencies' by imitating the very forms of mass manipulation, mass media, and mass culture it is committed to oppose? These two directions cannot be reconciled.

Our use of 'media', mobilizations, and actions must appeal to mind and to spirit, not to conditioned reflexes and shock tactics that leave no room for reason and humanity. In any case, the choice must be made now, before the ecology movement becomes institutionalized into a mere appendage of the very system whose structure and methods it professes to oppose. It must be made consciously and decisively – or the century itself, not only the decade, will be lost to us forever.

Third World Poverty

We have already seen how the *Limits to Growth* analysis leads to the conclusion that present rates of economic and population growth are unsustainable. In the indignant extract below, the Australian critic Ted Trainer endorses this conclusion and then applies it to the context of the Third World. He suggests that Third World poverty is a direct result of developed world affluence and concludes that the developed world has good moral and prudential reasons for embarking on what he calls a programme of 'de-development'. The moral reason is that it is not right for us to consume so conspicuously at the expense of the poverty of others, and the prudential reason is that 'business-as-usual' will bring about resource wars in which we will all be losers.

From Ted Trainer, *Abandon Affluence!* (London: Zed Books Ltd., 1985) pp. 1–9, 176–8.

The basic premise is that some of the core institutions and values of our society are seriously mistaken, and unless they are radically altered we will find ourselves sliding into more and more acute difficulties within the next few decades with an ever-increasing chance of catastrophic self-destruction. It is not that our intrinsically sound society has had the misfortune to run into serious problems – the claim is that by its very nature our society is inevitably generating problems such as resource and energy scarcity, the destruction of the global ecosystem, the poverty and underdevelopment of the Third World, the danger of international conflict and nuclear war, and a declining quality of life. These are direct consequences of our commitments to levels of material affluence that are far higher than can be sustained for all people, and to an economic system which obliges us to strive for continual increases in these material living standards regardless of how high they already are.

The problem:
our commitment to a way of life that is impossibly affluent

The characteristic way of life of people in the developed countries involves very high per capita rates of resource use. Typically, these are about fifteen times those of people in Third World countries.

The most glaring and objectionable aspects of this way of life are the high levels of unnecessary consumption and waste. The typical household possesses far more things, and far more sophisticated and expensive things, than are remotely necessary for a comfortable existence.

In addition to our high rates of personal consumption, we use extremely expensive systems for supplying food, water, energy, sewage services, housing and many goods. These systems tend to be centralized, based on sophisticated technology, and dependent on extensive transport and high inputs of energy, materials and capital. Most of our goods and services are produced commercially, as distinct from being produced in households and local neighbour-hoods, and this means that many non-renewable resource costs are much higher than they need be. We have organized production in ways that require an enormous amount of travel to and from work. We incur high distribution costs for water, electricity and goods because these tend to be produced in distant centralized locations.

Every year each American uses:

- 29 barrels of oil
- 27 times as much energy as the average for the poorest 2,300 million people
- 55 times as much energy as the average for people in the poorest 80 countries
- 617 times as much energy as the average for Ethiopians

It is because the way of life characteristic of the developed countries involves very high per capita material living standards that these countries consume the bulk of the resources used in the world each year. This is the origin of many of our most serious global problems. Hundreds of millions of people in desperate need must go without the materials and energy that could improve their conditions while these resources flow into developed countries, often to produce frivolous luxuries. . . .

Resources

Almost all discussions of 'whether we will run out of resources' have concerned themselves only with whether the few developed countries will be able to go on getting resources in the increased quantities they are likely to want over the next twenty to thirty years. The conclusions are usually optimistic, but these inquiries typically ignore the fact that the few rich countries, containing about one-quarter of the world's people, are using up about three-quarters of the world's annual resource production at a consumption rate per person that is fifteen times the rate for most individuals in the Third World. The most important question is whether there are enough resources for everyone to use them at this rate.

When we consider estimates of the total amount of potentially recoverable mineral and energy resources that exist in the earth's crust, we can see that if we had eleven billion people living on the per capita levels of resources use characteristic of Americans in the 1970s, the resource stocks of almost half the basic mineral items would be exhausted in about three decades. The most *optimistic* estimates suggest that our energy resources will last about seventy years; the most *plausible* estimates suggest a less than twenty-year lifetime. Even if we ignore any question of a fair distribution of global resource use, it is likely that in the early decades of the next century the industrialized nations will find it too expensive to provide a number of materials in anything like the quantities to which we have become accustomed.

Our way of life assumes an endless increase in affluence. If American per capita use of resources continued to increase by at least 2 per cent per annum, as it did in the period 1950–70, then by 2050 each American would be using four times as much each year as in the mid-1970s. If we are willing to endorse an already affluent society in which there is continued growth on this scale, then we are assuming that after 2050 something like *forty times* as many resources can be provided each year as were provided in the 1970s, and that it is in order for people in a few rich countries to live in this super-affluent way while the other 9.5 billion people in the world do not.

Some savage implications follow from this analysis. Unless extremely implausible assumptions are made *there is no chance of all people ever rising to the levels of material affluence enjoyed by Americans in the late 1970s*, let alone to the levels Americans will reach if growth in material living standards continues. The corollary is that people in developed countries today are affluent because they are hogging scarce and dwindling resources; our way of life is only possible for the few who live in developed countries as long as we go on securing and consuming most of the materials produced each year. If we shared world resources equally the average American would have to get by on less than one-sixth of the present average energy now used.

If these figures are at all accurate they show that our affluent living standards are grossly immoral, and extremely dangerous. They indicate that *our society does not constitute a model that can be achieved by all people, that it is only a possibility for a few so long as the majority of people in the world do not attain it*, and that determination on our part to retain our affluent way of life must eventually generate more and more serious resource conflicts. . . .

The problems of Third World poverty and underdevelopment

This is where we have to face the most disturbing indictments of our way of life. The core criticism here is not that the few rich nations are indifferent to the situation of the poor nations and have made insufficient effort to assist them, but that *our affluence is a direct cause of their poverty*, and that our commitments to high material living standards and to our sort of economic system cannot be realized without depriving the Third World of its fair share of the world's resources. Satisfactory development for most people in poor countries will not be possible until existing economic relations between rich and poor countries are radically altered. (This is as much an accusation of the Russians in their sphere of influence as it is of the developed western nations in theirs.). . . .

The reasons for Third World poverty are complex and include corruption, superstition and ignorance, but the main reasons derive from the determination of the developed countries to pursue ever-rising living standards and from the logic of the global economic system that provides them with their affluence. Their affluence would be much more difficult to achieve if they could not import resources from the Third World nor sell goods to it. Their superior effective demand enables them to secure many of the resources produced in the Third World and to ensure that the industries built there are industries that will produce the things we want, rather than the things the world's poor people need. If the underdeveloped nations were able to pursue a more self-sufficient development model, gearing their usually quite adequate resources directly to producing what their people need rather than to export markets, the rich countries would suffer the disastrous loss of most of their resource consumption and one third of their export markets. If on the other hand we were content with material living standards that were reasonably comfortable and convenient, if we produced only what was necessary for a satisfactory quality of life, if we produced things to last and to be repaired, if we eliminated the production of throw-away and unnecessarily elaborate goods, and if we had an economy which would allow us to cut total production and resource use to perhaps one fifth of what they are now, enough resources would be freed to enable the Third World to provide for itself the basic goods and services that would eliminate its most serious problems. Even more important, we would be much less inclined to draw the Third World into trade and investment relations, which generally tend to deliver much of its wealth to the rich few and do little or nothing for most of its people.

If these arguments are valid it follows that our affluent way of life is highly immoral and that we in rich countries must accept the idea of de-development; we should take immediate action towards reducing our material living standards in order to permit the Third World to have a fairer share of the available resources and to permit more of the Third World's productive capacity to be geared to the needs of its people. Above all, this means we should undertake fundamental change to types of economic systems that do not deliver most wealth to the already rich and do not oblige us to consume resources at anything like our present rates. The imperative is summed up neatly by the saying, 'The rich must live more simply so that the poor may simply live.'

The magnitude of the required redistribution could easily be under-estimated. If world wealth were to be equalized at present the average person in developed countries would have to get by on less than one third of the present resource use. Significant redistribution will therefore involve enormous changes in the living standards and the social systems of developed countries.

To refuse to contemplate de-development is to adopt what is clearly both a morally and prudentially unacceptable position. For three dollars an Indian village family could be provided with safe drinking water; yet Americans spend $800 million each year on chewing-gum. A mere five cents would buy enough Vitamin A to save the sight of one of the possibly 100,000 children who go blind through malnutrition each year; yet Australians have recently chosen to spend $100 million on an Opera House and to bring out one new car model costing the same amount. Sanitation could be brought to Third World rural areas for five dollars per person, and three dollars would immunize a child against the six most common diseases indicating that one year's expenditure by the US beauty industry could provide 1,600 million people with sanitation. According to UNICEF, seventeen million children died in 1980. The cost of saving them would have been about the price of one Trident submarine. One tonne of fertilizer would increase Third World food production sufficiently to feed ten people for a year; but each year Americans apply three million tons of fertilizer to their lawns and gardens. One tonne of grain could feed more than four Third World people for a year; but each year over 400 million tonnes of grain goes into the totally unnecessary practice of feedlot meat production in rich countries. The fact that we choose to lavish resources on ourselves and to glut our shops with masses of unnecessary gadgets, trinkets and luxuries when perhaps billions of people on earth go without bare necessities must rank with the most remarkable moral crimes in human history. The situation is remarkable because so few of those who perpetuate it and benefit from it have any idea of how morally obnoxious their behaviour is. How many are disgusted when millions of dollars are spent on a perfume advertising campaign or on America's Cup yacht challenge or colour TV or skiing holidays, or on the construction of revolving restaurants? Yet the energy and the steel and the talent that goes into these ventures could have gone into producing food, clothing, shelter and health services for people who literally die at a rate of perhaps 80,000 every day because they do not get these things. Our moral position would be appalling even if we owned and deserved our riches and were just being niggardly in helping others in need, but we are not only grabbing most of the available resources by outbidding the poor, we are also getting most of the resources that make us so rich from poor countries. All of us in developed countries can therefore be regarded as parties to the crime; we benefit from the maldistribution and we do little or nothing to challenge the systems that bring it about.

If moral appeals are pointless then perhaps prudential considerations might have more impact. By late next century people in the presently developed countries will probably be outnumbered six or eight to one by people in poor countries. According to the analyses given above the former will then be able to have affluent living standards only if they commandeer an even higher percentage of world resource production than they do now and import even more of their consumption from a Third World that will be even poorer than it is now. Struggles between developed countries for resources and conflicts between developed and underdeveloped countries are likely to reach critical levels long before then. If only in order to improve our own chances of surviving the twenty-first century it would seem to be very wise for the rich countries to commit themselves to significant de-development.

THE GREEN SOCIETY

Decentralization

The decentralization of social and political life is fundamental to the Green vision of a sustainable society. Most of the arguments in favour of such decentralization are deployed below: that face-to-face communities encourage a sense of social responsibility which is lacking in the anonymity of large-scale industrial and city life; that local production for local use with less trade and travel reduces a community's impact on its environment; that 'human-scale' forms of living are more congenial than their modern counterparts; and that decentralized forms of production and exchange satisfy a human demand for improvements in the quality of life rather than catering for the modern – and misplaced – emphasis on quantity. The 'we' in the text refers to Edward Goldsmith and the rest of the editorial board of *The Ecologist* magazine, whose members co-wrote the *Blueprint for Survival*. At the same time, thirty-four distinguished biologists, economists and doctors – such as Sir Julian Huxley, Peter Scott and Sir Frank Fraser-Darling – expressed support for the *Blueprint*'s basic principles.

From Edward Goldsmith *et al; (The Ecologist)*, *A Blueprint for Survival* (Harmondsworth: Penguin, 1972) pp. 50–3.

Possibly the most radical change we propose in the creation of a new social system is decentralization. We do so not because we are sunk in nostalgia for a mythical little England of fêtes, olde worlde pubs, and perpetual conversations over garden fences, but for four much more fundamental reasons.

1. While there is good evidence that human societies can happily remain stable for long periods, there is no doubt that the long transitional stage that we and our children must go through will impose a heavy burden on our moral courage and will require great restraint. Legislation and the operations of police forces and the courts will be necessary to reinforce this restraint, but we believe

that such external controls can never be so subtle or so effective as internal controls. It would therefore be sensible to promote the social conditions in which public opinion and full public participation in decision-making become as far as possible the means whereby communities are ordered. The larger a community the less likely this can be: in a heterogeneous, centralized society such as ours, the restraints of the stable society if they were to be effective would appear as so much outside coercion; but in communities small enough for the general will to be worked out and expressed by individuals confident of themselves and their fellows as individuals, 'us and them' situations are less likely to occur – people having learned the limits of a stable society would be free to order their own lives within them as they wished, and would therefore accept the restraints of the stable society as necessary and desirable and not as some arbitrary restriction imposed by a remote and unsympathetic government.

2. As agriculture depends more and more on integrated control and becomes more diversified, there will no longer be any scope for prairie-type crop-growing or factory-type livestock-rearing. Small farms run by teams with specialized knowledge of ecology, entomology, botany, etc. will then be the rule, and indeed individual small-holdings could become extremely productive suppliers of eggs, fruit and vegetables to neighbourhoods. Thus a much more diversified urban-rural mix will be not only possible but, because of the need to reduce the transportation costs of returning domestic sewage to the land, desirable. In industry, as with agriculture, it will be important to maintain a vigorous feedback between supply and demand in order to avoid waste, overproduction, or production of goods which the community does not really want, thereby eliminating the needless expense of time, energy and money in attempts to persuade it that it does. If an industry is an integral part of a community, it is much more likely to encourage product innovation because people clearly want qualitative improvements in a given field, rather than because expansion is necessary for that industry's survival or because there is otherwise insufficient work for its research and development section. . . .

3. The small community not only is the organizational structure in which internal or systemic controls are most likely to operate effectively, but its dynamic is an essential source of stimulation and pleasure for the individual. Indeed it is probable that only in the small community can a man or woman be an individual. In today's

large agglomerations he is merely an isolate – and it is significant that the decreasing autonomy of communities and local regions and the increasing centralization of decision-making and authority in the cumbersome bureaucracies of the state, have been accompanied by the rise of self-conscious individualism, an individualism which feels threatened unless it is harped upon. . . .

In the small, self-regulating communities observed by anthropologists, there is by contrast no assertion of individualism, and certain individual aspirations may have to be repressed or modified for the benefit of the community – yet no man controls another and each has very great freedom of action, much greater than we have today. At the same time they enjoy the rewards of the small community, of knowing and being known, of an intensity of relationships with a few, rather than urban man's variety of innumerable, superficial relationships. Such rewards should provide ample compensation for the decreasing emphasis on consumption, which will be the inevitable result of the premium on durability which we have suggested should be established so that resources may be conserved and pollution minimized. This premium, while not diminishing our real standard of living, will greatly reduce the turnover of material goods. They will thus be more expensive, although once paid for they should not need replacing except after long periods. Their rapid accumulation will no longer be a realizable or indeed socially acceptable goal, and alternative satisfactions will have to be sought. We believe a major potential source of these satisfactions to be the rich and variegated interchanges and responsibilities of community life, and that these are possible only when such communities are on a human scale.

4. The fourth reason for decentralization is that to deploy a population in small towns and villages is to reduce to the minimum its impact on the environment. This is because the actual urban superstructure required per inhabitant goes up radically as the size of the town increases beyond a certain point. . . .

Thus, if everybody lived in villages the need for sewage treatment plants would be somewhat reduced, while in an entirely urban society they are essential, and the cost of treatment is high. Broadly speaking, it is only by decentralization that we can increase self-sufficiency – and self-sufficiency is vital if we are to minimize the burden of social systems on the ecosystems that support them.

Although we believe that the small community should be the basic unit of society and that each community should be as self-sufficient and self-regulating as possible, we would like to stress that we are not proposing that they be inward-looking, self-obsessed or in any way closed to the rest of the world. Basic precepts of ecology, such as the interrelatedness of all things and the far-reaching effects of ecological processes and their disruption, should influence community decision-making, and therefore there must be an efficient and sensitive communications network between all communities. There must be procedures whereby community actions that effect regions can be discussed at regional level and regional actions with extra-regional effects can be discussed at global level. We have no hard and fast views on the size of the proposed communities, but for the moment we suggest neighbourhoods of 500, represented in communities of 5,000, in regions of 500,000, represented nationally, which in turn as today should be represented globally. We emphasize that our goal should be to create *community feeling* and *global awareness*, rather than that dangerous and sterile compromise which is nationalism.

Bioregionalism

Perhaps the most extreme form of Green decentralist theory is that which goes by the name of 'bioregionalism'. In the pieces below, the American journalist and writer Kirkpatrick Sale gives a succinct summary of the principles of bioregionalism and its implications for social, political, economic and cultural life. All Greens to a certain extent take their 'lessons from nature' as Sale would have them do, but not all will agree with the implications of his conclusions – e.g. that bioregions may have different political systems, and be organized around values which Greens find objectionable. Greens are most likely to extract the spirit from the bioregional project without necessarily following it to the letter.

From Kirkpatrick Sale, 'Mother of All' in Satish Kumar, *The Schumacher Lectures Vol. 2* (London: Abacus, 1974) pp. 224–34, 245–8.

To become 'dwellers in the land', to regain the spirit of the Greeks, to come to know the earth, fully and honestly, the crucial and perhaps only and all-encompassing task is to understand the place, the immediate, specific place, where we live: 'In the question of how we treat the land', as Schumacher says, 'our entire way of life is involved'. We must somehow live as close to it as possible, be in touch with its particular soils, its waters, its winds; we must learn its ways, its capacities, its limits; we must make its rhythms our patterns, its laws our guide, its fruits our bounty.

That, in essence, is bioregionalism.

Now I must acknowledge that 'bioregionalism' is not yet quite a household word . . .

But I believe bioregionalism to be a concept so accessible, so serviceable, so productive – and, after about five years, now so impelling as to have created a momentum of its own – that I feel quite confident in its use. For there is really nothing so mysterious about the components of the word – *bio*, from the Greek for life, *regional*, from the Latin for territory to be ruled, *ism*, from the Greek for doctrine – and nothing, after a moment's thought, so terribly strange in what they convey; and if initially it falls oddly on our ears, that may perhaps only be a measure of how far we have distanced ourselves from its wisdom – and how badly we need it now.

Let me spend a little time excavating this concept of bioregionalism a bit, baring and examining its several layers, as one might in looking at the strata of the earth.

All aspects of the bioregional society – and, one might imagine, a bioregional world – take their forms from that of Gaea herself. One of Gaea's many offspring, the first of all her daughters, was Themis, the goddess of the laws of nature and the mother of the seasons, and it is by a diligent study of her – her laws, her messages, her patterns as they have been established over these many uncounted millenia – that we can guide ourselves in constructing human settlements and systems. This is not, of course, an easy undertaking, for the lessons of nature can sometimes seem confusing and even contradictory; and perhaps I have read them wrong: perhaps only more time and more opportunity to be closer to nature, as close as the preliterate peoples who have twenty words for snow and distinguish thirty kinds of annual seasons, will allow us to learn them properly. But I think I have at least the outlines right, and I am bolstered by the knowledge that they seem to accord well with the findings of many others who have looked in this direction, not the least of whom was Fritz Schumacher himself. . . .

A bioregion is a part of the earth's surface whose rough boundaries are determined by natural rather than human dictates, distinguishable from other areas by attributes of flora, fauna, water, climate soils and landforms, and the human settlements and cultures those attributes have given rise to. The borders between such areas are usually not rigid – nature works with more flexibility and fluidity than that – but the general contours of the regions themselves are not hard to identify, and indeed will probably be felt, understood or sensed, in some way known to many of the inhabitants, and particularly those still rooted in the land, farmers and ranchers, hunters and fishers, foresters and botanists, and most especially, across the face of America, tribal Indians, those still in touch with a culture that for centuries knew the earth as sacred and its well-being as imperative. . . .

The widest region, taking its character from the broadest measures of native vegetation and soil contours, may be called the *ecore-*

gion and will generally cover several hundred thousands of square
miles over several states; it is possible to determine somewhere
between forty and fifty such areas across North America. But within
these ecoregions it is easy to distinguish other coherent territories
that define themselves primarily by their surface features – a water-
shed or river basin, a valley, a desert, a plateau, a mountain range
– and which we may call the *georegion*. And within these georegions,
in turn, one can often locate still smaller areas, of perhaps several
thousand square miles, discrete and identifiable with their own
topographies and inhabitants, their own variations of human culture
and agriculture, to which we may give the name *vitaregion*. . . .

The economy that comes into being within a bioregion also
derives its character from the conditions, the laws, of nature. Our
ignorance is immense, but what we can be said to know with some
surety after these many centuries of living on the soil has been
cogently summarized by Edward Goldsmith*, the editor of *The
Ecologist*, as the Laws of Ecodynamics – to be distinguished, of
course, from the scientistic Laws of Thermodynamics.

The first law is that conservation, preservation, sustenance, is the
central goal of the natural world – hence its ingenerate, fundamental
resistance to large-scale structural change; the second law is that,
far from being entropic (that's an image rightly belonging to physics,
errantly borrowed by scientistic ecologists), nature is inherently
stable, working in all times and places toward what ecology calls a
climax: that is, a balanced, harmonious, integrative state of maturity
which, once reached, is maintained for prolonged periods. From
this it follows that a bioregional economy would seem to maintain
rather than exploit the natural world, accommodate to the environment rather than resist it; it would attempt to create conditions for
a climax, a balance, for what some economists have recently taken
to calling a 'steady state', rather than for perpetual change and
continual growth in service to 'progress', a false and delusory goddess if ever there was one. It would, in practical terms, minimize
resource-use, emphasize conservation and recycling, avoid pollution
and waste. It would adapt its systems to the given bioregional
resources – energy based on wind, for example, where nature called
for that, or wood where that was appropriate, and food based on
what the region itself – particularly in its native, preagricultural
state – could grow.

And thus it would be based, above all, on the most elemental
and most elegant principles of the natural world, that of self-sufficiency. Just as nature does not depend on trade, does not create

elaborate networks of continental dependency, so the bioregion would find all its needed resources – for energy, food, shelter, clothing, craft, manufacture, luxury – within its own environment. And far from being deprived, far from being thus impoverished, it would gain in every measure of economic health. It would be more stable, free from boom-and-bust cycles and distant political crises; it would be able to plan, to allocate its resources, to develop what it wants to develop at the safest pace, in the most ecological manner. It would not be at the mercy of distant and uncontrollable national bureaucracies and transnational governments, and thus it would be more self-regarding, more cohesive, developing a sense of place, of community, of comradeship, and the pride that comes from stability, control, competence and independence. . . .

Political principles on a bioregional scale are also grounded in the dictates presented by nature, in which what is forever valued are not the imperatives of giantism, centralization, hierarchy and monolithicity, but rather, in starkest contraposition, those of scale, decentralization, division and diversity.

Nothing is more striking in the examination of a natural setting than the absence of the forms of authoritarianism, domination and sovereignty that are taken as inevitable in human governance; even the queen bee is queen only because we designate her so. In a healthy ecological niche, or 'econiche', the various sets of animals – whether themselves organized as individuals, families, bands or communal hives – get along with one another without the need of any system of authority or dominance – indeed, without structure or organization of any kind soever. No one species rules, not one even makes the attempt, and the only assertion of power has to do with territory, with a particular area to be left alone in. Each set, each species, in the system has its own methods of organization, but none attempts to impose them on any other or to set itself up as the central source of power or sovereignty. Far from there being contention and discord, the pseudo-Darwinian war of all-against-all, there is, for the most part, balance and adjustment, co-operation among communities, integration into the environment, variety, complexity and flexibility. . . .

I feel I must add here a note that may be painful for those whose allegiance to the precepts of fragmentation and diversification tend to crumble halfway through. Bioregional diversity means exactly that. It does not mean that every region of the north-east, or North America, or the globe, will construct itself upon the values of democracy, equality, liberty, freedom, justice, and other such like *desider-*

ata. It means rather that truly automonous bioregions will likely go their own separate ways and end up with quite disparate political systems – some democracies, no doubt, some direct, some representative, some federative, but undoubtedly all kinds of aristocracies, oligarchies, theocracies, principalities, margravates, duchies and palatinates as well. And some with values, beliefs, standards and customs quite antithetical to those that the people in this room, for example, hold dearest.

Schumacher somewhere quotes with favour Gandhi's remark that it is worthless to go 'dreaming of systems so perfect that no one will need to be good'. But that is exactly what I think is *necessary*. There's no point, it seems to me, in dreaming of systems where we can expect everyone is *going* to be good, not merely because that would produce a fairly vapid society, I should think, but because there's every reason to suppose that it is simply not likely to take place on this planet in this galaxy. We must dream of systems, rather, which allow people to be *people*, in all their variety, to be wrong upon occasion and errant and bad and even evil, to commit the crimes which as near as we know have always been committed – brutality, subjugation, even war – and yet where all social and civil structures work to minimize such errancies and, what is even more important, hold them within strict bounds should they occur. Bioregionalism, properly conceived, is such a construct, because it provides a scale at which misconduct is likely to be mitigated because bonds of community are strong and material, and social needs for the most part fulfilled; at which the consequences of individual and regional actions are visible and unconcealable, and violence can be seen to be a transgression against the environment and its people in defiance of basic ecological common sense; and at which even error and iniquity, should they happen, will not do irreparable damage beyond the narrow regional limits, and will not send their poisons coursing through the veins of entire continents and the world itself. Bioregionalism, properly conceived, not merely tolerates but thrives upon the diversities of human behaviour, and the varieties of political and social arrangements those give rise to, even if at times they may stem from the baser rather than the more noble motives. In any case, there is no other way to have it. . . .

It is a necessary part of any political construct that it offer an image of the future that can be regarded as positive and liberating and realistic and energizing. This, I submit, bioregionalism succeeds in doing.

For what the bioregional vision suggests is a way of living that not merely can take us away from the calamities of the present, the diseases of our quotidian lives, but can provide its own in-dwelling enrichments and satisfactions, a widening of human possibilities. Imagine, if you will, the joy of knowing, as we can imagine from the scholarly record, what the American Indians knew: the meaning of the changes of wind on a summer afternoon; the ameliorative properties of everyday plants; the comfort of tribal, clannish and community ties throughout life; the satisfaction of being rooted in history, in lore, in place; the excitement of a culture understandable because of its imminence in the simple realities of the surroundings. Imagine a life primarily of contemplation and leisure, where work takes up only a few hours a day – an average of less than four, according to the studies of non-literate societies – where conversation and making love and play become the common rituals of the afternoon, and there is no scramble for the necessities of life because they are provided regularly, equally, joyfully, and without charge. Imagine a life – and here I am paraphrasing an anthropologist's description of a California Indian tribe – where people feel themselves to be something other than independent, autonomous individuals . . . deeply bound together with other people and with the surrounding non-human forms of life in a complex interconnected web of being, a true community in which all creatures and all things can be felt almost as brothers and sisters . . . and where the principle of non-exploitation, of respect and reverence for all creatures, all living things, is as much a part of life as breathing.

But I think, however enchanting that image might be, the bioregional vision is even more important in that it actually has an air of the practical, the do-able, the achievable: it has the smell of reality about it. . . .

And finally, the bioregional vision does not demand elaborate wrenchings of either physical or human realities. It does not posit, on the one hand, the violent interference with nature that so many of the scientistic technofix visions of the future do – those, for example, that ask for icebergs to be floated into deserts, or the Great Plains to be given over to concentrated nuclear power plants (it does not, for that matter, have anything whatsoever to do with nuclear fission, the single most unnatural project humankind has ever devised), or rockets full of people to be fired millions of miles away into space colonies around the sun. And it does not imagine, on the other, the creation of some kind of unlikely and never-before-encountered superbeings, as do so many of the reformist and radical visions of the future – those, for example, that promise 'a new socialist man' without motives of greed or self-interest, or that plan by education or religion or therapy to evolve a populace living in aquarian harmony without human vices. On the contrary, bioregionalism insists on taking the world as it is – if anything, making it more 'as it is' – and taking people, as I indicated before, as they are.

Abandon Affluence!

As a conclusion to his book *Abandon Affluence!* Ted Trainer paints a picture of what he believes a just and sustainable society would look like. Trainer's picture is a radical one. He promotes frugality over affluence, darning socks ahead of buying new ones, close-knit neighbourhoods over cities, and backyard vegetable plots ahead of supermarkets. Not all Greens would go along with this to the letter (at least not in public), but they will all derive their inspiration from it, and in this sense Trainer provides us with an opportunity to peer into a Green future. Some of us will be pleased to see that we can keep our word processors.

From Ted Trainer, *Abandon Affluence!* (London: Zed Books, 1985) pp. 248–79.

The basic premise: the total rejection of affluence and growth

The most obvious requirement is that the alternative society must be one in which per capita rates of consumption of non-renewable resources are *far* lower than they are now in developed countries. The fundamental realization must be that a safe and just society cannot be an affluent society. We have been fooled by decades of cheap resources, principally oil, into believing that Los Angeles provides the appropriate development model for mankind. We have come to assume that the norm for all people can be an expensive house full of electrical gadgets with two cars in the garage, and that it is in order to drive 30 km to work and to jet 3,000 km for a holiday and to eat food produced on the other side of the world. We have seen that a few of us can live like this – but only if the rest do not. . . .

A materially frugal lifestyle

Our alternative society would involve a lifestyle in which a minimum of unnecessary items were produced. It is not easy to say where lines should be drawn, but there are huge numbers of items we could cease producing without significantly affecting anyone's quality of life. We would, in general, have to limit ourselves to acquiring what we needed or could derive a great deal of enjoyment or convenience from, which means we would have to give up the idea of buying things for fun, buying novelties and unnecessary gifts, buying more clothes than we need, buying more expensive and elaborate versions of things that we need, and so on. But would people limit themselves like this? Of course they would not if they continued to hold the values and perspectives most people now hold. The task is to help people to understand the reasons why it is wise to accept a frugal lifestyle and to understand that these reasons include the possibility of achieving a higher quality of life than derives from striving to become materially richer. Acquiring things is important to many of us today because there is not much else that yields interest and a sense of progress and satisfaction in life. In the alternative situation there would be far more important sources of satisfaction available to all.

It goes without saying that it would be a zealously conserving society. People would save, re-cycle, repair, wear out old clothes and look after things. They would be continually concerned to eliminate unnecessary use, to find more efficient ways, and to cut down on resource throughput. These concerns may strike the conventional housekeeper as inconvenient responsibilities; but in a conserver society they become an important part of the art of living. The conserver derives satisfaction from doing things in resource-efficient ways, in finding uses for things that once were thrown away, in making things last, in caring for tools, in improving designs or procedures. To a conventional outsider it would probably appear to be a somewhat drab and impoverished existence because people would spend much of their times in old and much-repaired clothes and houses, making do with worn and shabby appliances. Things would not gleam with freshly painted and polished surfaces and there would not be a premium on newness and fashion. But to the conserver, worn or makeshift or patched-up appearances are sources of considerable satisfaction since they represent important achievements. When one understands the shortage of resources in the world, making an old jumper last two more years through darning and careful use becomes a valuable and satisfying contribution. . . .

As much self-sufficiency as possible

Our high per capita resource-use rates are due in large part to the fact that households and neighbourhoods produce for themselves so few of the goods and services they consume. Commercially produced food not only requires a lot of energy to produce, but perhaps ten times as much energy has to be spent getting it from the farm gate to the kitchen. On the other hand, food grown in the backyard may not involve any cost in non-renewable resources. Our alternative society will achieve much of its saving through producing many goods and services at home and in the neighbourhood. We can make most of our own clothing and footwear, we can grow much of our own food, we can make most of our own furniture, solar panels and indeed our own housing. We can also provide many of the services we need, such as care of convalescents, handicapped and old people, and toddlers, using the non-professional human resources within our neighbourhood. Surpluses from one household could be exchanged for those from others nearby, through co-operatives or weekend bazaars, or simply by being left at the drop-in centre for others to take as they wish.

A high degree of self-sufficiency will require neighbourhoods to be permeated by small-scale productive devices, most obviously gardens, workshops, craft centres, animal pens, ponds for fish and ducks, re-cycling systems, storage sheds, greenhouses, and solar and wind systems. For many purposes, the block with its ten to twenty houses would be the appropriate unit for organization and interaction. These houses might all flush their wastes into the one garbage gas unit, which would also produce high quality garden fertilizer (at more than half a tonne per person per year, when kitchen scraps are included). They might all draw from the one windmill and heat storage tank, and make most use of the house on the block which has been converted to a group workshop, craft centre, library, computer terminal, store, drop-in centre and focal point for meetings, hobbies, leisure activities and entertainment. Where the back fences used to meet there might be a compact collection of jointly operated fowl pens, fish ponds, fruit trees and greenhouses. . . .

But would it not be far less efficient to produce things in back-yards than in factories? We would retain many large factories with sophisticated plant, and much more production would be carried out in the many small decentralized firms. But perhaps most of the important things we now consume could be produced by households. In many cases that efficiency would rival that of our present large-scale producers. This is especially so in primary industry. The peasant and the home gardener are usually much more efficient producers than agribusiness when energy and other non-labour inputs are considered. McRobie discusses small brickworks operating in the Third World producing bricks at half the unit price typical of normal plants with a hundred times the output. Nevertheless many of the things produced at home certainly would be much more costly in terms of labour time than factory produced items. A homemade chair may well be ten times as 'expensive'; but this might not matter at all if its home production is experienced as a satisfying activity. If our concern is simply to maximize the efficiency of production, where this is defined solely in dollar terms, then we should allow the transnational corporation to set up one or two super-technology factories in Taiwan to supply all the world's chairs; but along with the efficiency we will get non-repairable throwaway chairs, no control over the industry, and loss of jobs, and all chair-making labour will have been turned into a boring process of watching computerized machinery. . . .

Alternative technology

It should not need to be pointed out that a low resource-use society would make extensive use of alternative technologies. These are generally simple, exciting, ecologically sensible and in need of little or no research and development. There are many well-understood and widely practised alternative procedures for the production of food, clothing, housing, water and energy. Our houses and backyards could contain solar panels, ponds, re-cycling systems, compost heaps, windmills, and greenhouses. We would make maximum use of passive solar housing design. Above all we would convert to the use of the best, cheapest and most abundant building material known, namely, earth. Rammed earth or mud-brick technologies are ideal for house construction. These houses can be superior to conventional houses in durability, insulation capacity, fire resistance and especially in dollar and non-renewable resource costs. A family could build its own basic dwelling in a few months, gaining exercise and satisfaction in the process and incurring little or no debt. . . .

All wastes from the block would go into a garbage gas digester or compost heaps, and then into ponds and gardens, eliminating all need for sewage treatment works, mains, pumping for domestic wastes. All space heat would come from solar panels via the underground hot water storage tanks which double as the source of domestic water. Most of the water would be collected from roofs, eliminating the need for most water supply mains. Some fraction of electricity could come from windmills and photo-electric cells. On the national level, biomass could become the main source of liquid fuels. Some of these alternatives involve high capital costs, but they will not be needed in the quantities required to sustain an industrialized society and it is therefore probable that we will be able to afford sufficient capacity.

It is not necessary to devote much space here to outlining the technologies available since most of them are common knowledge. Some reference, however, should be made to permaculture. Even densely populated suburban areas could be planted with shrubs and herbs that in time form a largely self-maintaining permanent ecosystem supplying many food items and materials with little cost in labour or resource inputs. Whereas a great deal of energy is needed to sow and harvest a wheat field, a permaculture forest will look after itself year after year and provide fruits and materials that can be taken when needed. The many niches in the ecosystem can be filled with plants and animals which meet each other's needs and therefore do much of the 'work' required to maintain the system. Worms do most of the digging, fowls can feed themselves on fallen fruit, large trees can shelter herbs from the sun, fowls can cultivate shrubs while foraging for soil organisms. . . .

The decentralization of much production into backyards and factories within easy cycling distance of home will cut down the high distribution costs we now incur. We will cease to transport most food over large distances. We will reduce travel to centralized work places. We will make huge savings by dealing with sewage on the block rather than pumping it tens of kilometres to be thrown away through resource and energy-intensive treatment works. Some of the most spectacular savings will derive from the local production of energy. Electricity generated in a conventional power station represents only about one third of the energy in the power station fuel, but one sixth of the electricity is then lost in transit to your house and in running the Electricity Commission's workshops and offices. There will be hardly any losses of this sort when the energy comes from the solar panels and windmill on the block, which we can maintain without the need for an electricity bureaucracy or expert technicians.

A shift to more communal and co-operative ways

Some of the most valuable and generally unrecognized benefits of de-development would occur in the realm of community relations. Here we would become richer in 'spiritual' ways precisely because we had become poorer in material ways. De-development would force people together, it would require them to co-operate on important common goals, to share, to get to know each other, to depend on and to help each other and therefore to build the social relations that are so impoverished in affluent society.

The neighbourhood would have to take on the organization and running of many services now provided by centralized and resource-expensive agencies, notably councils and corporations. Because councils and central authorities would be much less extensive, small local groups would have to organize themselves to deal with many problems like maintenance of libraries and public parks. Rosters and responsibilities would have to be arranged for the care of small children, maintenance of the windmill, care of the old and of convalescents. There would have to be committees and meetings although most things might be attended to through informal and spontaneous discussion and co-operation. Neighbours would have to talk to each other about important things. After the roads had been dug up more communal property would exist so communal decisions would have to be made about the best uses to which it is to be put. Communities would have to take responsibility for themselves. . . .

A place for high technology

The tight energy budget underlying this discussion should permit all important high technology to continue. There is no reason why medical research, for instance, should be curtailed. Remember that perhaps half the world's scientists and technologists are now working on arms production and many of the remainder are working directly or indirectly on the production of unnecessary gadgets. When we cut back on the production of non-necessities we should be able greatly to increase research on projects that contribute to the quality of life.

Reducing resource consumption need not require much change in the availability of electronic media, computerized information services or the use of microprocessors, as these are not very expensive in terms of energy and resource use. The media would take on a significant responsibility in substituting for travel to different lands and to events such as theatre performances, and in keeping a less mobile population informed about what was happening in other places.

Green Defence

When the Green movement was still in the political wilderness it could afford to ignore some of the thornier problems of daily political existence. As its star has risen, though, these problems have demanded urgent attention, both in the face of prodding by established political parties and in response to calls for clarification from the public at large. The electorate has increasingly asked: is this a movement with a range of policies 'beyond the environment'? This is especially true of subjects which, on the face of it, are anathema to Green thinking, such as defence – the subject of the following piece by Brian Tokar. Tokar is a graduate from the Massachussets Institute of Technology and has worked in a number of fields, including environmental consultancy and computer programming. He is a founder member of the New England Committees of Correspondence and the Central Vermont Greens and lives part-time in a tepee.

From Brian Tokar, *The Green Alternative* (San Pedro, California: R. and E. Miles, © 1987) pp. 119–21.

The problem of defending our own [American] borders appears to be a relatively manageable one.

In Europe, however, the problem of defending one's own borders is much more real. All Europeans lost friends and relatives during the Second World War and memories of that war's destruction are still quite fresh. This has raised an important debate among European Greens about just what kind of defence is most compatible with Green principles. It is a debate North Americans can learn a great deal from.

One group of Greens, which includes several former NATO officers, has developed the concept of a decentralized, non-nuclear border defence. As nuclear weapons are dismantled and foreign troops are withdrawn, each country could line its frontiers with the heavy armour and defensive anti-aircraft weaponry necessary to deter an attack. In different regions of a country, defensive installations would be managed by militias of local volunteers intimately familiar with their region's terrain. All weapons capable of striking other lands and peoples would be dismantled, whether nuclear or conventional. The elimination of large military bases would remove the sorts of targets that invite massive military assaults.

At the same time, we could see a rise in locally-initiated popular diplomacy, helping break the current deadlocks on the road to peace. In the United States, there would be efforts by different regions of our country to engage in pacts of non-aggression and peace with other peoples, including the Soviet Union. One hundred and thirty localities in the United States, and many more in Europe, Japan and the South Pacific, have already voted to declare themselves Nuclear Free Zones. Genuine steps toward economic decentralization would eliminate huge industrial targets, in addition to explicitly military ones. Our 'national security' would be based upon the integrity of our own people, rather than the extended web of overseas 'security interests' and corporate investments that bind our government to its current interventionist policies.

For many Greens, however, this kind of an approach does not go far enough. They support local disarmament initiatives, but view even a decentralized military defence as a dangerous and short-sighted idea. They feel that it still legitimizes violent solutions to conflicts and does not sufficiently address the cultural roots of militarism. It could create a fortress mentality that sustains rather than dissolves national chauvinism. Even voluntary militias, bringing together and empowering those individuals who have a personal affinity for military weaponry and military ways of being, could actually help preserve our society's most aggressive tendencies.

Greens who profess a personal commitment to non-violence as a way of life have proposed a different solution. If we are to follow our opposition to the arms race to its conclusion, their argument goes, we should be willing to live our own lives, without the false protection afforded by any arsenals of weapons. Violence breeds violence and the ability of any occupying army, or any existing government, to control a population requires that most people passively acquiesce to being ruled. A people united in their desire for freedom and well-prepared in the methods of non-violent resistance should, in this view, be able to mount a non-military social defence against any potential invader.

Historical precedents for this include the successful resistance of people in the Scandinavian countries to the full consolidation of Nazi control during the Second World War and the widespread internal sabotage of the Polish economy in the months following the imposition of martial law in 1981. Gandhi and his supporters developed a full-fledged plan to prevent non-violently a German occupation of India during the Second World War. A high enough level of non-cooperation, civil disobedience and sabotage, it is argued, should be sufficient to render any country ungovernable. The awareness that a people is prepared to respond in this manner should discourage potential invaders, as the difficulty of mounting a successful occupation would quickly outweigh any possible benefits. Most of the repressive military regimes in the world today could not survive without constant infusions of military supplies and brutal counterinsurgency training, most often supplied by the United States. A Green decentralist outlook with a firm commitment to personal empowerment through non-violence, might be the key to breaking the habits of subservience that keep people from fully asserting their freedom.

In the industrialized world today, non-violent resistance is clearly the most important tool for opposing the arms and all forms of militarism. Non-violent action exposes the moral barrenness of the arms race in a society that believes it is committed to peace. Non-violent activists speak truth to power and help people realize all the ways they quietly support the arms race by simply carrying on their daily lives.

A Possible Utopia

The reflections of French social theorist André Gorz on Marxism in the modern age have led him into political-ecological territory and he has meditated at length on issues close to Green hearts, such as the decline of the working-class as a political force, the nature of work in post-industrial societies and the political implications of scarcity. The following extract is called 'A Possible Utopia' and while it would not be endorsed by all Greens, its advocacy of communitarian living, self-reliance, public transport and something like a basic income*, together with its assertion that economic growth does not necessarily result in an improvement in the quality of life, all make this – at least in parts – a recognizably Green Utopia. Some Greens, though, will baulk at the highly automated future which Gorz envisages as well as the centralized political system he seems to think necessary. Some have even suggested that his 'social labour' proposals take us into the dystopian realms of totalitarianism rather than into a Green Utopia, properly speaking.

From André Gorz, *Ecology as Politics* (London: Pluto Press, 1983) pp. 42–50.

When they woke up that morning, the citizens asked themselves what new turmoil waited them. After the elections, but during the period of transition to the new administration, a number of factories and enterprises had been taken over by the workers. The young unemployed, who for the previous two years had been occupying abandoned plants in order to engage in 'wildcat production' of various socially useful products, were now joined by a growing number of students, older workers who had been laid off recently, and retired people. In many places, empty buildings were being transformed into communes, production cooperatives, or 'alternative schools'. In the schools themselves, the older pupils were taking the lead in practising skills for self-reliance and, with or without the collaboration of the teachers, establishing hydroponic gardens and facilities for raising fish and rabbits; in addition, students were beginning to install equipment for woodworking, metalworking, and other crafts which had for a long time been neglected or relegated to marginal institutions.

The day after the new government came into office, those who set out for work found a surprise awaiting them: during the night, in most of the larger cities, white lines had been painted on all the major thoroughfares. Henceforth these would have a corridor reserved for buses, while on the sidestreets similar corridors were set aside for bicyclists and motorcyclists. At the major points of entry to each city, hundreds of bicycles and mopeds were assembled for use by the public, and long lines of police cars and army vans supplemented the buses. On this morning, no tickets were being sold or required on the buses or suburban trains.

At noon, the government announced that it had reached the decision to institute free public transportation throughout the country, and to phase out, over the next twelve months, the use of private automobiles in the most congested urban areas. Seven hundred new tramway lines would be created or reopened in the major metropolitan centers, and twenty-six thousand new buses would be added to city fleets during the course of the year. The government also announced the immediate elimination of sales tax on bicycles and small motorbikes, thus reducing their purchase price by 20 per cent.

That evening, the President of the Republic and the Prime Minister went on nationwide television to explain the larger design behind these measures. Since 1972, the President said, the GNP per person in France has reached a level close to that of the United States – the difference varying between 5 and 12 per cent according to the fluctuations in the value of the franc, which has been notoriously undervalued. 'Indeed, my fellow citizens,' the President concluded, 'we have nearly caught up with the US. But,' he added soberly, 'this is not something to be proud of.'. . .

'Economic growth has brought us neither greater equity nor greater social harmony and appreciation of life. I believe we have followed the wrong path and must now seek a new course.' Consequently, the government had developed a programme for 'an alternative pattern of growth, based on an alternative economy and alternative institutions.' The philosophy underlying this programme, the President stated, could be summed up in three basic points:

1. 'We shall work less.' Until now, the purpose of economic activity was to amass capital in order to increase production and sales, and to create profits which, reinvested, would permit the accumulation of more capital, and so on. But this process must inevitably reach an impasse. Beyond a certain point, it could not continue unless it destroyed the surplus which it had created. 'We have reached that point today,' the President said. 'It is, in fact, only by wasting our labour and our resources that we have managed in the past to create a semblance of the full employment of people and productive capacities.'

In the future, therefore, it was necessary to consider working less, more effectively, and in new ways. He said that the Prime Minister would spell out the details of proposed measures for change in this direction. Without going into them, the President nevertheless stated that they would give substance to the following principle: 'Every individual will, as a matter of right, be entitled to the satisfaction of his or her needs, regardless of whether or not he or she has a job.' He argued that once the productive machinery reaches the level of technical efficiency where a fraction of the available workforce can supply the needs of the entire population, it is no longer possible to make the right to a full income dependent on having a full-time job. 'We have earned,' the President concluded, 'the right to free work and to free time.'

2. 'We must consume better.' Until now, products have been designed to produce the greatest profit for the firms selling them. 'Henceforth,' the President said, 'they will be designed to produce the greatest satisfaction for those who use them as well as for those who produce them.'

To this end, the dominant firms in each sector would become the property of society. The task of the great firms would be to produce, in each area, a restricted number of standardized products, of equal quality and in sufficient amounts, to satisfy the needs of all. The design of these products would be based on four fundamental criteria: durability, ease of repair, pleasantness of manufacture, and absence of polluting effects.

The durability of products, expressed in hours of use, would be required to appear alongside the price. 'We foresee a very strong foreign demand for these products,' the President added, 'for they will be unique in the world.'

3. 'We must re-integrate culture into the everyday life of all.' Until

now, the extension of education had gone hand in hand with that of generalized incompetence.

Thus, said the President, we unlearned how to raise our own children, how to cook our own meals and make our own music. Paid technicians now provide our food, our music, and our ideas in prepackaged form. 'We have reached the point,' the President remarked, 'where parents consider that only state-certified professionals are qualified to raise their children adequately.' Having earned the right to leisure, we appoint professional buffoons to fill our emptiness with electronic entertainment, and content ourselves with complaining about the poor quality of the goods and services we consume.

It had become urgent, the President said, for individuals and communities to regain control over the organization of their existence, over their relationships and their environment. 'The recovery and extension of individual and social autonomy, is the only method of avoiding the dictatorship of the state.'

The President then turned to the Prime Minister for a statement of the new programme. The latter began by reading a list of twenty-nine enterprises and corporations whose socialization would be sought in the National Assembly. More than half belonged to the consumer goods sector, in order to be able to give immediate application to the principles of 'working less' and 'consuming better'.

To translate these principles into practice, the Prime Minister said it was necessary to rely on the workers themselves. They would be free to hold general assemblies and set up specialized groups, following the system devised by the workers of Lip, where planning is done in specialized committees, but decisions are taken by the general assembly. The workers should allow themselves a month, the Prime Minister estimated, to define, with the assistance of outside advisers and consumer groups, a reduced range of product models and new sets of quality standards and production targets. New management systems had already been devised by a semi-clandestine group of Ministry of Finance officials.

During this first month, said the Prime Minister, production work should be done only in the afternoons, the mornings being reserved for collective discussion. The workers should set as their goal the organizing of the productive process to meet the demands for essential goods, while at the same time reducing their average worktime to twenty-four hours a week. The number of workers would evidently have to be increased. There would, he promised, be no shortage of women and men ready to take these jobs. . . .

The government's economic aim, the Prime Minister stated, was gradually to eliminate commodity production and exchange by decentralizing and scaling down production units in such a way that each community was able to meet at least half its needs. The source of the waste and frustration of modern life, the Prime Minister noted, was that 'no one consumes what he or she produces and no one produces what he or she consumes'.

As a first step in the new direction, the government had negotiated with the bicycle industry an immediate 30 per cent increase in production, but with at least half of all the bicycles and motorcycles being provided as kits to be put together by the users themselves. Detailed instruction sheets had been printed up, and assembly shops with all the necessary tools would be installed without delay in town halls, schools, police stations, army barracks, and in parks and parking lots.

The Prime Minister voiced the hope that in the future local communities would develop this kind of initiative themselves: each neighbourhood, each town, indeed each apartment block, should set up studios and workshops for free creative work and production; places where, during their free time, people could produce whatever they wished thanks to the increasingly sophisticated array of tools which they would find at their disposal (including stereo equipment or closed-circuit television). The twenty-four hour week and the fact that income would no longer depend on holding a job would permit people to organize so as to create neighbourhood services (caring for children, helping the old and the sick, teaching each other new skills) on a co-operative or mutual-aid basis, and to install convenient neighbourhood facilities and equipment. 'Stop asking, whenever you have a problem, "What is the government doing about it?"' the Prime Minister exclaimed. 'The government's vocation is to abdicate into the hands of the people.' . . .

'Defending our territory,' the Prime Minister said, 'requires first of all that we occupy it. National sovereignty depends first of all on our capacity to grow our own food.' For this reason the government would do everything possible to encourage a hundred thousand people a year to establish themselves in the depopulated regions of the country, and to reintroduce and improve organic farming methods and other 'soft' technologies. All necessary scientific and technical assistance would be provided free for five years to newly established rural communities. This would do more to overcome world hunger, he added, than the export of nuclear power stations or insecticide factories.

The Prime Minister concluded by saying that, in order to encourage the exercise of imagination and the greater exchange of ideas, no television programmes would be broadcast on Fridays and Saturdays.

Ecofeminism

Ecofeminism is hardly a household word, but it has begun to make an impression both on the Green movement and also on the feminist movement at large. Its aims are not the same as those associated with the dominant liberal feminist position. This means that ecofeminists do not seek equality with men, as such, but rather want us to recognize that women's liberation means liberation for women *as women*. They have a specific understanding of what 'being a woman' involves, and they believe that women's liberation will require a positive revaluation of those activities and sites of activity traditionally associated with women – giving birth, nurturing and the domestic arena. This has led other feminists to baulk at the ecofeminist project, seeing it as reinforcing the stereotypes which are used to oppress women. Below, the Canadian ecofeminist Judith Plant sets out the main principles: the closeness of women to nature (with the implication that women are potentially in the political-ecological vanguard); the belief that the domination of women and the despoliation of nature have the same root cause: patriarchy; and the need to re-establish for nature the organic metaphor over the machine metaphor (Fritjof Capra*). Finally, Plant suggests that the bioregional project* comes closest to providing the socio-political context within which ecofeminism's schemes could best be carried out.

From Judith Plant 'Women and Nature', *Green Line* (Oxford) offprint, not dated, pp. 1–8.

Women have long been associated with nature – metaphorically, as in 'Mother Earth', for instance. Our language says it all: a 'virgin' forest is one awaiting exploitation, as yet untouched by man. In society, too, women have been associated with the physical side of life. Our role has been 'closer to nature', our natural work centred around human physical requirements: eating, sex, cleaning, the care of children, and sick people. We have taken care of day-to-day life so that men have been able to go 'out into the world', to create and enact methods of exploiting nature, including other human beings. Then to return to a home-life which waits in readiness. (A man's home is his castle.)

Historically, women have had no real power in the outside world, no place in decision-making. Intellectual life, the work of the mind, has traditionally not been accessible to women – due in part to society's either/or mentality, coupled with a valuing of the spiritual over the natural. Women have been generally passive, as has been nature. Today, however, ecology speaks for the earth, for the 'other' in human/environmental relationships; and feminism speaks for the 'other' in female/male relations. And ecofeminism, by speaking for the original others, seeks to understand the interconnected roots of all domination, and ways to resist and change. . . .

Before the world was mechanized and industrialized, the metaphor that explained self, society and the cosmos was the image of organism. This is not surprising since most people were connected with the earth in their daily lives, being peasants and living a subsistence existence. The earth was seen as female. And with two faces: one, the passive, nurturing mother; the other, wild and uncontrollable. Thus the earth, giver and supporter of life, was symbolized by woman, as was the image of nature as disorder, with her storms, droughts, and other natural disasters.

These images served as cultural constraints. The earth was seen to be alive, sensitive; it was considered unethical to do violence towards her. Who could conceive of killing a mother, or of digging into her body for gold, or mutilating her? In relation to mining, people believed that minerals and metals ripened in the uterus of the earth; they compared mines to Mother Earth's vagina, and metallurgy itself was an abortion of the metal's natural growth cycle. So rituals were carried out by miners: offerings to the gods of the soil and the subterranean world, ceremonial sacrifices, sexual abstinence and fasting were conducted and observed before violating what was considered to be the sacred earth. . . .

The organic metaphor that once explained everything was replaced by mechanical images. . . .

The new images were of controlling and dominating: having power over nature. Where the nurturing image had once been a cultural restraint, the new image of mastery allowed the clearing of forests and the damming of rivers. Nature as unlimited resource is epitomized today by scarred hillsides, uranium mine tailings poisoning river systems, toxic waste, and human junk floating in space.

One theory bases this propensity for domination over nature on the human fear that nature is more powerful than human beings. By subduing and controlling nature, society thus can assume power over life. Women, with their biological connection with life-giving, are a constant reminder of the reality of human mortality. Thus patriarchal society, based on a view that subjugated nature to the spirit of man (*sic*), also subjugated woman. . . .

Once we understand the historical connections between women and nature and their subsequent oppression, we cannot help but take a stand on war against nature. By participating in environmental stand-offs against those who are assuming the right to control the natural world, we are helping to create an awareness of domination at all levels. From this perspective, consensus decision making and non-hierarchical organization become accepted facts of life.

Ecofeminism gives women and men common ground. While women may have been associated with nature, this does not mean that somehow they have been socialized in a different world from men. Women have learned to think in the same dualities as men, and we feel just as alienated as do our brothers. The social system isn't good for either – or both – of us. Yet, we are the social system. We need some common ground from which to be critically self-conscious, to enable us to recognize and affect the deep structure of our relations, with each other and with our environment.

In addition to participating in forms of resistance, such as non-violent civil disobedience, we can also encourage, support and develop within our communities a cultural life which celebrates the many differences in nature, and which encourages reflection on the consequences of our actions, in all our relations. . . .

Women's values, centred around life-giving, must be revalued, elevated from their once-subordinate role. What women know from experience needs recognition and respect. We have had generations of experience in conciliation, dealing with interpersonal conflicts daily in domestic life. We know how to feel for others because we have been socialized that way.

At the same time, our work – tending to human physical requirements – has been undervalued. As discussed earlier, what has been considered material and physical has been thought to be 'less than' the intellectual, the 'outside' (of home) world. Women have been very much affected by this devaluation and this is reflected in our images of ourselves and our attitudes towards our work. Men too have been alienated from child-care and all the rest of daily domestic life which very much nurtures all who participate. Our society has devalued the source of its humanness. Home is the theatre of our human ecology, and it is here that we can effectively think feelingly. Bioregionalism, essentially, is attempting to rebuild human and natural community. We know that it is non-adaptive to repeat the social organization which left women and children alone, at home, and men out in the world doing the 'important' work. The real work is at home. As part of this process, woman and nature, indeed humans and nature, need a new image of ourselves, as we mend our relations with each other and with the earth. Such an image will surely reflect what we are learning through the study of ecology, what we are coming to understand through feminism, and what we are experiencing by participating in the bioregional project. Much depends on us, on our determination to make things different and to take a stand.

The Spiritual Dimension

For a public which has been brought up on the belief that Green politics involves nothing more profound or onerous than buying the right petrol or aerosols (green consumerism*), the idea of 'green spirituality' will seem particularly irrelevant. Not so. In private, if not yet in public, Greens will make a point of saying that their project involves much more than winning a few seats in national legislatures; rather, it involves a remaking of our relationship with the natural world. This remaking will be spiritual, in recognition of our being part of something greater than ourselves – something so inscrutably complex that it transcends understanding and demands respect. From this point of view (sometimes called 'deep green') a sustainable relationship with our environment will be built in the spirit rather than in the supermarket. Besides being a useful introduction to the spiritual dimension, the paragraphs below, from Walter and Dorothy Schwarz (Walter Schwarz is the religious affairs correspondent for the British newspaper *The Guardian*), also reveal how hard it will be for Greens to get this message across to a predominantly sceptical, secular and materialistic public.

From Walter and Dorothy Schwarz, *Breaking Through* (Bideford: Green Books, 1987) pp. 235, 237–8, 245–6.

Human-scale thinking must have spiritual content. If we are to move from partial, fragmented, compartmentalized living towards completeness and wholistic living, we have to put back what our dominant industrial-materialist-scientific world view leaves out. That world view is not wrong, any more than science is wrong or capitalism or socialism are wrong; its shortcoming is in what it omits. That omitted area is what we mean by spiritual.

In that sense, the spiritual is not identified with any actual religion, nor confined to religious sentiment; it includes the intuitive, the non-measurable, the aesthetic, the caring and the loving.

All these aspects of our consciousness have been progressively relegated in our world to the domain of the private, subjective, even secret world of the individual. They are not considered to have direct relevance to society, except in churches. They have been demoted to the second class of values, after demand and supply, freedom and mobility, comfort and welfare, education and health. . . .

░░░░░░░

Another requirement for human survival, as our own book has shown, is a deeper awareness of the natural environment. And here, too, there can be no awareness which is not spiritual; otherwise we are talking yet again, of a quantifiable commodity called environment and of a department of life instead of life itself. The American ecological writers make this point with the greatest eloquence. Robinson Jeffers wrote:

> I believe that the Universe is one being, all its parts are different expressions of the same energy, and they are all in communication with each other, therefore parts of one organic whole. (This is physics, I believe, as well as religion.) . . . This whole is in all its parts so beautiful, and if felt by me to be so intensely in earnest, that I am compelled to love it, and to think of it as divine. It seems to me that this whole alone is worthy of the deeper sort of love; and that there is peace, freedom, I might say a kind of salvation, in turning one's affections outward towards this one God, rather than inwards on one's self, or on humanity, or on human imaginations and abstractions – the world of spirits. I think that it is our privilege and felicity to love God for his beauty, without claiming or expecting love from him. We are not important to him, but he to us. I think that one may contribute (ever so slightly) to the beauty of things by making one's own life and environment beautiful, so far as one's power reaches.

We are talking about attention to spiritual needs which is ecologically aware, but not necessarily linked to an established religion. Those who agree do not normally start from revelation or from mystic experience; they start from the material world of people, animals, plants and landscape. They find, as Schumacher did on a visit to Leningrad, that our official map of reality is woefully incomplete. Everywhere in Leningrad, Schumacher saw churches; but these large landmarks, so obvious to his eye, had not been included on his Intourist map. He was reminded of the missing landmarks on the official maps of our civilization. Everything which is subjective, which cannot be proved, is left out. . . .

⁂

Do we need a new religion for the post-industrial age? There are indeed many signs of restiveness within established religions, and some of these imply dissatisfaction with an image of God that has become unacceptable in a scientific context. Theologians and scientists have tried to re-define God in such phrases as 'the source of your ultimate concern, what you take seriously without reservation'. Einstein suggested: 'the central order of things and events'.

Many green-thinking people who identify themselves with a new age spirituality, notably in the influential Findhorn Foundation in northern Scotland, practise a personal faith that is rooted in nature and has echoes of vitalism and even pantheism. Findhorn began semi-miraculously in 1962 by 'communion with nature' that produced forty-pound cabbages and eight-inch delphiniums in almost barren soil. Caroline Hall, a member, sums up her faith by analogy with a hologram, an idea widely used in wholistic thought. A hologram is a representation in which every detail contains a picture of the whole, unlike a photograph which produces an effect through individual dots meaningless in isolation.

> Every part of our universe is a hologram. Each cell, each plant, each person contains a picture of the whole. So every time I experience God a little more, the universe experiences God a little more; each time I dissolve a negative thought form and replace it with knowledge of abundance, so I bring a bit more awareness of abundance into the planet. This is the central message of the Findhorn Foundation: you and I as individuals are vitally important to the growth and development of our world. The way I live my life, both inner and outer, can bring the world closer to God, or move us further away.

Frugality and Freedom

Two of the objections people often raise when they think of living in a Green society are that life would be more boring and less free. They believe it would be more boring because, as the American writer and lecturer William Ophuls says below: 'men whose ambition it is to conquer the stars for the human race and undertake equally great deeds will find frugality a little humdrum'. And they believe it will be less free both because we shall not to be able to consume as voraciously as we do at present, and because government will need to impose restrictions upon us in the name of sustainability. In this extract, Ophuls grasps the nettle of both objections. First, he states that fulfilment can take many more forms than those provided for by our high-speed, modern society. Second, he accepts that 'certain kinds of rights' would have to be given up, but follows standard Green thinking by saying that these restrictions should be self-imposed rather than demanded by government diktat. Ophuls makes one other important distinction: between a sustainable society and a *just* sustainable society. In principle a sustainable society could take many political forms, and in their desire to get across the message of sustainability, Greens may not have said enough about what they consider the desirable political and economic relations between people to be.

From W. Ophuls, 'The Politics of the Sustainable Society' in D. Pirages (ed), *The Sustainable Society: Implications for Limited Growth* (New York and London: Praeger, 1977) pp. 164–70.

The frugal sustainable state

. . . the alternative to the maximum-feasible society would involve a sharp break with the principles of the modern era, for the simpler frugal sustainable society would be characterized by a relatively low-throughput, income-energy economy designed to elicit an optimal amount of material goods from nature – in other words, a modicum or a sufficiency of material well-being rather than a maximum. Although many different varieties of frugal sustainable society are conceivable, it seems likely that they would all share more or less completely certain basic features (relative to the maximum-feasible society) – decentralization and local autonomy; a simpler, smaller-scale, face-to-face life closer to nature; labour-intensive modes of production; a de-emphasis on material things; individual self-sufficiency (versus dependence on complex systems for the fulfilment of basic needs); and cultural diversity.

The political constitutions of 'frugal' societies would be a matter of social choice. Such societies could be either sacred or secular, cosmopolitan or provincial, open or closed, according to the wishes of the local population, so it is difficult to be precise about what form their politics could or should take. However, for Americans, the political ideas of Rousseau and Jefferson would seem particularly appropriate for such circumstances, unlike the Lockean and Hamiltonian ideas that have dominated US history so far. Also, any set of political institutions that aims to be ecologically viable over the long term would be very likely to have many features that Edmund Burke would approve of, for ecology is a profoundly conservative doctrine in its social implications. . . .

To obviate any possible misunderstanding, it is necessary to insist that most, if not all, of the dangers inherent in classical politics are avoidable in a well-ordered frugal society. As noted previously, most Americans are likely to see potential tyranny lurking behind any suggestion that the rights we now enjoy be curtailed in the slightest amount or that citizens should embrace moderation and self-restraint in the name of the common good; any concession of liberty seems to place us on a 'slippery slope' toward fascist dictatorship. This is an understandable but quite irrational reaction. In fact, classical politics have run the entire political gamut, and we have equal latitude of choice. Moreover, as the previous discussion of the maximum-feasible state ought to have made clear, it is precisely the rejection of frugality that will create inexorable pressures toward totalitarianism.

Indeed, the great political virtue of the frugal society is that, even though we must accept certain restrictions, we can in principle retain most of our cherished liberties. For instance, there is absolutely no reason why a frugal society cannot be a constitutional polity in which all the key civil rights are upheld. What is not possible in a frugal society is a free-for-all system of wealth-getting and unrestricted property rights. Thus, although citizens can be made secure in their political liberty and in the ownership of their personal possessions or means of livelihood in a well-ordered frugal state, they probably cannot be allowed to use private property as capital, except in the most restricted fashion, or to treat land and other basic resources as commodities divorced from their critical ecological and environmental role. So, certain kinds of rights that we now enjoy will indeed have to be given up. But once we self-consciously adopt limits for the good of the whole and posterity, we would readily discover many humane yet effective means for operating a society of moderation and self-restraint. Provided only that we accept the concept of self-imposed limits and plan to optimize our political values within those limits, nothing politically necessary for a full and dignified life need be yielded up.

Moreover, the wise use of technology would allow even 'frugal' societies to enjoy a high level of material well-being relative to pre-modern societies. Thus, choosing this path need not constitute a regression in any important respect – unless any diminution of private affluence is regarded as intolerable. Indeed, with the technology that we now have or that we could readily develop without any fundamental breakthroughs, we could have societies that were quite Utopian by historical standards. That is, ecological scarcity is not equivalent to classical scarcity, even though many of the political implications are the same. The greater penury of classical scarcity seems inevitably to have produced inequality along with the oppression necessary to maintain it (and to have made slavery over-whelmingly attractive as a source of energy). Ecological scarcity need not be so stringent. Solar energy and other technological possibilities denied to our ancestors will make the frugal society a radically new form of civilization, not just a reversion to past patterns.

Utopian or not, however, life clearly will seem frugal in many important respects. To take just one example, it seems evident that in the long run agriculture will become more labour-intensive, both because labour will be cheaper than energy in a frugal society and because horticultural agriculture as practised in many parts of Asia is less ecologically damaging than our current extensive, industrial agriculture. This is likely to mean that a larger proportion of the population will have to be 'peasants' in a low-energy steady-state society (or, alternatively, that most of the population will have to be at least part-time peasants along Maoist lines), and this is a situation that will seem unpalatable and regressive to most moderns, for whom toil has always been an enemy, even though Marx's 'idiocy of rural life' would not be inevitable with wise use of advanced technology. . . .

The picture of the frugal society that thus emerges resembles something like a return to the city-state form of civilization, but on a much higher and more sophisticated technological base, especially in the area of communications, which makes possible a simple yet ample and humane life for all (but, of course, real life can only approximate such an ideal).

As with classical scarcity in the past, however, ecological scarcity would create the potential for conflict between locally autonomous city states, 'Utopian' or not, so that microautonomy must inevitably be accompanied by some form of macroauthority capable of preventing warfare or anti-ecological acts likely to produce the 'tragedy of the commons'. Thus, local polities would have to exist within a regional or global empire of some kind.

Arguments for the frugal society are basically the inverse of arguments against the maximum-feasible society. Naturally, it is ecologically viable, for the frugal state is by definition one that restrains its material demands on nature to an optimal level that nature can tolerate and that does not depend on the near-perfect operation of artificial systems. In the area of values, it is clear that almost any form of the frugal society would permit individuals greater freedom, because there would be no necessity to plan and control all areas of life in order to make the system work and because the kind of psycho-social conditioning that Huxley describes would therefore not be necessary to make individuals fit into the system. Furthermore, although some kind of macroauthority will be needed to keep ecological and civil peace among local communities, there is no intrinsic reason why its authority could not be limited solely to these essential tasks, leaving local communities to proceed toward heaven or hell as their own customs, predilections, and standards of religious or social morality dictated. . . .

Naturally, there are some drawbacks. For example, precisely to the extent that government was limited and local communities were free to govern themselves, the latter would be likely to contain many of the ills that agitate reformers and revolutionaries. Of course, certain standards of justice could be imposed by the macroauthority, but this dilution of limited government has its dangers, and exactly where to make the trade-offs between ecological values, social justice, and liberty will obviously be a major problem for the political theorists of the frugal state. Nevertheless, it is clear that total equality and social justice are at least conceivable in a total, centralized regime; just as clearly, they are not attainable in the basically decentralized frugal society. As compensation for this, however, the plane would be characterized by a certain spicy variety absent from the maximum-feasible variety.

Another possible drawback for many will be the very modesty of the frugal society. Naturally, men whose ambition it is to conquer the stars for the human race and undertake other equally great deeds will find frugality a little humdrum, but even the ordinary man of today might be reluctant to give up his power over the 'energy slaves' that now do his bidding. On the other hand, the corrupting potential of power is well known, and so renunciation may be the better part of wisdom. In any event, frugality would inhibit only external conquest; there is no intrinsic reason why those living in frugal societies should ever lack for new fields to conquer in the arts and sciences and in the realm of spirit. Indeed, once we cease to be preoccupied with what John Stuart Mill, surely one of liberty's greatest friends, pejoratively called 'getting on', then we should experience a considerable expansion of our possibilities in these areas. . . .

It thus appears that we do have a significant choice. Although in one sense the politics of the maximum-feasible and the frugal state converge – either way we will get a more authoritarian, communalistic, and ideological set of political institutions – there are clearly vast differences between the two basic paths to the sustainable state. For the reasons given, my own sympathies lie almost entirely with the frugal alternative, and I am convinced that it is what we must necessarily arrive at eventually, even if we start out in the opposite direction. Unfortunately, the frugal alternative is alien to our current way of thinking and threatens many of the material and psychological vested interests we all have in the current order, so it is quite 'unrealistic' to believe that we shall choose simplicity and frugality except under ecological duress.

Small or Appropriate?

Despite the title of his famous book, Fritz Schumacher didn't actually think that 'small is beautiful'. He developed the much more challenging idea that in questions of size, *appropriateness* is the essential rule of thumb. In the extract below he points out that it is only because giantism is presently so much the rage that the virtues of smallness need to be stressed so strongly. The important thing, he writes, is to be aware of what is *needed* in any given situation, and this idea bears most fruit in his notion of appropriate, or intermediate, technology*.

From E. F. Schumacher, *Small is Beautiful* (London: Abacus, 1974) pp. 52–5.

I was brought up on an interpretation of history which suggested that in the beginning was the family; then families got together and formed tribes; then a number of tribes formed a nation; then a number of nations formed a 'Union' or 'United States' of this or that; and that, finally, we could look forward to a single world government. Ever since I heard this plausible story I have taken a special interest in the process, but could not help noticing that the opposite seemed to be happening: a proliferation of nation-states. The United Nations Organization started some twenty-five years ago with some sixty members; now there are more than twice as many, and the number is still growing. In my youth, this process of proliferation was called 'Balkanization' and was thought to be a very bad thing. Although everybody said it was bad, it has now been going on merrily for over fifty years, in most parts of the world. Large units tend to break up into smaller units. This phenomenon, so mockingly the opposite of what I had been taught, whether we approve of it or not, should at least not pass unnoticed.

Second, I was brought up on the theory that in order to be prosperous a country had to be big – the bigger the better. This also seemed quite plausible. Look at what Churchill called 'the pumpernickel principalities' of Germany before Bismarck; and then look at the Bismarckian Reich. Is it not true that the great prosperity of Germany became possible only through this unification? All the same, the German-speaking Swiss and the German-speaking Austrians, who did not join, did just as well economically, and if we make a list of all the most prosperous countries in the world, we find that most of them are very small; whereas a list of all the biggest countries in the world shows most of them to be very poor indeed. Here again, there is food for thought.

And third, I was brought up on the theory of the 'economies of scale' – that with industries and firms, just as with nations, there is an irresistible trend, dictated by modern technology, for units to become ever bigger. Now, it is quite true that today there are more large organizations and probably also bigger organizations than ever before in history; but the number of small units is also growing and certainly not declining in countries like Britain and the United States, and many of these small units are highly prosperous and provide society with most of the really fruitful new developments. Again, it is not altogether easy to reconcile theory and practice, and the situation as regards this whole issue of size is certainly puzzling to anyone brought up on these three concurrent theories. . . .

Let us now approach our subject from another angle and ask what is actually *needed*. In the affairs of men, there always appears to be a need for at least two things simultaneously, which, on the face of it, seem to be incompatible and to exclude one another. We always need both freedom and order. We need the freedom of lots and lots of small, autonomous units, and, at the same time, the orderliness of large-scale, possibly global, unity and co-ordination. When it comes to action, we obviously need small units, because action is a highly personal affair, and one cannot be in touch with more than a very limited number of persons at any one time. But when it comes to the world of ideas, to principles or to ethics, to the indivisibility of peace and also of ecology, we need to recognize the unity of mankind and base our actions upon this recognition. Or to put it differently, it is true that all men are brothers, but it is also true that in our active personal relationships we can, in fact, be brothers to only a few of them, and we are called upon to show more brotherliness to them than we could possibly show to the whole of mankind. We all know people who freely talk about the brotherhood of man while treating their neighbours as enemies, just as we also know people who have, in fact, excellent relations with all their neighbours while harbouring, at the same time, appalling prejudices about all human groups outside their particular circle.

What I wish to emphasize is the *duality* of the human requirement when it comes to the question of size: there is no *single* answer. For his different purposes man needs many different structures, both small ones and large ones, some exclusive and some comprehensive. Yet people find it most difficult to keep two seemingly opposite necessities of truth in their minds at the same time. They always tend to clamour for a final solution, as if in actual life there could ever be a final solution other than death. For constructive work, the principal task is always the restoration of some kind of balance. Today, we suffer from an almost universal idolatry of giantism. It is therefore necessary to insist on the virtues of smallness – where this applies. (If there were a prevailing idolatry of smallness, irrespective of subject or purpose, one would have to try and exercise influence in the opposite direction.) . . .

What scale is appropriate? It depends on what we are trying to do. The question of scale is extremely crucial today, in political, social and economic affairs just as in almost everything else. What, for instance, is the appropriate size of a city? And also, one might ask, what is the appropriate size of a country? Now these are serious and difficult questions. It is not possible to programme a computer and get the answer. The really serious matters of life cannot be calculated. We cannot directly calculate what is right; but we jolly well know what is wrong! We can recognize right and wrong at the extremes, although we cannot normally judge them finely enough to say: 'This ought to be 5 per cent more; or that ought to be 5 per cent less.'

Take the question of size of a city. While one cannot judge these things with precision, I think it is fairly safe to say that the upper limit of what is desirable for the size of a city is probably something of the order of half a million inhabitants. It is quite clear that above such a size nothing is added to the virtue of the city. In places like London, or Tokyo, or New York, the millions do not add to the city's real value but merely create *enormous* problems and produce human degradation. So probably the order of magnitude of 500,000 inhabitants could be looked upon as the upper limit. The question of the lower limit of a real city is much more difficult to judge. The finest cities in history have been very small by twentieth-century standards. The instruments and institutions of city culture depend, no doubt, on a certain accumulation of wealth. But how much wealth has to be accumulated depends on the type of culture pursued. Philosophy, the arts and religion cost very, very little money.

Other types of what claims to be 'high culture' – space research or ultra-modern physics – cost a lot of money, but are somewhat remote from the real needs of men.

Organic Farming

A fundamental feature of any Green sustainable society would be its organic farms. Greens oppose what they call industrialized farming because of its use of artificial fertilizers, herbicides and pesticides, its over-mechanization, its monocultural landscapes, and its tendency to erode the soil. At the same time, say the Greens, the industrial farmer's technological and manipulative relationship with the land is wholly at odds with the principle of responsible trusteeship required for long-term sustainability. How we farm the land is an indication of our relationship with it. Lady Eve Balfour has long been associated with the development of the theory and practice of organic farming, and her classic book, *The Living Soil* (1943), has been reprinted and re-edited on a number of occasions. The extract below is taken from a paper given at the International Federation of Organic Agricultural Movements (IFOAM) conference in 1977, in which Lady Balfour sets out the aims of sustainable agriculture, the principles of organic farming, and the need to embed them in a wider philosophy of reverence for life.

From Lady Eve Balfour, 'Towards a Sustainable Agriculture: the Living Soil'. Paper given at the IFOAM conference of 1977.

Now I want to put forward what I believe our aims should be in evolving a sustainable agriculture, and then . . . pass on to you some thoughts on organic farming as I see it.

The criteria for a sustainable agriculture can be summed up in one word – *permanence*, which means adopting techniques that maintain soil fertility indefinitely; that utilize, as far as possible, only renewable resources; that do not grossly pollute the environment, and that foster life energy (or if preferred biological activity) within the soil and throughout the cycles of all the involved food-chains.

This is what biological husbandry sets out to attempt – with an

increasing degree of understanding and success among its prac-
titioners. Throughout the world, as a result of their own experience,
these sincerely believe that they can offer a genuine and viable
alternative agriculture, capable of solving many of the problems of
mankind. This possibility, as well as the need for it, is becoming
increasingly recognized in academic and scientific circles.

I am often asked how, in a broad sense, I define organic farming
as opposed to conventional farming. Though I prefer the term
biological husbandry because of its emphasis on life, the short
answer is *balance*; however I think it is necessary to amplify a little.

Contrary to the views held by some, I am sure that the techniques
of 'organic farming' cannot be imprisoned in a rigid set of rules.
They depend essentially on the outlook of the farmer. Without a
positive and ecological approach it is not possible to farm organi-
cally. The approach of the modern conventional farmer is negative,
narrow and fragmentary, and consequently produces imbalance. His
attitude to 'pests' and 'weeds', for example, is to regard them as
enemies to be killed – if possible exterminated. When he attacks
them with lethal chemicals he seldom gives a thought to the effect
this may have on the food supply or habitat of other forms of
wildlife among whom he has many more friends than foes. The
predatory insects and the insectivorous birds are obvious examples.

The attitude of the organic farmer, who has trained himself to
think ecologically, is different. He tries to see the living world as a
whole. He regards so-called pests and weeds as part of the natural
pattern of the biota, probably necessary to its stability and permanence, to be *utilized* rather than attacked. Throughout his operations
he endeavours to achieve his objective by co-operating with natural
agencies in place of relying on man-made substitutes. He studies
what appear to be nature's rules – as manifested in a healthy wilderness – and attempts to adapt them to his own farm needs, instead
of flouting them. One of the first things he will notice about a
natural eco-system such as a wilderness or a natural forest is balance
and stability. The innumerable different species of fauna and flora
that go to make up such a community, achieve, as a result of their
interdependence, whether in co-operation or competition, collective
immortality. Seldom, if ever, is any species eliminated; seldom, if
ever, does any species multiply to pest proportions.

Thus the organic farmer, if he has a crop badly attacked by some
pest, let us say (and this can happen, even to organic farmers!),
recognizes that this is a symptom of imbalance in his local environment, and he first looks to see if some faulty technique of his own

has been responsible – often it has. This does not mean that he can always avoid emergency remedial measures but these he employs only when there is a real emergency, not as a routine. He strives instead to bring about biological balance, and it is remarkable the extent to which organic farmers and growers do in fact achieve this. I could give you several examples, but one must suffice.

Some years ago a large scale organic commercial grower of my acquaintance, growing vegetables, fruit and flowers was visited by a team of scientists from Cambridge University – they included plant pathologists and entomologists. They knew it was an unsprayed holding and they came looking for disease and pests. They found isolated examples of everything they expected to find, but, as they put it, they failed to find a single case of crop damage.

Besides biological balance, the ecologically-minded organic farmer takes note of, and tries to apply, other apparent biological rules. For example, nature's diversity of species he adapts through rotations, under-sowing, and avoiding monoculture of crops or animals. Nature's habit of filtering sunlight and rain through some form of protective soil cover he adapts by such practices as cover-cropping and mulching. Top soil on the top appears to be nature's plan. Organic matter is always deposited on the surface. It is left to the earthworms and some insects to take it below. The organic farmer also put his compost and farmyard manure on, or very near, the surface, and in carrying out mechanical cultivations keeps soil-inversion to a minimum, the tine cultivator being preferred to the plough.

Nature's highly efficient re-cycling system ensures provision of living food for all organisms in the food chain from soil bacteria and fungi to large fauna; the organic farmer therefore lays great stress on the conservation and return to the soil of all organic residues. His aim is to feed and to assist proliferation of the soil population and to leave it to feed the crop.

Finally, and of equal importance, he notes, and tries to reproduce, the almost perfect structure of a biologically active soil which alone ensures the three most important characteristics of a fertile soil – good aeration, water-holding capacity, and free drainage.

It is quite astonishing the extent to which this all-important property of good soil is neglected in modern agriculture. Poor soil structure leads to imbalance between water and air in the pore spaces of the soil. Many apparent mineral or trace mineral deficiencies in the soil turn out to be oxygen deficiencies. When that is corrected the others disappear. In most agriculture soils there is really plenty of mineral plant food for the nutritional requirements of plants, even when continuously cropped, if their roots are allowed to exploit it downwards. They key to this is good soil structure which is greatly influenced by the activity of earthworms. The techniques of modern farming tend to destroy good structure in a number of ways, such as by the impaction of heavy implements, by carrying out culti- vations in unsuitable weather conditions, and by failure to provide sufficient organic food and/or a suitable lime status for the earth- worm population.

All these faults are the outcome of failure to think ecologically – they are symptoms of a degree of fragmentation in our approach to the living world which has become a real threat to our survival. Throughout biological evolution, starting from single-celled organ- isms right up to the complexity of rain forests, the process has been characterized by increasing diversity among species lengthening of the food chains, and progressive enrichment of the environment. For the first time in the history of the plant the actions of modern man appear to be putting this process into reverse. Whole species of fauna and flora are being eliminated, the food-chains are becoming shorter, and the environment progressively impoverished. It only takes a little imagination to picture what could happen if the trend continues. . . .

There are two motivations behind an ecological approach – one is based on self interest, however enlightened, i.e. when consideration for other species is taught solely because on that depends the sur- vival of our own.

The other motivation springs from a sense that the biota is a whole, of which we are a part, and that the other species which compose it and helped to create it, are entitled to existence in their own right. This is the wholeness approach and it is my hope and belief that this is what we, as a federation, stand for.

If I am right, this means that we cannot escape from the ethical and spiritual values of life for they are part of wholeness. To ignore them and their implications would be to pursue another form of fragmentation.

Therefore, I hold that what we have to teach is the attitude defined by Aldo Leopold as 'A Land Ethic'.* This requires that we extend the concept of community to include all the species of life with which we share the planet. We must foster a reverence for *all* life, even that which we are forced to control, and we must, as Leopold put it – 'Quit thinking about decent landuse as solely an economic problem, but examine each question in terms of what is ethically and esthetically right, as well as what is economically expedient. A thing is right when it tends to preserve the integrity, stability and beauty of the biotic community. It is wrong when it tends otherwise'.

The quotation expresses what I believe should be our guidelines.

Soft Energy Paths

Alternative sources of energy such as wind, sun and wave –
the 'renewables' – have become so intimately linked with Green
politics that for some people they are what Green politics is all
about. While this is a distortion, there is no doubt that alternative energy would bulk large in the practice of a sustainable
society. Amory Lovins gives a classic summary below of what
he calls 'soft technologies' (as opposed to the 'hard technologies'
associated with coal, oil, gas and uranium), and there is every
likelihood that as governments look for ways of grafting
environmental concern onto their policies, Lovins' call for soft
technology adoption will be taken ever more seriously. In the
second extract, entitled 'Socio-politics', Lovins argues that soft
technologies not only make for a healthier environment but
also have a more benign politics built into them than do hard
technologies. He suggests that the politics of hard technologies
are characterized by centralization, secret decision-making,
threats to civil liberties and loss of local control. Soft technologies, on the other hand, are said to be less coercive, more
participatory and more 'convivial', and for these reasons they
ideally suit the political aspirations of the Green sustainable
society.

From Amory Lovins, *Soft Energy Paths: towards a durable
peace* (Harmondsworth: Penguin, 1977) pp. 38–9, 42–5, 54–7,
148–52.

Soft energy technologies

There exists today a body of energy technologies that have certain
specific features in common and that offer great technical, economic,
and political attractions, yet for which there is no generic term. For
lack of a more satisfactory term, I shall call them 'soft' technologies:
a textural description, intended to mean not vague, mushy, speculative, or ephemeral, but rather flexible, resilient, sustainable, and
benign. . . .

These are defined by five characteristics:

1. They rely on renewable energy flows that are always there whether we use them or not, such as sun and wind and vegetation: on energy income, not on depletable energy capital.

2. They are diverse, so that as a national treasury runs on many small tax contributions, so national energy supply is an aggregate of very many individually modest contributions, each designed for maximum effectiveness in particular circumstances.

3. They are flexible and relatively low technology – which does not mean unsophisticated, but rather, easy to understand and use without esoteric skills, accessible rather than arcane.

4. They are matched in *scale* and in geographic distribution to end-use needs, taking advantage of the free distribution of most natural energy flows.

5. They are matched in *energy quality* to end-use needs. . . .

⁂

Many genuine soft technologies are now available and are now economic. What are some of them?

Solar heating and, imminently, cooling head the list. They are incrementally cheaper than electric heating, and far more inflation-proof, practically anywhere in the world. In the United States (with fairly high average sunlight levels), they are cheaper than present electric heating virtually anywhere, cheaper than oil heat in many parts, and cheaper than gas and coal in some. Even in the least favourable parts of the continental United States, far more sunlight falls on a typical building than is required to heat and cool it without supplement; whether this is considered economic depends on how the accounts are done. The difference in solar input between the most and least favourable parts of the lower forty-nine states is generally less than twofold, and in cold regions, the long heating season can improve solar economics. . . .

Second, exciting developments in the conversion of agricultural, forestry, and urban wastes to methanol and other liquid and gaseous fuels now offer practical, economically interesting technologies sufficient to run an efficient US transport sector. Some bacterial and enzymatic routes under study look even more promising, but presently proved processes already offer sizable contributions without the inevitable climatic constraints of fossil fuel combustion. Organic conversion technologies must be sensitively integrated with agriculture and forestry so as not to deplete the soil; most current methods seem suitable in this respect, though they may change the farmer's priorities by making his whole yield of biomass (vegetable matter) salable. . . .

Additional soft technologies include wind hydraulic systems (especially those with a vertical axis), which already seem likely in many design studies to compete with nuclear power in much of North America and Western Europe. But wind is not restricted to making electricity: it can heat, pump, heat-pump, or compress air. Solar process heat, too, is coming along rapidly as we learn to use the 5,800°C potential of sunlight (much hotter than a boiler). Finally, high and low temperature solar collectors, organic converters, and wind machines can form symbiotic hybrid combinations more attractive than the separate components.

Energy storage is often said to be a major problem of energy income technologies. But this 'problem' is largely an artifact of trying to recentralize, upgrade and redistribute inherently diffuse energy flows. Directly storing sunlight or wind – or, for that matter, electricity from any source – is indeed difficult on a large scale. But it is easy if done on a scale and in an energy quality matched to most end-use needs. Daily, even seasonal, storage of low and medium temperature heat at the point of use is straightforward with water-tanks, rock beds, or perhaps fusible salts. Neighbourhood heat storage is even cheaper. In industry, wind-generated compressed air can easily (and, with due care, safely) be stored to operate machinery: the technology is simple, cheap, reliable, and highly developed. (Some European cities even used to supply compressed air as a standard utility.) Installing pipes to distribute hot water (or compressed air) tends to be considerably cheaper than installing equivalent electric distribution capacity. Hydro-electricity is stored behind dams, and organic conversion yields readily stored liquid and gaseous fuels. On the whole, therefore, energy storage is much less of a problem in a soft energy economy than in a hard one. . . .

⁞⁞⁞⁞⁞⁞

Sociopolitics

Perhaps the most profound difference between the soft and hard paths – the difference that ultimately distinguishes them – is their domestic socio-political impact. Both paths, like any fifty-year energy path, entail significant social change. But the kinds of social change needed for a hard path are apt to be much less pleasant, less plausible, less compatible with social diversity and personal freedom of choice, and less consistent with traditional values than are the social changes that could make a soft path work.

It is often said that, on the contrary, a soft path must be repressive; and coercive paths to energy conservation and soft technologies can indeed be imagined. But coercion is not necessary and its use would signal a major failure of imagination, given the many policy instruments available to achieve a given technical end. Why use penal legislation to encourage roof insulation when tax incentives and education (leading to the sophisticated public understanding now being achieved in Canada and parts of Europe) will do? Policy tools need not harm lifestyles or liberties if chosen with reasonable sensitivity.

In contrast to the soft path's dependence on pluralistic consumer choice in deploying a myriad of small devices and refinements, the hard path depends on difficult, large-scale projects requiring a major social commitment under centralized management. We have noted in section 2.3 the extraordinary capital intensity of centralized, electrified high technologies. Their similarly heavy demands on other scarce resources – skills, labour, materials, special sites – likewise cannot be met by market allocation, but require compulsory diversion from whatever priorities are backed by the weakest constituencies. Quasi-warpowers legislation to this end has already been seriously proposed. The hard path, sometimes portrayed as the bastion of free enterprise and free markets, would instead be a world of subsidies, $100 billion bailouts, oligopolies, regulations, nationalization, eminent domain, corporate statism.

Such dirigiste autarchy is the first of many distortions of the political fabric. While soft technologies can match any settlement pattern, their diversity reflecting our own pluralism, centralized energy sources encourage industrial clustering and urbanization. While soft technologies give everyone the costs and benefits of the energy system he or she chooses, centralized systems inequitably allocate benefits to suburbanites and social costs to politically weaker rural agrarians. Siting big energy systems pits central authority against local autonomy in an increasingly divisive and wasteful form of centrifugal politics that is already proving one of the most potent constraints on expansion.

In an electrical world, your lifeline comes not from an understandable neighbourhood technology run by people you know who are at your own social level, but rather from an alien, remote, and perhaps humiliatingly uncontrollable technology run by a faraway, bureaucratized, technical élite who have probably never heard of you. Decisions about who shall have how much energy at what price also become centralized – a politically dangerous trend because it divides those who use energy from those who supply and regulate it. Those who do not like the decisions can simply be disconnected.

The scale and complexity of centralized grids not only make them politically inaccessible to the poor and weak, but also increase the likelihood and size of malfunctions, mistakes, and deliberate disruptions. A small fault or a few discontented people become able to turn off a country. Even a single rifleman can probably black out a typical city instantaneously. Societies may therefore be tempted to discourage disruption through stringent controls akin to a garrison state. In times of social stress, when grids become a likely target for dissidents, the sector may be paramilitarized and further isolated from grassroots politics.

If the technology used, like nuclear power, is subject to technical surprises and unique psychological handicaps, prudence or public clamour may require generic shutdowns in case of an unexpected type of malfunction: one may have to choose between turning off a country and persisting in potentially unsafe operation. Indeed, though many in the $100 billion quasi-civilian nuclear industry agree that it could be politically destroyed if a major accident occurred soon, few have considered the economic or political implications of putting at risk such a large fraction of societal capital. How far would governments go to protect against a threat – even a purely political threat – a basket full of such delicate, costly, and essential eggs? Already in individual nuclear plants, the cost of a shutdown – often many dollars a second – weighs heavily, perhaps too heavily, in operating and safety decisions.

Any demanding high technology tends to develop influential and dedicated constituencies of those who link its commercial success with both the public welfare and their own. Such sincerely held beliefs, peer pressures, and the harsh demands that the work itself places on time and energy all tend to discourage such people from acquiring a similarly thorough knowledge of alternative policies and the need to discuss them. Moreover, the money and talent invested in an electrical programme tend to give it disproportionate influence in the councils of government, often directly through staff swapping between policy- and mission-oriented agencies. This incestuous position, now well developed in most industrial countries, distorts both social and energy priorities in a lasting way that resists political remedy.

For all these reasons, if nuclear power were clean, safe, economic, assured of ample fuel, and socially benign *per se*, it would still be unattractive because of the political implications of the kind of energy economy into which it would lock us. But fission technology also has unique socio-political side effects arising from the impact of human fallibility and malice on the persistently toxic and explosive materials in the fuel cycle. For example, discouraging nuclear violence and coercion requires some abrogation of civil liberties; guarding long-lived wastes against geological or social contingencies implies some form of hierarchical social rigidity or homogeneity to insulate the technological priesthood from social turbulence; and making political decisions about nuclear hazards that are compulsory, remote from social experience, disputed, unknown, or unknowable may tempt governments to bypass democratic decision in favour of élitist technocracy.

Even now, the inability of our political institutions to cope with nuclear hazard is straining both their competence and their perceived legitimacy. There is no scientific basis for calculating the likelihood or the maximum long-term effects of nuclear mishaps, or for guaranteeing that those effects will not exceed a particular level; we know only that all precautions are, for fundamental reasons, inherently imperfect in essentially unknown degree. Reducing that imperfection would require much social engineering whose success would be speculative. Technical success in reducing the hazards would not reduce, and might enhance, the need for such social engineering. The most attractive political feature of soft technologies and conservation – the alternatives that will let us avoid these decisions and their high political costs – may be that, like motherhood, everyone is in favour of them. . . .

In short, hard technologies are oriented toward abstract economic services for remote and anonymous consumers, and therefore can neither command nor allow personal involvement by people in the community they serve. Soft technologies, on the other hand, use familiar, equitably distributed natural energies to meet perceived human needs directly and comprehensibly, and are thus, in Illich's sense, 'convivial' to choose, build, and use. . . .

Soft technologies, then, are inherently, structurally more participatory than hard technologies. Conversely, soft technologies are also less coercive. In a nuclear society, nobody can opt out of nuclear risk. In an electrified society, everyone's lifestyle is shaped by the homogenizing infrastructure and economic incentives of the energy system, and, from the viewpoint of the consumer, diversity becomes a vanishing luxury. Like purchasers of Model T Fords, the consumer can have anything he or she wants so long as it is electrified. But in a soft path, people can choose their own risk-benefit balances and energy systems to match their own degree of caution and involvement. The stakes are smaller, the choices wider, the mistakes more forgiving. Few decisions are irreversible, none compulsory. Preference rules over pattern. People who want to drive big cars or inhabit uninsulated houses will be free to do so – and to pay the social costs. People can choose to live in city centres, remote countryside, or in between, without being told their lifestyle is uneconomic. People can choose to minimize what Robert Socolow calls their 'consumer humiliation' – their forced dependence on systems they cannot understand, control, diagnose, repair, or modify – or can continue to depend on traditional utilities.

In a soft path, then, dissent and diversity are not just a futile gesture but a basis for political action and a spur to individual enterprise. Some action by central and local government is of course necessary to get the ball rolling, but then it's mostly downhill: the first push and any later mid-course correction, however laborious they may seem, are slight and brief compared to the uphill struggle otherwise needed to manage the ever-increasing autarchy of a hard path.

Intermediate Technology

Greens are suspicious of the path of development which is followed by industrial nations because they believe it to be unsustainable. But when they see the massive countries of the industrializing Third World being encouraged along the same path they object not only to its unsustainability, but also to its inappropriateness. This idea owes much to Fritz Schumacher's work on appropriate, or intermediate, technology which is explained in the extract below. Schumacher argues that developing countries need technologies which are appropriate to their stage of development, rather than state-of-the-art technologies imported from the developed world. It is worth noting that Schumacher is not criticising western-style development as such, although many Greens would now do so – he is merely calling into question the rate at which development takes place. The idea of intermediate technology has had a strong influence on the issue of alternative technology in the developed world, particularly in the field of alternative energy sources. Once again, the guiding principle is appropriateness – but this time, in the context of a Green sustainable society.

From E. F. Schumacher, *Small is Beautiful* (London: Abacus, 1974) pp. 150–9.

If we define the level of technology in terms of 'equipment cost per workplace', we can call the indigenous technology of a typical developing country – symbolically speaking – a £1–technology, while that of the developed countries could be called a £1,000–technology. The gap between these two technologies is so enormous that a transition from the one to the other is simply impossible. In fact, the current attempt of the developing countries to infiltrate the £1,000–technology into their economies inevitably kills off the £1–technology at an alarming rate, destroying traditional workplaces much faster than modern workplaces can be created, and thus leaves the poor in a more desperate and helpless position than ever before.

If effective help is to be brought to those who need it most, a technology is required which would range in some intermediate position between the £1–technology and the £1,000–technology. Let us call it – again symbolically speaking – a £100–technology.

Such an intermediate technology would be immensely more productive than the indigenous technology (which is often in a condition of decay), but it would also be immensely cheaper than the sophisticated, highly capital-intensive technology of modern industry. At such a level of capitalization, very large numbers of workplaces could be created within a fairly short time; and the creation of such workplaces would be 'within reach' for the more enterprising minority within the district, not only in financial terms but also in terms of their education, aptitude, organizing skill, and so forth. . . .

The intermediate technology would also fit much more smoothly into the relatively unsophisticated environment in which it is to be utilized. The equipment would be fairly simple and therefore understandable, suitable for maintenance and repair on the spot. Simple equipment is normally far less dependent on raw materials of great purity or exact specifications and much more adaptable to market fluctuations than highly sophisticated equipment. Men are more easily trained; supervision, control, and organization are simpler; and there is far less vulnerability to unforeseen difficulties.

Objections raised and discussed

Since the idea of intermediate technology was first put forward, a number of objections have been raised. The most immediate objections are psychological: 'You are trying to withhold the best and make us put up with something inferior and outdated.' This is the voice of those who are not in need, who can help themselves and want to be assisted in reaching a higher standard of living at once. It is not the voice of those with whom we are here concerned, the poverty-stricken multitudes who lack any real basis of existence, whether in rural or in urban areas, who have neither 'the best' nor 'the second best' but go short of even the most essential means of subsistence. One sometimes wonders how many 'development economists' have any real comprehension of the condition of the poor. . . .

The central concern of development policy, as I have argued already, must be the creation of work opportunities for those who, being unemployed, are consumers – on however miserable a level

– without contributing anything to the fund of either 'wages goods' or 'capital'. Employment is the very precondition of everything else. The output of an idle man is nil, whereas the output of even a poorly equipped man can be a positive contribution, and this contribution can be to 'capital' as well as to 'wages goods'. The distinction between those two is by no means as definite as the econometricians are inclined to think, because the definition of 'capital' itself depends decisively on the level of technology employed.

Let us consider a very simple example. Some earth-moving job has to be done in an area of high unemployment. There is a wide choice of technologies, ranging from the most modern earth-moving equipment to purely manual work without tools of any kind. The 'output' is fixed by the nature of the job, and it is quite clear that the capital/output ratio will be highest, if the input of 'capital' is kept lowest. If the job were done without any tools, the capital/output ratio would be infinitely large, but the productivity per man would be exceedingly low. If the job were done at the highest level of modern technology, the capital/output ratio would be low and the productivity per man very high. Neither of these extremes is desirable, and a middle way has to be found. Assume some of the unemployed men were first set to work to make a variety of tools, including wheelbarrows and the like, while others were made to produce various 'wages goods'. Each of these lines of production in turn could be based on a wide range of different technologies, from the simplest to the most sophisticated. The task in every case would be to find an intermediate technology which obtains a fair level of productivity without having to resort to the purchase of expensive and sophisticated equipment. The outcome of the whole venture would be an economic development going far beyond the completion of the initial earth-moving project. With a total input of 'capital' from outside which might be much smaller than would have been involved in the acquisition of the most modern earth-moving equipment, and an input of (previously unemployed) labour much greater than the 'modern' method would have demanded, not only a given project would have been completed, but a whole community would have been set on the path of development.

I say, therefore, that the dynamic approach to development, which treats the choice of appropriate, intermediate technologies as the central issue, opens up avenues of constructive action, which the static, econometric approach totally fails to recognize. . . .

Two further arguments have been advanced against the idea of intermediate technology – that its products would require protection within the country and would be unsuitable for export. Both arguments are based on mere surmise. In fact a considerable number of design studies and costings, made for specific products in specific districts, have universally demonstrated that the products of an intelligently chosen intermediate technology could actually be cheaper than those of modern factories in the nearest big city. Whether or not such products could be exported is an open question; the unemployed are not contributing to exports now, and the primary task is to put them to work so that they will produce useful goods from local materials for local use.

Applicability of intermediate technology

The applicability of intermediate technology is, of course, not universal. There are products which are themselves the typical outcome of highly sophisticated modern industry and cannot be produced except by such an industry. These products, at the same time, are not normally an urgent need of the poor. What the poor need most of all is simple things – building materials, clothing, household goods, agricultural implements – and a better return for their agricultural products. They also most urgently need in many places: trees, water, and crop storage facilities. Most agricultural populations would be helped immensely if they could themselves do the first stages of processing their products. All these are ideal fields for intermediate technology. . . .

The idea of intermediate technology does not imply simply a 'going back' in history to methods now outdated, although a systematic study of methods employed in the developed countries, say, a hundred years ago could indeed yield highly suggestive results. It is too often assumed that the achievement of western science, pure and applied, lies mainly in the apparatus and machinery that have been developed from it, and that a rejection of the apparatus and machinery would be tantamount to a rejection of science. This is an excessively superficial view. The real achievement lies in the accumulation of precise knowledge, and this knowledge can be applied in a great variety of ways, of which the current application in modern industry is only one. The development of an intermediate technology, therefore, means a genuine forward movement into new territory, where the enormous cost and complication of production methods for the sake of labour saving and job elimination is avoided and technology is made appropriate for labour surplus societies. . . .

In summary we can conclude:

1. The 'dual economy' in the developing countries will remain for the foreseeable future. The modern sector will not be able to absorb the whole.
2. If the non-modern sector is not made the object of special development efforts, it will continue to disintegrate; this disintegration will continue to manifest itself in mass unemployment and mass migration into the metropolitan areas; and this will poison economic life in the modern sector as well.
3. The poor can be helped to help themselves, but only by making available to them a technology that recognizes the economic boundaries and limitations of poverty – an intermediate technology.
4. Action programmes on a national and supranational basis are needed to develop intermediate technologies suitable for the promotion of full employment in developing countries.

Sustainable Development

Most people associate playing the environmental card with the politics of northern, or industrially developed, countries. So when the word 'sustainability' is mentioned we think of problems such as acid rain, leaded petrol and storing nuclear waste. But the vast majority of people on the planet is afflicted by environmental problems of a different – and perhaps even more fundamental – type: problems involving deforestation and soil erosion, for example. Traditionally, the development of poorer countries has involved following the paths of development of northern nations, but much quicker. Only now is it becoming clear that these forms of development are often inappropriate and can cause such environmental havoc that the very livelihoods of people are put at risk. In response to this, a whole new field of theory and practice called 'sustainable development', related to the Third World, has sprung up and some of its themes are described below. The idea is that aid from developed countries should fulfil two functions: first, that it should enhance the sustainability of the natural resource base; and second, that it should be tied to projects which are appropriate to the culture in question. As Czech Conroy points out, this involves development professionals doing at least as much listening as talking, as well as understanding that inequitable distribution of wealth is a major source of environmental degradation. Some would argue that this applies as much to the First as to the Third World.

From Czech Conroy and Miles Litvinoff, *The Greening of Aid* (London: Earthscan, 1988) pp. xi–xiv.

There is a new jargon phrase in the development business – 'sustainable development'. It stems from a concern that many activities undertaken in the name of development have actually squandered the resources upon which development is based. In the industrialized countries the rapid consumption of finite materials such as fossil fuels and metals is the main concern. In the least developed countries overexploitation of natural biological resources is usually the major threat to sustainability.

Resource consumption can also have damaging environmental side-effects. In the north, chemical pollutants lead to acid deposition, ozone depletion and, lead poisoning. In the south the main environmental costs are usually associated with degradation of the natural resource base – deforestation, soil erosion and salinization are occurring at alarming rates. When rural livelihoods are undermined people migrate to the cities, where inadequate water and sewage services, and the degraded sites on which the poor are forced to live, pose other major environmental problems.

Definitions of sustainable development usually talk of improving people's material well-being through utilizing the earth's resources at a rate that can be sustained indefinitely, or at least over several decades, living off nature's interest rather than depleting the capital. The World Commission on Environment and Development (WCED) defined it as 'development that meets the needs of the present without compromising the ability of future generations to meet their own needs' (WCED, 1987). The Commission particularly stressed the importance of meeting the essential needs of the world's poor.

General definitions are important, but they do not tell us what actions are needed to achieve sustainable development in practice. This book should help to fill that gap in the field of overseas aid. It provides specific and practical guidance to aid agencies and all those interested in ensuring that overseas aid supports countries' long-term development. It is based on papers produced for an international conference on sustainable development that the International Institute for Environment and Development (IIED) organized in April 1987 at Regent's College, London.

The people and economies of most Third World countries are heavily dependent on indigenous natural resources. Food production is a major activity for most rural people; and timber, paper, rubber and cotton textiles are but a few of the other industries based on natural resources. Thus, degradation or overexploitation of these resources directly affects economic development and human well-being.

Many of the world's most valuable fisheries have been overexploited, reducing catches to well below their previous levels. The export of timber from tropical forests can be an important source of foreign exchange, but for how long? Tropical forests are hardly ever harvested on a sustainable basis, and reforestation is uncommon.

People in the north are concerned about the huge scale of environmental destruction in the south. This has raised the question of what their governments can do to help alleviate these problems. The answer is: a lot.

They can start by putting their own economies on a sustainable development path so that their impact on the global environment (the atmosphere and the oceans), and particularly on Third World countries, is minimized. They need to reduce the vast quantities of the world's non-renewable resources that they are consuming, and to change their policies if they are having harmful effects on people in the south. They can help to change international economic relations between north and south so that they are more equitable. Finally, they can take steps to ensure that their $40 billion spent annually on overseas aid supports sustainable development and does not undermine it.

Unfortunately, there are many examples of aid projects that have disrupted the lives of local people and done serious damage to the environment; this is a second factor that has aroused public concern about aid and the environment. Also, a large proportion of aid projects that were intended to help conserve and enhance the productivity of natural resources have failed to do so. For instance, one report concluded that most conservation programmes in Africa 'have been unsuccessful . . . structures and activities introduced are not maintained . . . most programmes have been too expensive and too complex to be replicable'. The record of other kinds of project, such as community tree-planting and new energy-efficient stoves, has also been disappointing.

Public discussion in the 1970s and early 1980s repeatedly emphasized these negative aspects of aid and the environment, to the point where some people must have wondered whether aid had ever benefited the environment and natural resource base. In fact, many projects *have* made a positive contribution to sustainable development, and IIED decided to gather information on some of the best and to see what lessons could be learned from them. . . .

Many development projects have failed to produce their intended benefits because of the 'mindset' of the people who designed and/or managed them. Development professionals tend to share certain biases that add up to what Robert Chambers has called 'normal professionalism'. These biases 'start with things rather than people, the rich rather than the poor, men rather than women and numbers rather than qualities . . . Poor rural children, women and men have been treated as residual not primary, as terminal problems not starting-points'. Consequently, normal professionals have often misunderstood the 'problem' and misspecified the 'solution'.

Many soil and water conservation projects, as their very name suggests, fall into this trap. Development professionals saw soil erosion as the problem, rather than the associated reduction in people's well-being, and designed technical solutions that people were then pressed to adhere to. The people's views were not sought, nor was much thought given as to whether these 'solutions' would be compatible with their way of living. Often they were not compatible, which is why the project activities were not maintained by the intended beneficiaries.

The rural poor, in their struggle to survive, are sometimes driven to doing environmental damage. Their herds overgraze; their shortened fallows on steep slopes and fragile soils induce erosion; they are forced to cultivate and degrade marginal lands.

There is much greater awareness now that poverty and environmental degradation are often interlinked. But there has been a tendency to portray the poor as stupid and short-sighted, and in need of education on the importance of conserving natural resources. The factors that force poor people to degrade their environments are frequently overlooked. Population growth is often, and sometimes incorrectly, given as the main factor. Other factors may be more important, such as inequitable land distribution; appropriation of poor people's lands by the rich; no security of tenure; and the unavailability of credit for new and more efficient technologies.

The increased awareness of how poverty can affect the environment is welcome, but it should not distract from the harmful environmental impacts of the rich. The high resource consumption of developed countries and the wealthier groups in Third World countries place heavy pressures on natural resources (on forests, fisheries, etc.). Some people argue that this is the world's 'main source of environmental destruction'.

Improving the livelihoods of the poor is essential if pressures on the natural environment are to be reduced. Secure resources and adequate livelihoods lead to good husbandry and sustainable management; and by combating poverty they help to slow population growth. For these reasons, most of the projects described in the following chapters are ones that have involved some of the poorest people. Although few of them are explicitly aimed at slowing population growth, many may do so indirectly.

IIED and the contributors to this book have tried to break out of the old paradigm of 'normal professionalism' and to put people and their livelihoods first. We hope that this book will be a valuable contribution to the debate on how the poorest of this planet's five billion people can secure a fulfilling and sustainable living.

Ecosocialism

When Green politics first appeared on the scene, people on the left tended to be hostile towards it because they thought that it ignored the most important divisions in society – class divisions. Likewise, they didn't take kindly to being told that capitalism and socialism were basically the same thing from an 'industrialist' point of view (see Porritt*). Others, though, have felt that socialism and ecology have more in common than first meets the eye and ecologists, from one side, and socialists, from the other, have tried to pull each other towards a meeting point which has come to be called 'ecosocialism'. In the extracts below Martin Ryle (himself an ecosocialist) sets out the terms of debate: a socialist acceptance of the need to rein in the profligate habits of industrialized countries, and an ecological acceptance that it speaks in the language of socialism (equality and social justice) and will need to draw on socialist defences of the state to put its project into action.

From Martin Ryle, *Ecology and Socialism* (London: Radius, 1988) pp. 6–8, 19–20, 60.

The limits of ecology as politics

I do not believe that anyone can read the extensive literature on the ecology crisis without concluding that its impact will oblige us to make changes in production and consumption of a kind, and on a scale, which will entail a break with the lifestyles and expectations that have become habitual in industrialized countries. . . .

However, the mere invocation of 'ecology', crucial as it is, does not in itself determine in a positive sense the future development of social and economic reality. A society adapted to ecological constraints – and that adaptation might come about by the sheer impact of scarcity and environmental catastrophe, quite as well as by way of democratic debate and planning – could take widely varying forms. . . .

One can imagine an authoritarian capitalist or post-capitalist society, with rigid and marked hierarchies of wealth and power, in which those at the top enjoyed ecologically profligate lifestyles amidst 'unspoiled' surroundings, protected by armed police from the mass of the people, who would endure an impoverished and 'sustainable' material standard of living in dangerously polluted habitats: many lineaments of such a society were found in nineteenth-century industrial cities, exist on a world scale today, and are visible (both as actuality and as growing potentiality) even within modern First-world countries. One can imagine a 'barrack socialism' in which an ecologically well-informed, bureaucratic élite directed the economy in accordance with environmental and resource constraints, but in which the population participated as more or less reluctant helots, rather than as enfranchised and responsible citizens: tendencies in that direction might emerge in 'actually existing socialism' as the ecology crisis sharpens. Or perhaps the political and economic institutions of both market and state socialist societies will prove incapable of mediating the pressures of unmet need and disappointed greed engendered by ecological scarcity (when, maybe, the 'period of reduced oil supplies and higher prices' sets in), and we shall have a kind of anarchy – not necessarily a pacific and libertarian kind. Tightening ecological limits will certainly affect relations between states, and the rich nations may well seek (are already seeking) to 'resolve' such a crisis 'independently of' – that is, at the continuing expense of – poorer countries. Some countries may retreat into autarkic self-preservation, others may seek closer ties of dependence on powerful allies. . . .

A variety of visions, most of them dystopian, can be entertained, all of them feasible in ecological terms – and none of them particularly green. Ecological limits may limit political choices, but they do not determine them. The green movement may attempt to assess every option against ecological criteria, and may claim that all its proposals are compatible with sustainability; but we should not make the mistake of thinking that no other proposals, and no other outcomes, could be compatible. We should not assume that 'ecology' can satisfactorily define the new politics we are trying to develop.

Social interests, ecological interests and the general interest

The fundamental tension between socialist and ecological perspectives lies in the fact that, while political ecology starts from the relation of humanity to nature, and with the general interest in ensuring that this relation is sustainable, socialism has concerned itself primarily with the distribution of power and wealth within societies, and specifically with the interests of a particular class, the working class, under capitalism. The socialist analysis of the relations of capitalist production discloses who benefits and who is oppressed, and envisages the ending of that oppression. The ecological critique, by contrast, focuses on the impact of a given level and pattern of material production on the ecosystem: changes which affect only the internal relations between classes are irrelevant from this point of view. This disparity of perspectives can amount to a directly contradictory diagnosis, and give rise to opposed political and economic programmes, when – as has usually been the historical case – socialist parties and administrations have made the objective of higher overall productivity a key part of their project, and have regarded capitalist social relations as an obstacle to the achievement of a more rationally ordered *because more productive* economy.

I have argued that green politics cannot adopt a 'purely ecological' approach: relations between people and classes are at stake the moment one begins to talk about structural economic and social change, even if change is originally advocated because of 'ecological' desires and fears. Moreover, as the green movement develops out of eco-protest and formulates comprehensive programmes, it finds itself asking not just what kinds of social relations are ecologically viable, but what kinds are good; and so confronts the questions about justice, autonomy and hierarchy, public and private spheres which have constituted political discourse since antiquity. It does so, what is more, in societies where many means and forces exist for the expression and mediation of social *interests*: trade unions, military-industrial lobbies, legal and financial institutions, elected assemblies, political parties.

Ecological politics cannot fail to recognize that we are social/political animals as well as denizens of an organic biosphere. Its historical importance, and the tensions which it embodies and to which it gives rise in politics generally, derive from the 'double vision' which this dual realization entails.

The state and the environment

The green movement has a strong decentralist and libertarian orientation, and anti-statism is also found, though not of course universally, on the Left. Much of my own argument hitherto, and especially my criticisms of the green emphasis on 'the local economy', runs counter to this anti-statist current. Most ecosocialists, myself included, doubtless *prefer* to imagine a decentralized federation of autonomous communities, producers' collectives and the like, co-operating on the basis of freely entered mutual association. If one is honest, however, about the objectives which an ecologically enlightened society would set for itself, it is difficult to avoid concluding that the state, as the agent of the collective will, would have to take an active law-making and -enforcing role in imposing a range of environmental and resource constraints. More problematically, an ecosocialist transformation, which I regard as necessary if we are to transcend the contradiction between ecological imperatives and market 'laws', implies the necessity of replacing the current, highly centralized institutions of capitalist finance and production, and here the state must play an active role also.

GREEN ECONOMICS

The Steady-State Economy

The American academic and economist Herman Daly produced some of the most influential early thinking on the nature of the sustainable economy. Here he describes the general features of a 'steady-state' economy, as he calls it, as well as the reasons for why we need one. The Laws of Thermodynamics play a large part in this, but Daly also suggests a series of 'moral' principles which point towards the desirability of such an economy. The date of this text (1977) and the fact that most members of the Green movement would still agree with its basic line of argument, is some indication of the consistency and durability of the Green position.

From H. Daly, 'The Steady-State Economy: What, Why, and How?' in D. Pirages, *The Sustainable Society: Implications for Limited Growth* (New York and London: Praeger, 1977) pp. 107–14.

What is a steady-state economy?

The steady-state economy is a physical concept. It is characterized by constant stocks of people and physical wealth maintained at some chosen, desirable level by a low rate of throughput. Throughput flow begins with depletion (followed by production and consumption) and ends with an equal amount of waste effluent or pollution. Benefits come from the services rendered by the stock of wealth (and people). This service or psychic income is unmeasurable, but it is clearly a function of the stock, not of the throughput flow. One cannot ride to town on the maintenance flow of the stock of automobiles, but only in an existing automobile that is a current member of the stock. Stocks yield services and require maintenance and replacement. The throughput flow is the maintenance cost of the stock. As such it should be minimized for any given stock size. . . .

Once a steady state is attained at some level of population and wealth, it would not be forever frozen at that level. As values and technology evolve, different levels might become both possible and desirable. But the growth (or decline) required to get to the new level would be seen as a temporary adjustment process, not a norm. The momentum of growth in population and capital currently creates our technological and moral development. In the steady state, technological and moral evolution would be autonomous rather than growth-induced. They would precede and pull growth in the most desirable direction, rather than being pushed down the path of least resistance by the pressure of autonomous growth. Growth (positive or negative) would always be seen as a temporary passage from one steady state to another.

Why? Assumption and values underlying the steady-state view

The steady-state view is based on physical, biological, and moral first principles and is immediately deductable from them without the aid of computer simulations.

The physical first principles are the laws of thermodynamics. . . .

From the first law (conservation of matter-energy) it is obvious that we do not produce or consume anything, we merely rearrange it. From the second law (increasing entropy) it is clear that our rearrangement implies a continual reduction in potential for further use within the system as a whole. In mining concentrated ores we convert usable energy to unusable energy. We concentrate and refine the material ores in 'production', but then by way of 'consumption' or depreciation we eventually, through friction, rust, accident, loss, decay, and so on, disperse the once-concentrated minerals all over the face of the earth so that they become forever useless. Entropy applies to materials as well as energy. For materials it means that order turns to disorder, the concentrated tends to be dispersed, the structured becomes unstructured. It is true that materials can be recycled and energy cannot, but materials recycling can never be 100 per cent complete. Some fraction of useful materials will be irrevocably lost during each cycle of use. For energy, entropy means that usable energy is always diminishing, and useless (equilibrium temperature) energy is always increasing. The distinction between useful and useless is an anthropomorphic one – in fact an economic distinction. Thus the relevance of entropy to economics is built into the very concept of entropy and requires no further demonstration. The concept itself originated with an economic problem: the maximum efficiency of heat engines. Entropic constraints are not abstractions far off in the future. We are not talking about the ultimate heat death of the universe. The effect of the entropy law is as immediate and concrete as the facts that you can't burn the same tank of gasoline twice, that organisms cannot live in a medium of their own waste products, and that efficiencies cannot reach, much less exceed, 100 per cent. The low entropy of highly organized stocks of wealth and human bodies must be maintained by the continual importation of low-entropy inputs from the environment and the continual exportation of high-entropy outputs back to the environment, where through the agency of solar-powered biogeochemical cycles they are transformed into low-entropy forms on varying timescales. The entropic flow, beginning with depletion and ending with population (the throughput), is the necessary cost of maintaining the stocks of commodities and people. Too large a throughput can disrupt the biosphere and impair its capacity to assimilate wastes. The world's sources of useful (low-entropy) matter and energy become depleted, while the sinks for waste high-entropy matter and energy become polluted. We live off of the depletion-pollution throughput and cannot exist or enjoy life without it. It is a necessary cost of existence and plentitude. But the entropic degradation is a cost and must be reckoned as a cost and minimized for any chosen level of population and per capita wealth. Unfortunately, it seems that our present economic institutions and theories are more attuned to maximizing throughput than to minimizing it. This results from the close association of throughput with GNP, which is taken as an index of welfare, and from our failure to recognize any concept of a mature or sufficient level of stocks.

It is true that we have a continual input of new low entropy in the form of sunlight (our earth system is open with respect to solar energy), so that it is possible to maintain and increase the order and complexity of the earth, via photosynthesis and life processes, at the expense of increasing the entropy of the sun. Solar energy only arrives at a fixed rate independent of man's will, and the entire biosphere has, over millions of years of evolution, adapted itself to living off this fixed income of solar energy. But in the last two centuries (a mere instant in the history of the biosphere) man has ceased to live within the annual solar budget and has become addicted to living off his capital of terrestrial stocks of low entropy (fossil fuels, minerals). Terrestrial stocks of fossil fuels represent a minute fraction of the energy available from the sun, but unlike the sun these stocks can be used at a rate of a man's own choosing that is, we cannot mine the sun, but we can mine, and rapidly deplete, terrestrial stocks. As population grew, man needed more food and undertook the work necessary to produce it, employing draft animals to help. As population continued to grow man became more reluctant to share his food-producing land to grow fodder for draft animals. Instead he began to feed tractors with fossil fuels and increased the ability of the land to support a larger population. Also, new products were produced and standards of individual consumption increased along with population, further increasing man's addiction to living off his terrestrial capital.

Some big problems emerge from this addiction. Our terrestrial capital will clearly become more and more scarce, and then for all practical purposes available non-renewable resources will be used up. Our national income accounts treat consumption of geological capital as current income, thus sanctifying the addiction. Substitution will extend the life of all resources, but will not 'create new resources' as metaphorically stated by many people. Whenever the net energy yield becomes zero (that is, it costs as much energy to mine a ton of coal as can be got from a ton of coal) then it becomes nonsensical to continue mining that energy source. This consideration is unaffected by prices and clearly shows that we will never be able to use all the resources in the earth's crust. Second, since man is the only species living beyond the solar budget, it is clear that such behaviour will throw the human species out of balance with the rest of the biosphere which, because of evolution over eons, has become ever more elaborately adapted to the fixed solar flow. Man is the only member of the biosphere who has broken this evolutionary budget constraint. It is only natural that this unique expansionary behaviour should cause repercussions and feedbacks from the rest of the system in the unhappy form of pollution and breakdown of local life-support systems. These systems are unable to accommodate man-made energy and material flows that constitute significant additions either to the local solar flux, or to that part of the solar flux trapped by photosynthesis, or to the natural volumes of solar-powered material cycles. The surprising thing is not that these breakdowns occur, but that they have not occurred to a greater degree. The ecosystem evidently has considerable slack, redundancy, and resilience. But the slack is being used up in one dimension after another – no one doubts that man has the capacity to destroy the biosphere, whether directly by war or indirectly through the growing commercialization of chemical and radioactive poisons (DDT and plutonium), with which the biosphere has had no evolutionary experience and to which it is consequently unadapted. . . .

The physical and biological first principles just discussed (that is, the first and second laws of thermodynamics, and the evolutionary adaption of the biosphere to solar energy) point toward the eventual necessity of a stabilized economy (that is, ignoring the first and second laws results in excessive depletion and pollution, which in turn provoke ecological disruption).

Independently, there are also some ethical first principles indicating the desirability of a steady state. Nearly all traditional religions teach man to conform his soul to reality by knowledge, self-discipline, and restraint on the multiplication of desires, as well as on the lengths to which one will go to satisfy a desire. The modern religions of technological scientism, magic, and economic growth seek to subjugate reality and bend it to the uninstructed will and whim of some men, usually to the uncounted detriment of other men. C. S. Lewis has reminded us that what we call the increasing dominance of 'man' over nature is really the increasing dominance of some men over other men with knowledge of nature serving as the instrument of domination. This may not be intentional or always a bad thing, but it should be recognized for what it is. There is a limit beyond which the extra costs of surrendering control over one's environs and activities to the experts becomes greater than the extra benefits. This is not anti-science – it is merely a warning against the idolatry of science by some of its zealous fanatics who are consecrated to redoubling their efforts while forgetting their purposes. . . .

For scientism and growth-mania there is no such thing as 'enough' even on the material plane. Indeed the whole idea seems to be to try to fill a spiritual void with material commodities. The usual objection to limiting growth, made in the name of the poor, only illustrates the extent of the void because it defends growth as an alternative to sharing, which is considered 'unrealistic', if not inconceivable. For the traditional attitude there is such a thing as material sufficiency, and beyond that admittedly vague and historically changing amount the goal of life becomes wisdom, enjoyment, cultivation of the mind and soul, and of community. It may be that community requires a certain degree of scarcity, without which cooperation, sharing, and friendship would have no organic reason to be, and hence community would atrophy. Witness the self-sufficiency and lack of community of middle-class suburbs.

Another ethical first principle is a sense of stewardship for all of creation, and an extension of some degree of brotherhood to future generations and to subhuman life. Clearly the first demands on brotherhood are those of presently existing human beings who do not enjoy material sufficiency. The answer to this failure of brotherhood is not simply more growth, but is mainly to be found in more sharing and more population control, both of which are necessary. Without population control, sharing will simply make everyone equally poor. Without sharing, population control will at best reduce the number of the poor, but will not eliminate poverty. If, as often happens, the rich limit their numbers and the poor do not, then birth control worsens the distribution of income. Both sharing and population control are basically moral problems whose solutions require sound values far more than clever techniques.

The virtue of humility is also high on the list of moral first principles. Much of the drive to convert the ecosphere into one big technosphere comes from the technological hubris of ordinary men who think that the scientific method has somehow transfigured them into little godlings who can collectively accomplish anything – if only society will give them more and more research funds. At a more basic level the drive comes from the need for doing and controlling as a verification of knowledge. There is no reason why we must do everything we know how to do, but there is a sense in which we cannot be sure we know how to do something unless we have done it. If we are going to avoid doing certain things we will have to sacrifice the forbidden knowledge that would have been gained.

Another important virtue is 'holism', the attitude that recognizes that the whole is greater than the sum of its parts, that reductionist analysis never tells the whole story, and that the abstractions necessary to make mechanistic models always do violence to reality. Those who habitually think in terms of abstract, reductionist models are especially prone to the 'fallacy of misplaced concreteness' – that is, applying to one level of abstraction conclusions arrived at from thinking on a different (higher) level of abstraction.

In sum the moral first principles are some concept of 'enoughness', stewardship, humility, and holism. In social science today one hears little of moral values or ethics (even though historically economics began as a branch of moral philosophy). Appeals to moral solutions, to a change in values, are considered as an admission of intellectual defeat, as a retreat from the rules of the game – as cheating. The quest is for clever mechanistic technical solutions, not straightforward moral solutions. Power-yielding techniques have been assiduously sought for, while the cultivation of right purposes has been neglected – some even consider the latter 'a meaningless question'. We now have growing power in search of shrinking purpose.

If one accepts these biophysical and moral first principles, then it will be hard for him to reject the ideal of a steady-state economy. If one rejects the moral first principles, he may still be convinced by arguments of necessity arising from the biophysical first principles. If one rejects the biophysical premises, he may still be led to accept the steady state for reasons of desirability arising from the moral premises. If one accepts both sets of first principles then he should be doubly convinced.

The Basic Income Scheme

The following extract comprises a comprehensive introduction to what is often regarded as the flagship of Green economic policy – the Basic Income Scheme. The idea is that present systems of benefits would be done away with and that, instead, every woman, man and child would receive a weekly payment as of right, non-means-tested and sufficient to cover basic needs. In the arguments in favour of such a scheme, below, first the problems with the present benefit system are identified, then the essential principles of the scheme are set out together with its advantages both to employers and employees. Finally, some criticisms of the scheme are noted and dealt with.

From Paul Ekins (ed.), *The Living Economy* (London: Routledge and Kegan Paul, 1986) pp. 225–32.

Given the invalidity of these key Beveridge assumptions[1], it is not surprising that the benefit system based on them is close to collapse. First there is the poverty trap, by which a pay rise for someone on a low wage can actually result in loss of income through the withdrawal of benefit. Even where there is a net income gain, the effective marginal tax rate (defined as the amount of income forfeited by the wage earner from each extra £1 earned, on account of tax or benefit withdrawal) can be greater than that experienced even in the highest income brackets. Then there is the unemployment trap, whereby if only low-income jobs are available, working at all can entail a drop in income for some people due to withdrawal of their benefits. There is also an idleness trap, involving the effective prohibitions on unemployed people doing voluntary work or anything else except 'looking for a job', even when there are obviously no jobs, which is a recipe for despair, alienation and depression. And there is the spendthrift trap, which discourages from saving people who think they might become unemployed, because sup-

---

[1] based on the premise that full employment is both possible and desirable.

plementary benefit is denied to those who have financial assets of more than £3,000.

In addition, the present system often involves means-testing, always a repugnant process, and sometimes involving the investigation of the most intimate of people's private lives, as with the cohabitation rule. Moreover, the system is so complicated that many of those who need the benefits most miss out on them, because they do not know their entitlements nor how to claim them.

There is no point trying to tinker with the superstructure of a system with such fundamental structural flaws. It needs to be rebuilt from first principles that have their roots in the realities, lifestyles and aspirations of the present day. Such a rebuilt system is the Basic Income Scheme:

> A Basic Income Scheme would aim to guarantee to each man, woman and child the unconditional right to an independent income sufficient to meet basic living costs. Its main purpose would be the prevention of poverty, as opposed to mere poverty relief.

These are the opening sentences of the Constitution of the Basic Income Research Group (BIRG), based in London, which seeks to encourage an informed debate about the desirability and practicability of the Basic Income idea. . . .

The Basic Income Scheme does not start from Beveridge's discredited assumptions. It grants an unconditional right to an independent income to all citizens, irrespective of other income, work status, sex or marital status. It advocates that such income should be adequate to meet basic living costs. For the sake of fairness, consistency and simplicity, it further advocates that it should replace existing benefits and tax-relief, being administered through an integrated tax-benefit system. . . .

The beneficial effects of a Basic Income Scheme are wide-ranging and profound. It would obviously abolish the poverty, unemployment, idleness and spendthrift traps: because the basic income is not withdrawn, people are free to take what work they can find, earn what they can and save what they wish. This would positively encourage the flexible working patterns discussed earlier, doing much to break down the distinction between the present stark alternatives of 'employed' or 'unemployed' and so diminishing the stigma of the latter. . . .

Much work that is currently not done, because of its inability to compete with benefits, would become viable, because even the low wage involved would represent an addition to the basic income. Some marginal employers who find difficulty paying the subsistence component of income would be able to employ people at a wage-rate determined purely by the value added by the work involved. From the point of view of labour, a worker would be able to negotiate a wage with subsistence already assured, so that people would not be forced by hardship into unpleasant work, but could hold out for the decent pay that such work should entail. A real choice would exist as to the mix between paid, unpaid, voluntary and domestic work which people wished to do, and the basic income would also make a reality of wages for housework, giving financial independence for the first time to those who were rearing children, keeping house or caring for dependent relatives. It would be society's acknowledgment of the vital importance of these tasks, without undermining their human, social component by seeking to bring them formally into the monetary economy as such. The lack of means-testing would end investigations of personal circumstances, and the simplicity of the scheme should ensure that no one slips through the net because of ignorance or confusion.

Given these advantages, which are largely uncontested, one must look at the objections which have so far prevented the implementation of Basic Income Schemes. The first is that a basic income, being a universal payment, is thought to be impossibly expensive and to entail very high tax rates, if it is to give adequate help to those who need it. Yet the alternative of selective payments can involve very high marginal tax rates on low-income earners. . . .

Even the present system in the UK is intended to give a guaranteed income (though with many strings attached and with the notable exception of five million married women) to those who cannot earn one. Formalizing this in a Basic Income Scheme need not entail any increase in taxation, if the basic income is set low enough. . . .

Notwithstanding the redistribution potential of Basic Income Schemes, some, especially on the political left, resent a scheme that guarantees an income to the rich as well as the poor. This is a peculiar blind spot, for those with high incomes will more than pay for their basic incomes through the higher tax rates involved in schemes such as those above.

A potentially more potent criticism is that the payment of a basic income would erode the incentive to work, at the low-wage end of the scale, by encouraging idleness, and at the high-wage end through the disincentive of high tax rates. In countering this suggestion, it must be pointed out again that, for those currently on unemployment benefit or on low pay, the payment of a basic income would significantly increase the incentive to work by abolishing the poverty and unemployment traps. For the rest, there are probably few people who would relish a life of idleness on £28 per week, and the basic income could always be indexed to the national income if this proved to be necessary. Higher incomes are already subject to higher tax rates and, in any case, the necessity to share work, especially highly paid work, which was emphasized at the end of the last chapter, means that it may be no bad thing if over-stressed executives were given some encouragement by high tax rates to work less hard at their jobs and spend more time with their families in their informal economies.

Buddhist Economics

Work is a sensitive issue for Greens. Some of them (probably a minority) think that economic systems should be geared to reduce the amount of work that needs to be done (through labour-saving machinery, for example), while others think that doing work enhances the human being in a number of important ways. In the extract below, from a chapter from *Small is Beautiful* with the unlikely title of 'Buddhist Economics', Fritz Schumacher argues for the latter point of view. He then goes on to suggest some of the wider implications of a Buddhist economics, all of which coincide with typical Green thinking: that standards of living are not best judged by counting consumption, that local production for local use should be the norm, and that resource-use must take into account long-term sustainability as well as short-term profit.

From E. F. Schumacher, *Small is Beautiful* (London: Abacus, 1974) pp. 44–51.

'Right Livelihood' is one of the requirements of the Buddha's Noble Eightfold Path. It is clear, therefore, that there must be such a thing as Buddhist economics. . . .

There is universal agreement that a fundamental source of wealth is human labour. Now, the modern economist has been brought up to consider 'labour' or work as little more than a necessary evil. From the point of view of the employer, it is in any case simply an item of cost, to be reduced to a minimum if it cannot be eliminated altogether, say, by automation. From the point of view of the workman, it is a 'disutility': to work is to make a sacrifice of one's leisure and comfort, and wages are a kind of compensation for the sacrifice. Hence the ideal from the point of view of the employer is to have output without employees, and the ideal from the point of view of the employee is to have income without employment.

The consequences of these attitudes both in theory and in practice are, of course, extremely far-reaching. If the ideal with regard to work is to get rid of it, every method that 'reduces the work load' is a good thing. The most potent method, short of automation, is the so-called 'division of labour' and the classical example is the pin factory eulogised in Adam Smith's *Wealth of Nations*. Here it is not a matter of ordinary specialization, which mankind has practised from time immemorial, but of dividing up every complete process of production into minute parts, so that the final product can be produced at great speed without anyone having had to contribute more than a totally insignificant and, in most cases, unskilled movement of his limbs.

The Buddhist point of view takes the function of work to be at last threefold: to give a man a chance to utilize and develop his faculties; to enable him to overcome his egocentredness by joining with other people in a common task; and to bring forth the goods and services needed for a becoming existence. Again, the consequences that flow from this view are endless. To organize work in such a manner that it becomes meaningless, boring, stultifying, or nerve-racking for the worker would be little short of criminal; it would indicate a greater concern with goods than with people, an evil lack of compassion and a soul-destroying degree of attachment to the most primitive side of this wordly existence. Equally, to strive for leisure as an alternative to work would be considered a complete misunderstanding of one of the basic truths of human existence, namely that work and leisure are complementary parts of the same living process and cannot be separated without destroying the joy of work and the bliss of leisure. . . .

The very start of Buddhist economic planning would be a planning for full employment, and the primary purpose of this would in fact be employment for everyone who needs an 'outside' job: it would not be the maximization of employment nor the maximization of production. Women, on the whole, do not need an 'outside' job and the large-scale employment of women in offices or factories would be considered a sign of serious economic failure. In particular, to let mothers of young children work in factories while the children run wild would be as uneconomic in the eyes of a Buddhist economist as the employment of a skilled worker as a soldier in the eyes of a modern economist.

While the materialist is mainly interested in goods, the Buddhist is mainly interested in liberation. But Buddhism is 'The Middle Way' and therefore in no way antagonistic to physical well-being. It is not wealth that stands in the way of liberation but the attachment to wealth; not the enjoyment of pleasureable things but the craving for them. The keynote of Buddhist economics, therefore, is simplicity and non-violence. From an economist's point of view, the marvel of the Buddhist way of life is the utter rationality of its pattern – amazingly small means leading to extraordinary satisfactory results.

For the modern economist this is very difficult to understand. He is used to measuring the 'standard of living' by the amount of annual consumption, assuming all the time that a man who consumes more is 'better off' than a man who consumes less. A Buddhist economist would consider this approach excessively irrational: since consumption is merely a means to human well-being, the aim should be to obtain the maximum of well-being with the minimum of consumption. Thus, if the purpose of clothing is a certain amount of temperature comfort and an attractive appearance, the task is to attain this purpose with the smallest possible effort, that is, with the smallest annual destruction of cloth and with the help of designs that involve the smallest possible input of toil. The less toil there is, the more time and strength is left for artistic creativity. It would be highly uneconomic, for instance, to go in for complicated tailoring, like the modern west, when a much more beautiful effect can be achieved by the skilful draping of uncut material. It would be the height of folly to make material so that it should wear out quickly and the height of barbarity to make anything ugly, shabby or mean. What has just been said about clothing applies equally to all other human requirements. The ownership and the consumption of goods is a means to an end, and Buddhist economics is the systematic study of how to attain given ends with the minimum means.

Modern economics, on the other hand, considers consumption to be the sole end and purpose of all economic activity, taking the factors of production – land, labour, and capital – as the means. The former, in short, tries to maximize human satisfactions by the optimal pattern of consumption, while the latter tries to maximize consumption by the optimal pattern of productive effort. It is easy to see that the effort needed to sustain a way of life which seeks to attain the optimal pattern of consumption is likely to be much smaller than the effort needed to sustain a drive for maximum consumption. We need not be surprised, therefore, that the pressure and strain of living is very much less in, say, Burma than it is in the United States, in spite of the fact that the amount of labour-saving machinery used in the former country is only a minute fraction of the amount used in the latter.

Simplicity and non-violence are obviously closely related. The

optimal pattern of consumption, producing a high degree of human
satisfaction by means of a relatively low rate of consumption, allows
people to live without great pressure and strain and to fulfil the
primary injunction of Buddhist teaching: 'Cease to do evil; try to
do good.' As physical resources are everywhere limited, people
satisfying their needs by means of a modest use of resources are
obviously less likely to be at each other's throats than people
depending upon a high rate of use. Equally, people who live in
highly self-sufficient local communities are less likely to get involved
in large-scale violence than people whose existence depends on
world-wide systems of trade.

From the point of view of Buddhist economics, therefore, production from local resources for local needs is the most rational way
of economic life, while dependence on imports from afar and the
consequent need to produce for export to unknown and distant
people is highly uneconomic and justifiable only in exceptional cases
and on a small scale. Just as the modern economist would admit
that a high rate of consumption of transport services between a
man's home and his place of work signifies a misfortune and not a
high standard of life, so the Buddhist economist would hold that to
satisfy human wants from faraway sources rather than from sources
nearby signifies failure rather than success. The former tends to
take statistics showing an increase in the number of ton/miles per
head of the population carried by a country's transport system as
proof of economic progress, while to the latter – the Buddhist
economist – the same statistics would indicate a highly undesirable
deterioration in the *pattern* of consumption.

Another striking difference between modern economics and
Buddhist economics arises over the use of natural resources.
Bertrand de Jouvenel, the eminent French political philosopher,
has characterized 'western man' in words which may be taken as a
fair description of the modern economist:

'He tends to count nothing as an expenditure, other than human
effort; he does not seem to mind how much mineral matter he
wastes and, far worse, how much living matter he destroys. He does
not seem to realize at all that human life is a dependent part of an
ecosystem of many different forms of life. As the world is ruled
from towns where men are cut off from any form of life other than
human, the feeling of belonging to an ecosystem is not revived.
This results in a harsh and improvident treatment of things upon
which we ultimately depend, such as water and trees.'

The teaching of the Buddha, on the other hand, enjoins a reverent and non-violent attitude not only to all sentient beings but also, with great emphasis, to trees. Every follower of the Buddha ought to plant a tree every few years and look after it until it is safely established, and the Buddhist economist can demonstrate without difficulty that the universal observation of this rule would result in a high rate of genuine economic development independent of any foreign aid. Much of the economic decay of South-East Asia (as of many other parts of the world) is undoubtedly due to a needless and shameful neglect of trees.

Modern economics does not distinguish between renewable and non-renewable materials, as its very method is to equalize and quantify everything by means of a money price. Thus, taking various alternative fuels, like coal, oil, wood, or water-power: the only difference between them recognized by modern economics is relative cost per equivalent unit. The cheapest is automatically the one to be preferred, as to do otherwise would be irrational and 'uneconomic'. From a Buddhist point of view, of course, this will not do; the essential difference between non-renewable fuels like coal and oil on the one hand and renewable fuels like wood and water-power on the other cannot be simply overlooked. Non-renewable goods must be used only if they are indispensable, and then only with the greatest care and the most meticulous concern for conservation. To use them heedlessly or extravagantly is an act of violence, and while complete non-violence may not be attainable on this earth, there is none the less an ineluctable duty on man to aim at the ideal of non-violence in all he does. . . .

It is in the light of both immediate experience and long-term prospects that the study of Buddhist economics could be recommended even to those who believe that economic growth is more important than any spiritual or religious values. For it is not a question of choosing between 'modern growth' and 'traditional stagnation'. It is a question of finding the right path of development, the Middle Way between materialist heedlessness and traditionalist immobility, in short, of finding 'Right Livelihood'.

The Problems with GNP

Building on the idea that there are limits to growth, Green economics – as the extracts which follow show – calls traditional 'growth is good' assumptions into question. Green economists suggest that the link between economic growth and increased welfare is by no means obvious (extracts 1 and 2), and that new ways of assessing the desirability of growth are required. They argue that traditional Gross National Product (GNP) indicators are hopelessly loose and inadequate for this task and illustrate the kinds of factors that would need to be taken into account to produce a life-enhancing indicator of the health of an economy (extracts 3 and 4).

From Paul Ekins (ed.), *The Living Economy* (London: Routledge and Kegan Paul, 1986) pp. 8–9, 38, 128–9, 132–3.

Most current economic policy, indeed the very orientation of economic theory, boils down to the pursuit of economic growth, as indicated by an increasing Gross National Product (GNP). An economy that is growing at 3 per cent per annum is thought to be performing adequately, more growth is splendid, less growth is worrying, no growth or negative growth indicates widespread economic failure. The assumption is that growth is good and more is better. It is as if economists had never heard of cancer. It is extraordinary that an entire social science, and the dominant discipline in today's world at that, can effectively have come to be based on such a simplistic assumption. It is the rejection of this assumption that the 'new economics' parts company most decisively from conventional economic theory.

The assumption is rejected on three main grounds. The first is that it confuses means with ends. The end purpose of economic activity is to increase human welfare. One way of doing this *may be* through some form of economic growth. But a *growth equals welfare* equation has no logical validity at all, for it begs three vital questions: growth of what? growth for whom? growth with what side-effects?

The answers to these questions have far more to do with the growth/welfare relation than the mere fact of economic growth itself. It is only by:

- showing that the growth has taken place through the production of goods and services that are inherently valuable and beneficial;
- demonstrating that these goods and services have been distributed widely throughout society;
- and proving that these benefits outweigh any detrimental effects of the growth process on other parts of society

that one can arrive at any sort of assessment as to whether a particular instance of economic growth is in fact a good or bad thing. Such an evaluation will vary, depending on personal attitudes and on the political perspective, and will still say nothing about economic growth in general. In time, perhaps, certain patterns of economic growth might come to be recognized as benign and life-enhancing, while others are perceived as wasteful, polluting or inequitable, as the case may be. Conventional economic thinking makes little or no attempt to make this assessment, nor has it developed the conceptual or political tools for such a task. For the 'new economics' their development and implementation is of the most fundamental importance.

The second flaw in the growth assumption, explored later in more detail, lies in its failure to appreciate the reality of a finite planet. A 3 per cent growth rate implies a doubling of production and consumption every twenty-five years. In the last twenty years, the decline in the resource base and global environmental degradation that are the result of growth economics have been impeccably documented, as will be seen. But growth economists and the politicians they advise still assume that economic growth on an indefinite basis is both possible and desirable, and hasten on towards environmental bankruptcy. The 'new economics', in contrast, is rooted in the recognition that human life and economic activity are an interdependent part of the wider ecological process that sustain life on earth and will either operate sustainably within those processes or bring about their own demise.

The third main ground for rejecting economic growth as the overriding policy objective is that its pursuit is actually likely to intensify the very economic problems which it is meant to solve, chief among them inflation and unemployment. This is because of the pattern of resource allocation to which the pursuit of economic growth inevitably seems to give rise. . . .

⁞⁞⁞⁞⁞⁞

The pursuit of growth in industrialized countries has been linked to a model of western industrial development, which has been applied in most countries and all continents. Even in its heyday, many of the poorest people in developing countries failed to benefit from the process. Now, after some years of recession, it is clear that only a handful of developing countries round the world have really taken off industrially, many of those that have tried are burdened with unserviceable levels of debt, the number of people in absolute poverty has risen and the global environment has taken a hammering that threatens the foundations of the biosphere.

With their money-based indicators and targets, oriented almost exclusively towards the formal economy, economists have consistently misread the situation and many of their prescriptions and remedies have actually caused it to deteriorate. Among other failings, these indicators are inclined to confuse costs and benefits, leave social and environmental factors out of account, and ignore the informal economy altogether as a source of work and wealth.

It is an awesome catalogue of failure and misconception, which the development of the new economic theory that follows seeks to remedy. . . .

⁞⁞⁞⁞⁞⁞

A large proportion of the outcome of the production process expressed each year in GNP does not represent any benefit to the quality of life and of the environment. On the contrary, it is an actual cost of production and consumption. The deficiency of the GNP concept becomes particularly obvious when it is recognized that GNP can be increased by methods of production which involve environmental destruction and social costs. The more environmentally damaging and spatially concentrated the production process, the greater the price to be paid in environmental protection and social costs, called here 'defensive expenditures'. These costs are then added into GNP and this higher level is hailed by economists, politicians and the business community as an achievement.

For the interest groups who see no future economic strategy other

than the pursuit of growth, the expansion of defensive costs offers
a new and certain growth mechanism in the context of industrial
decline, allowing the problem-generating industries to be comp-
lemented by the new problem-solving industries. The damage-con-
trol and damage-repair sector thus becomes a new opportunity for
growth for national economies, but, far from indicating an increase
in human well-being, this sector could be interpreted as representing
a decline in the quality of life to a level which now made defensive
expenditures essential.

A more appropriate perspective for the future can be described
as differentiated development, in which different sectors would
experience either growth or contraction depending on the substan-
tive goals of an ecologically- and socially-sound economic development. Such development would no longer be the chance result of
following a profit-oriented policy of non-selective growth.

In order to organize this qualitative development, differentiated
criteria of measurement are needed. More specifically, ways must
be found of differentiating within GNP, and identifying defensive
production and consumption activities, so as to arrive at an empirical
demonstration of the full costs of industrial activity. In this way it
will be possible to differentiate between types of production in
terms of the concepts of defensive and autonomous, i.e. beneficial,
expenditures. . . .

It should by now be becoming clear what constitutes economic
progress in the context of the new economic framework described
in this book:

- increasing satisfaction of the whole range of human needs,
  with the emphasis on personal development grounded in
  social justice; good health for all, conceived as the ability of
  the individual or group to satisfy their needs, achieve their
  personal aspirations and change or cope with their environment;
- more equitable sharing of work both in the formal and informal economies, with due value being given to each and with
  a new emphasis being put on the quality of work (the skills
  it uses and develops, the satisfaction it gives and its social
  usefulness) and on the quality of the technology which helps
  a person to do it;

- greater economic self-reliance at the individual, local, provincial, national and regional levels;
- conservation and ecological enhancement of the environment and sustainable use of natural resources, based on the realization that increased consumption in a context of sustainability can only be achieved by making better, more efficient use of a sustainable quantity of resources, rather than by increasing overall throughput.

It need hardly be further stressed that conventional economic indicators are both inadequate and inappropriate for measuring progress towards these complex, multi-dimensional goals. Enough has already been said about how the panacea commitment to economic growth cannot succeed even in its own terms; far less can GNP indicate the sort of economic achievement described above. New indicators are needed, especially tailored to measure the kind of progress that is being sought, and this chapter both defines the sort of indicators now required and elaborates some of them in more detail. It examines in turn:

- resource indicators and resource accounting;
- a new indicator of national product, called here the Adjusted National Product (ANP), basically consisting of GNP with the social and environmental costs deducted from it, rather than added to it;
- indicators of health;
- social indicators;
- ways of taking the informal economy into economic account, so that its contribution to the national economy can be fully appreciated and valued.

Improvement across this range of indicators really would show that overall progress in terms of wealth, health, well-being, economic security and the fulfilment of obligations to future generations had been achieved.

Local money

Local money schemes loom large in the thought of some Green economists. In the extract below, Guy Dauncey explains the workings of a local money system with a difference – no money circulates at all. The aims of the LETSystem are, though, the same as those of any local money scheme: to keep money local, and to provide the incentive for, and the possibility of, work in areas which are economically depressed. The LETSystem described here was set up by Michael Linton on Vancouver Island, Canada, in 1983.

From Guy Dauncey, *After the Crash: the emergence of the rainbow economy* (Basingstoke: Green Print, 1988) pp. 52–64.

The recession of the early 1980s had brought an enormous increase in unemployment, and a lot of local people, Michael included, were having problems with their income. Michael tried bartering his own skills in bodywork (being a trained teacher of the Alexander Technique), but found that it was a hopelessly slow method of trading. So he sat down and invented a new kind of money.

The result of his late-night ponderings was the 'Local Employment and Trade System', or 'LETSystem'. The LETSystem puts barter on to a non-profit, multi-centred, community-wide basis. It does this by inventing a new kind of local money called the 'Green Dollar', which facilitates local trade.

Unlike other money, the Green Dollar is invisible. You can't hold it, or stash it in a box under your bed. Nor can you lose it, steal it or accidentally send it to the laundry in the back pocket of your jeans. It only exists as information. The LETSystem has various other special qualities which we will consider later. But first – how does it work?

A number of people who live locally and who want to trade together get together, agree to the LETSystem rules, and give themselves account numbers. Each person then makes out two lists, one of 'wants' and one of 'offers', with prices attached (following normal market prices). A joint list is made up and circulated to everyone. Then the members look down the list, phone whoever has what they want, and start trading. Trading can also happen through newspaper advertisements, or personal contacts. The limits of one-to-one barter are eliminated, as you can now trade with the people in the system as a whole: barter is now a collective proposition.

Green Dollars don't exist as tangible money, and no notes are printed, or coins minted. When people trade, the purchaser calls up the central office and leaves a message on an answering machine saying: 'This is Elspeth Simpson, No 54. Please credit Jock MacIntosh, No 273, with $100 in Green for computer lessons'. At the LETSystem office, someone enters this information into the books, and also into a computer. Jock acquires a $100 credit, and Elspeth a $100 'commitment' or debit, like an overdraft or 'minus account'. Elspeth's debit carries no interest, as the whole system is interest-free, both credits and debits.

And so the trading goes on. Every month, a trades bulletin is sent out to the members. Elspeth didn't have to have $100 Green in her account before she spent it – and Jock, confident that he can earn more Green Dollars from giving computer lessons, can go out and purchase the beat-up old Volkswagon van that he has seen listed for $1,000 Green, thus putting himself $900 Green into commitment . . .

The LETSystem that Michael invented in Courtenay started trading in 1983. By 1985 it had 500 members who had done over $300,000 worth of trading up to that time, in everything from vegetables and goats' milk to dentistry, building work and room rental. By 1990, although the original Courtenay LETSystem had effectively wound up (see below) around fifty systems were operating world-wide, including twenty-six in Australia. . . .

As soon as people learn about the LETSystem they start asking questions to test it for snags, and to attempt to find its Achilles heel.

Do you have to pay taxes on Green Dollar earnings?

In Canada, the tax authorities have ruled that Green Dollar earnings in the pursuit of your normal profession are taxable, but that other Green Dollar earnings are not. Thus if you are a carpenter by trade, you will have to pay taxes if you earn $1,000 Green for fixing someone's attic; but if your basic trade is anything else, you will not. The tax situation in each country would have to be ascertained. . . .

What happens if someone accumulates a large commitment (debit) by spending lots of Green Dollars, and then leaves town, or simply refuses to honour their commitment?

This is a risk, and if it happens, the cost of the default is spread among the whole community, as that much energy is no longer circulating reciprocally. Instead of flowing on, the energy represented by the loss stagnates, and can introduce a sluggishness into the system. There are several possible solutions as follows:

1. Information on a person's accounts can be requested, so if you have doubts about someone's willingness to work off their commitment, you can see a statement of their balance before agreeing to trade. This is the normal LETS arrangement so far.
2. A graph showing all the balances in the system can be circulated each month with the newsletter, allowing people to form their own decisions about how far they should put themselves in credit by earning Green. Other options are also possible, such as setting general limits, publishing information about extreme accounts, or establishing an elected council to discuss solutions. . . .

How can unemployed people make use of the scheme, when the law says that people receiving welfare can only earn a very limited amount of money before their earnings are deducted from their welfare?

So far, there are no clear answers to this question. In Canada, Green Dollar earnings are counted in the same way as normal earnings, and deducted from benefit. . . .

Is there any limit to the number of people who can join?

Probably – but it has not been reached yet in any current LETSystem. Ideally, a LETSystem should remain small enough for an individual to understand how it works, and be limited to a geographical area local enough for people to meet each other personally. Five thousand people is probably the natural limit for any one system. If it grew too big, it would lose its human qualities.

Can I sell my services for (say) half Green and half ordinary money?

Yes. The dentist in Courtenay gives many treatments on this basis, and many other people trade in this manner.

What about shops? Can they buy and sell goods in Green Dollars?

Yes – they just need to ensure that they cover their costs in cash. Some shops sell locally-produced goods in Green Dollars and imported goods in ordinary dollars, while others offer an overall '10 per cent Green' policy, meaning '90 per cent normal money, 10 per cent Green'. The basic guideline is 'costs in cash, value-added in Green'. . . .

Surely, if a local economy only used Green Dollars,
people wouldn't be able to buy things like new cars or video cameras?

The LETSystem is not meant to replace ordinary money – it is meant to be used alongside it. There will always be ordinary money as well. If the circulation of ordinary money in the economy dries up, however, because of unemployment or recession, the LETSystem will keep on flowing. That's why it is so valuable. Green money will be preferred for local trading, and ordinary money saved for the import/export part of the community economy. . . .

What kind of opposition has the LETSystem received?

Plenty. In the early days, before it started getting national publicity, left-wingers thought it was right-wing stuff and right-wingers thought it was a communist takeover. Local businessmen thought it must be some kind of scam (con-trick) – it really worried them that they couldn't see any way to lose. They see life like a poker game, and can't accept a win-win situation. Where the men were suspicious, the women were generally much more pragmatic – they said 'Let's see if it works, and then get on with it'. . . .

The Green Dollar system has seven essential qualities.

The first is its *inherent simplicity*, and ease of operation. It represents the first complete break with the old idea of tangible 'money'. It is effectively self-regulating because of built-in constraining factors to do with local relationships, trust, and people's desire to have friends. It is compatible with the existing system of money, and above all, it works.

The LETSystem's second quality is that *it enables money to remain exactly what it is – information.* Money is simply pieces of paper which inform you about the values they represent. Once it becomes 'solid' it takes on a life of its own, and all sorts of strange things happen as people begin to deal in money for its own sake. Because Green Dollars have no tangible existence, they cannot be forged, devalued, hoarded, stolen or lost. No one can get a corner on the money supply, bringing trade to a halt and then leasing it out at a high interest, which is how some banks have behaved in the past. Nor can anyone control its flow, and then make a loan dependent on your having material collateral of some kind as security. No one owns the money in the first place, so no one can lend it to you.

Its third quality is its *total decentralization*. New Green money is created in a natural, organic way – by someone creating something of real value, and trading it with someone else. There are no board meetings when the governors sit down and discuss how much money they should create. Its creation is related directly to its source, which is our own creativity as people.

Its fourth quality is that *every transaction is a personal one*, which brings you new friends and relationships. A LETSystem enables a community to discover itself, perhaps for the first time. . . .

From these new relationships come many important invisible wealths – friendships, childcare arrangements, parties, greater recognition on the local streets, increased security, and a general broadening of the sense of community.

Fifth, *it encourages initiative and creative energy, and builds self-esteem and self-reliance*, both in individuals and in families. It removes the straitjacket of the full-time job which binds people's self-esteem to the job they have and causes many unemployed people to feel worthless. The monthly listing of wants and offers says to a discouraged worker 'Look at all these different ways in which people are earning Green Dollars. Maybe I am good for some of that, too.' It re-awakens the natural creativity of initiative which we all possess, but which many people lose touch with when they receive a regular salary or welfare-cheque. It begins to address some of the unmet needs that so many people have. . . .

Its sixth quality is that *the Green Dollar is limited to local circulation within the local economy*, and cannot leave the local economy to buy carpets from Samarkand to Toyotas from Korea, taking the wealth and the purchasing power that it represents with it. Because it *must* circulate locally, every trading transaction necessarily stimulates another, and in this way, the talent and creativity of local people is drawn out. . . .

In the ordinary economy, there is no commitment to the local community built into the patterns of trading. In return, it offers the freedom of the global market, which is also important. The LETSystem does not deny the value of the global economy or of free global trading – it is a complementary, not an alternative system. It simply says that if a local economy becomes too dependent on such trading, it becomes very vulnerable to the vagaries of international trade winds, and that too much global trading undermines community stability and sustainability. Many local economies risk becoming forgotten backwaters far away from the ocean of the global economy, with local people dependent on welfare, if they play all their cards in the global game. In addition to the global marketplace, communities must therefore also set up more limited local marketplaces, through which essential community needs can be met and local self-reliance strengthened.

In fostering community self-reliance, the LETSystem also helps to ground a local economy in its own resources, encouraging local production for local need, and strengthening the resources base and the ecological stability of the area.

Finally, the LETSystem *restores the quality of the gift economy to the modern trading economy*. People in Courtenay who trade in Green Dollars say that they experience an uncommon 'lightness of being' in their trading relationships. Normal trading relationships are often impersonal, reflecting the lack of personal contact between the people concerned. People who use the LETSystem have been surprised at how good it feels to trade in it. The system encourages trust and friendship, not suspicion, and this quality seems to permeate the transactions that occur within it. If you repair Phil's roof, you give him your energy and your craftsmanship, as well as a new roof; if you do the work with love, you are giving him an even bigger gift.

This is not to say that this cannot also happen in the ordinary economy – but when it does, it is the exception, not the rule. In the LETSystem, it seems to become the rule.

Author's footnote:

The Courtenay system wound up in 1989, chiefly because of organizational problems stemming from the lack of a locally-elected steering committee. Other LETSystems are blossoming, particularly in Australia, thanks largely to the organizational skills of Jill Jordan, who trained with Michael Linton in 1987 and subsequently took a LETSystem Roadshow around the country. One of these successfully operating Australian systems is the Maleny LETSystem which has about 240 members, and a monthly turnover of some 5,500 'Bunyas' (named after a local tree).

Valuing the environment

Having finally taken on board the environmentalists' message that 'there's no such thing as a free lunch' in environmental terms, economists are now faced with the problem of how to cost the lunch. In the summer of 1989 David Pearce, professor of economics at University College London, was appointed economics adviser to Chris Patten, Minister for the Environment in Margaret Thatcher's Conservative Party cabinet. He, together with Anil Markandya and Edward Barbier, produced the Pearce Report in which principles for costing the environment were laid out, and a flavour of the report is captured in the passage below. The importance of these principles extends far beyond the British context as they are likely to provide the direction in which any market economy which takes the environment seriously will move. It is of interest to read, then, that 'unaffected markets fail to allocate resources efficiently', especially when we consider that this report was written for a government which has staked its reputation on free market economics. The basic strategy is to modify markets so that environmental services are costed and taken into account, and two examples – pollution charges/taxes and a carbon tax – are described. A basic problem faced by 'market modifiers' is what value to put on various bits of the environment in the first place. Confidence is not increased when we discover that a Washington University economist gave as one reason for pricing Kenya's elephants at $25 million that the figure was 'easy to remember'.

From David Pearce, Anil Markandya, Edward B. Barbier, *Blueprint for a Green Economy* (London: Earthscan, 1989) pp. 5–7, 154–5, 162–5.

Valuing the environment

One of the central themes of environmental economics, and central to sustainable development thinking also, is the need to place proper values on the services provided by natural environments. The central problem is that many of these services are provided 'free'. They have a zero price simply because no market place exists in which their true values can be revealed through the acts of buying and selling. Examples might be a fine view, the water purification and storm protection functions of coastal wetlands, or the biological diversity within a tropical forest. The elementary theory of supply and demand tells us that if something is provided at a zero price, more of it will be demanded than if there was a positive price. Very simply, the cheaper it is the more will be demanded. The danger is that this greater level of demand will be unrelated to the capacity of the relevant natural environments to meet the demand. For example, by treating the ozone layer as a resource with a zero price there never was any incentive to protect it. Its value to human populations and to the global environment in general did not show up anywhere in a balance sheet of profit or loss, or of costs and benefits.

The important principle is that resources and environments serve economic functions and have positive value. To treat them as if they had zero value is seriously to risk overusing the resource. An 'economic function' in this context is any service that contributes to human well-being, to the 'standard of living', or 'development'. *This simple logic underlines the importance of valuing the environment correctly and integrating those correct values into economic policy.*

It is this argument that leads us to reject the first line of reasoning against the emphasis on environmental quality. We have a sound *a priori* case for supposing that the environment has been used to excess. Its degradation results, in part at least, from the fact that it is treated as a zero-priced resource when, in fact, it serves economic functions that have positive value.

Notice that this does not mean we should automatically introduce actual, positive prices for environmental functions wherever we can. There is a case for 'making the user pay', as we shall see. But for the moment the important principle to establish is that in our economic accounting, in the weighing up of the pros and cons of capital investments and economic policies, we should try, as best we can, to record the economic values that natural environments provide. It is, after all, something of an accident that some goods and services and some natural resources have markets whereas others do not. Even if it is possible to argue that, eventually, all natural resources will generate their own markets, we have no assurance at all that those markets will evolve before the resource is extinguished or irreparably damaged. . . .

Market and prices

The most desirable feature of the price mechanism is that it signals to consumers what the cost of producing a particular product is, and to producers what consumers' relative valuations are. In a nutshell, this is the elegance and virtue of free markets which economists have (generally) found so attractive since the time of Adam Smith.

As Chapter 1 noted, however, many environmental products, services and resources do not get represented in the price mechanism. This effectively amounts to them being treated as 'free goods', i.e. they have zero prices. It follows that an *unfettered* price mechanism will use too much of the zero-priced goods. Resources and environments will become degraded on this basis alone, i.e. because the price mechanism has wrongly recorded environmental goods as having zero prices when, in fact, they serve economic functions which should attract positive prices.

But economic goods and services themselves 'use up' some of the environment. Trace gases 'use' the atmosphere and troposphere as a waste sink; municipalities use rivers and coastal waters as cleaning agents for sewage, and so on. The cost of producing any good or service therefore tends to be a mixture of priced 'inputs' (labour, capital, technology) and unpriced inputs (environmental services). The market price for goods and services does not therefore reflect the true value of the totality of the resources being used to produce them. Unfettered markets fail to allocate resources efficiently. Or, in the economists' language, there is a divergence between private and social cost.

There are of course, ways in which freely functioning 'unfettered' markets will achieve improvements in environmental quality. If consumers change their tastes in favour of less polluting products and against more polluting forces, market forces will lead to a change in the 'pollution content' of final products and services. This is the 'green consumerism'* argument. For green consumerism to be effective consumers must be *informed* about the pollution profile of the products they buy. Government has a role, with other agencies, in extending the amount and quality of this information.

Green consumerism may do little to alter *production processes* since the consumer (a) is generally less well-informed about these processes and (b) is less able to impact on the choice of process. Process changes will occur if industry also becomes environmentally conscious, and/or the cost signals to industry alter.

There are two ways in which markets can be restructured so as to ensure that environmental services enter into the market system more effectively.

First, we could create markets in previously free services: all natural areas could charge entrance fees, coastal zones could be placed under private ownership with the owners charging for the use of coastal waters as sewage dumps, and so on. This is the *full privatization* option.

Second, we could 'modify' markets by centrally deciding the value of the environmental services and ensuring that those values are incorporated into the prices of goods and services. We refer to this regulatory approach as using the market, or establishing *market-based incentives*.

In what follows we explore the latter option and not the former. Apart from our terms of reference, the rationale here is simply that many environmental functions cannot be handed over to private ownership – the ozone layer, the oceans, the atmosphere are examples. Moreover, a market-based system of regulation can be shown to be more efficient than one based on 'command-and-control', i.e. one which simply sets environmental standards and enforces them without the aid of market-based incentives.

How then would a market-based incentive system work so as to contribute to sustainable development? . . .

What are market-based incentives?

Pollution charges/taxes

Market-based incentives are almost self-explanatory: they are incentive systems that operate, generally through establishing *prices* for environmental services, via a market. The markets in question are either established ones, for example existing markets in goods and services or in labour and capital equipment. Or the market may be 'created', usually with some form of encouragement from government.

The simplest conceptual form of a market-based incentive is the *pollution charge or tax*. Essentially what happens here is that a charge is set on the product (or the inputs used to make the product) so as to raise the cost of producing the product. The charge should then bear some relationship to the value of the environment services used in production. Ideally, the charge would equal the value of the MEC [Marginal External Cost] in the basic price equation established previously. But it is also the case that even where the PPP [Polluter Pays Principle] is modified to mean that the polluter bears the initial cost of meeting a pre-ordained standard, a charge can be very useful. Above all, it can be shown that charges often produce lower compliance costs – the costs that polluters bear in meeting the standard – than would be the case if the standard was simply set and polluters were legally obliged to honour it however best they see fit.

The basic reason why charges are likely to be better than 'command-and-control' techniques is that charges enable a polluter to choose how to adjust to the environmental quality standard. Polluters with high costs of abating pollution will prefer to pay the charge. Polluters with low costs of abatement will prefer to install abatement equipment. By making abatement something that 'low cost' polluters do rather than 'high cost' ones, charges tend to cut down the total costs of compliance.

Note, once again, there is no question of the charging mechanism reducing the environmental quality standard. It is the *same* standard as would be achieved by command-and-control. The charge simply introduces flexibility into the compliance mechanism. Command-and-control, because of its rigidities, does not do this.

The first proposition, then, is that pollution charges are generally better than 'command-and-control'. Such a blanket statement disguises many problems with taxes, but for current purposes the general implication is correct. A tax adjusts market prices to reflect the use of environmental services which are otherwise erroneously treated as being free. Command-and-control policies adopt a regulatory stance which ignores the efficiencies of the market mechanism. . . .

A carbon tax

A tax on carbon fuels is widely discussed as a means of combating
global warming through the release of greenhouse gases. A carbon
tax would be graduated according to the carbon content of fuels.
Thus coal would attract a higher tax than oil which in turn would
attract a higher tax than natural gas. Electricity would not be taxed
directly but would pay the taxes on the carbon fuels. In this way
the electricity sector would alter its fuel mix to a less carbon-
polluting form.

As noted above, any tax on an input such as fuel will be partly
borne by producers, partly by consumers. This is consistent with
the PPP.

What is the effect on consumers? If consumers have a choice of
heating systems for households one would expect some substitution
of less polluting heating systems (e.g. gas) for more polluting systems (e.g. oil). Many households, however, are 'locked in' to existing heating technologies. The effect of a carbon tax on these consumers, as on those who have a choice of systems, is to encourage
conservation, i.e. the reduction in the total amount of energy consumed.

Thus, a carbon tax would encourage:

1. a switch in the fuel mix of the industrial and electricity
   sector;
2. a switch in the fuel mix of the household sector;
3. energy conservation in all energy-using sectors.

These advantages of a carbon tax need to be set against possible
disadvantages. First, an energy tax tends to be regressive in so far
as the poor and aged respond less in terms of energy conservation
than do the better off and younger sections of society. But many
taxes are regressive and mechanisms to offset the regressiveness do
exist, e.g. through other tax or benefit concessions.

Second, a carbon tax may appear to add to the tax base of the
taxing country. New taxes tend to be treated with suspicion. One
possibility for encouraging wider acceptance is to couple the carbon
tax with reductions in other taxes. A carbon tax associated with
other tax offsets obviously generates no gain in net revenue to
government, but it still serves the important function of correcting
the resource misallocation arising from the failure to charge the full
social cost of energy use.

Third, a carbon tax *in one country alone* is likely to have negligible impact on the problem of global warming. The reasons for this are that (a) carbon gases are only one of the gases contributing to the 'greenhouse effect' (CO_2 maybe accounts for 50 per cent of all greenhouse gases), and (b) any one country tends to contribute small amounts to the overall CO_2 global emission level. A third possible reason for limited impact would arise if the demand for energy is 'price inelastic', i.e. if demand is comparatively unresponsive to price. This suggests that a carbon tax is one instrument for consideration in a *global convention* on carbon emissions.

The principles underlying a carbon tax are the same for any energy source: the full social costs of energy use should be reflected in the price of energy. The greenhouse gas problem is only one environmental issue. 'Acid rain' pollution tends to reinforce the idea of taxing carbon fuels. In the same way, while nuclear power is free of a carbon tax, its own social costs need to be reflected in electricity prices. Such costs include waste disposal, decommissioning, routine radiation and the costs of accidents.

Depletion Quotas vs. Pollution Taxes

As governments around the world, in the face of increasing public pressure, strive to green their rhetoric and – sometimes – their policies, pollution taxes* are becoming an ever more popular option. While Greens are obviously not opposed to pollution taxes as such, they are keen to make us aware of the danger of concentrating on them to the exclusion of other measures. Even more seriously, the American academic and economist Herman Daly here suggests that pollution taxes work at the wrong end of the extraction-production-waste process, and argues in favour of 'depletion quotas' instead. For Greens the most important thing is to reduce extraction rates – first, to make our resources last longer; and second, because reducing extraction is an absolute guarantee of reducing production and therefore waste and pollution too. Greens may have trouble converting the public and their governments to depletion quotas, as these mean not only cleaning up the production process, but reducing production – and therefore consumption – itself.

From Herman Daly, 'The Steady-State Economy: What, Why, and How?' in D. Pirages, *The Sustainable Society: Implications for Limited Growth* (New York and London: Praeger, 1977) pp. 121–4.

The strategic point at which to impose control on the throughput flow seems to me to be the rate of depletion of resources, particularly non-renewable resources. If we limit aggregate depletion, then by the law of conservation of matter and energy we will also indirectly limit aggregate pollution. Entropy is at its minimum at the input (depletion) end of the throughput pipeline, and at its maximum at the output (pollution) end. Therefore it is physically easier to monitor and control depletion than pollution – there are fewer mines, wells, and ports than there are smokestacks, garbage dumps, and drainpipes, not to mention such diffuse emission sources as run off of insecticides and fertilizers from fields into rivers and lakes, and auto exhausts. Given that there is more leverage in intervening at the input end, should we intervene by way of taxes or quotas? Quotas, if they are auctioned by the government rather than allocated on non-market criteria, have an important net advantage over taxes in that they definitely limit aggregate throughput, which is the quantity to be controlled. Taxes exert only an indirect and very uncertain limit. It is quite true that given a demand curve, a price plus a tax determines a quantity. But demand curves shift and are subject to great errors in estimation, even if stable. Demand curves for resources could shift up as a result of population increase, change in tastes, increase in income, and so on. Every time we increase a price (internalize an externality) we also increase an income, so that in the aggregate the economy can still purchase exactly as much as before. Say the government seeks to limit throughput by taxing it. It then spends the tax. On what? On throughput. If government expenditures on each category of throughput were equal to the revenues received from taxing that same category, then the limit on throughput would be largely cancelled out. If the government taxes resource-intensive items and spends on time-intensive items there will be a one-shot reduction in aggregate physical throughput, but not a limit to its future growth. A credit expansion by the banking sector, an increase in velocity of circulation of money, or deficit spending by the government for other purposes could easily offset even the short-run reduction induced by taxes. Taxes can influence the amount of depletion and pollution (throughput) per unit of GNP, but taxes provide no limit to the increase in the number of units of GNP (unless the government runs a growing surplus), and no limit to aggregate throughput. The fact that a tax levied on a single resource could by inducing substitution usually reduce the throughput of that resource very substantially should not mislead us into thinking that a general tax on all or most resources will reduce aggregate throughput (fallacy of composition). First, it is quantity that affects the ecosystem, not price, and therefore it is ecologically safer to let errors and unexpected shifts in demand result in price fluctuations rather than in quantity fluctuations. Hence quotas.

Pollution taxes also provide a much weaker inducement to resource-saving technological progress than do depletion quotas, since in the former scheme resource prices do not necessarily have to rise, and may even fall. The inducement of pollution taxes is to 'pollution avoidance', and thus to recycling. But increased competition from recycling industries, instead of reducing depletion, might spur the extractive industries to even greater competitive efforts. Intensified search and the development of technologies with still larger jaws (for example, strip mining) could speed up the rate of depletion and thereby lower resource prices. Thus new extraction might once again become competitive with recycling, leading to less recycling and more depletion and pollution – exactly what we wish to avoid. This perverse effect could not happen under a depletion quota system.

The usual recommendation of 'pollution taxes' would seem, if the above is correct, to intervene at the wrong end with the wrong policy tool. Intervention by pollution taxes also tends to be micro-control, rather than macro. There are, however, limits to the ability of depletion quotas to influence the qualitative nature and spatial location of pollution, and at this fine-tuning level pollution taxes would be a useful supplement, as would a bureau of technology assessment. Depletion quotas would induce resources-saving technological change, and the set of resource-saving technologies probably overlaps to a great degree with the set of socially benign technologies. But the coincidence is not complete and there is still a need, though a diminished one, for technology assessment.

How might a depletion quota system function? Let there be quotas set on new depletion on each of the basic resources, both renewable and non-renewable, during a given time period. Let legal rights to deplete up to the amount of the quota for each resource be auctioned off by the government, at the beginning of each time period, in conveniently divisible units, to private firms, individuals, and public enterprises. After purchases from the government the quota rights are freely transferable by sale or gift, and can be retained for use in subsequent time periods. As population growth and economic growth press against resources the prices of the depletion quotas will be driven higher and higher. Reduction of quotas to lower levels in the interest of conservation of non-renewables and sustainable exploitation of renewables would drive the price of the quotas still higher. The increasing windfall rents resulting from increasing pressure of demand on fixed supply would be captured by the government through the auctioning of the depletion rights. The government spends the revenues, let us say, by paying a social dividend. Even though the monetary flow is therefore undiminished, the real flow (throughput) has been physically limited by the resource quotas. All prices of resources and of goods increase, with the prices of resource-intensive goods increasing relatively more. Total resource consumption (depletion) is reduced. Moreover, by the law of conservation of matter-energy, if ultimate inputs are reduced so must ultimate output (pollution) be reduced. The aggregate throughput is reduced and with it the gross stress it puts on the ecosystem.

With depletion now more expensive and with higher prices on final goods, recycling becomes more profitable. As recycling increases, effluents are reduced even more. Also higher prices make consumers more interested in durability and careful maintenance of wealth. The extra burden on the poor of increased prices can be more than offset via the distributist institution. Most importantly there is now a strong price incentive to develop new resource-saving technologies and patterns of consumption. If there is any static efficiency loss in setting the rate of depletion outside the market (a very doubtful point), it seems to be more than offset by the dynamic benefits of greater inducements to resource-saving technological progress.

GREEN POLITICAL STRATEGIES

Changing to Green

Very few writers on Green politics have taken a systematic look at the issue of social change, or how to bring about the kind of sustainable society which they believe to be necessary for survival. Brian Tokar, of the United States, is an exception to this general rule and in the extract reproduced below he raises most of the important questions, such as: can sustainability be brought about by tinkering with the present system or is more fundamental change required?; can local action bring about global change?; what is the role of direct action in the Green movement?; can change by example (co-operatives, communes, individual lifestyle) bring about sustainability?; is electoral politics a realistic option or a dead-end?; at what point on the road to a sustainable society will governments, perhaps violently, call a halt, and how should the Green movement react?

From Brian Tokar, *The Green Alternative* (San Pedro, California: R. and E. Miles, © 1987) pp. 137–47.

Greens in the United States are working today in many different spheres and using many different approaches. Some people are focusing their attention on specific issues of local and regional concern. They are working to curb the excesses of industrialism and to head off the social and ecological disruptions rooted in our present way of life. This current is basically oppositional in nature, embracing political methods such as community organizing, lobbying for legislative reforms and a variety of direct non-violent efforts to protest or obstruct especially threatening policies and projects.

The second major current is reconstructive in its approach. It includes a wide variety of efforts to create living alternatives to our present ways – a wealth of experiments in co-operation and local democracy – both in the community and the workplace. It includes the development of alternative technologies and the raising of bioregional* awareness. For a Green movement to develop and grow in North America, there will need to be a merging of oppositional and reconstructive strategies that allows these two currents to support and strengthen each other.

Issue-oriented politics without an alternative vision can be politically limiting and personally frustrating. Many people are uncomfortable with the way things are, but are not motivated to act on their beliefs because they see no other way. Others might choose to work on a particular issue of concern, but are easily exhausted as each small victory reveals new complications. One might work for many months to block a particularly devastating project or to achieve a particular reform in the system, only to find that new injustices crept in the back door while your attention was focused on one small piece of the problem. The ecological crisis cannot be simply controlled within the limits of the existing system. In fact, some Greens believe that reformist efforts merely forestall the impending collapse of the industrial economies, a collapse which may need to occur before the real work of reconstruction can begin.

It can be equally limiting to work to create new institutions without actively seeking to understand and oppose the injustices of our present ways. Such efforts can be slowly bought off and accommodated into the service of the present system. One can point to food co-ops that have become more involved in elaborately marketing their goods than in fully challenging the limitations of the existing food supply system. A once-vibrant alternative energy movement in New England has become tied to the ecologically-devastating vacation home industry, as solar builders have drifted toward affluent resort areas in their search for steady employment and the freedom to experiment. Should healthy food and solar-heated homes become the luxury goods of an affluent minority seeking to purchase an ecological 'lifestyle'? How can a Green sensibility guide us toward a better way?

The West Germans have borrowed a phrase (originally attributed to the ecologist René Dubos) that has become a slogan for the world-wide peace movement: 'Think globally, act locally'. Local ecological problems, local symbols of the military-industrial complex, and local attempts to create alternatives in housing, food distribution and other basic needs all offer a focus for local activities that carry a global message. By working primarily on the local level, Greens are demonstrating the power of people really to change things and creating the grass-roots basis for a real change in consciousness.

In local issue-oriented work, a Green sensibility offers new opportunities to link specific issues together. For example, local weapons industries fuel the arms race, distort employment patterns in a region, and often produce the largest quantities of toxic wastes. Campaigns aimed toward converting such facilities to peaceful uses can raise questions of community and worker control and the nature of economic and technological change. Large development projects often destroy prime farmland, wildlife habitats and people's homes, while centralizing the control of a local economy in fewer hands. A Green anti-development campaign can fully integrate these closely related concerns. . . .

Another new model for environmental politics, one grounded in a more sweeping ecological vision, is offered by the Earth First!* organization. The founders of Earth First! (always spelled with a '!') were inspired by author Edward Abbey, whose writings embody the rhythms of the land and people of the south-western deserts and prairies. His popular novel, *The Money Wrench Gang*,* describes the often comic adventures of a band of renegades committed to reversing the commercial exploitation of their beloved desert by all means of disruption and sabotage.

Begun as a loose network of people committed to environmental direct action in the south-west, Earth First! has grown to include over fifty affiliated groups all across the continent. 'Monkey wrench' tactics are still very much a topic for discussion, but the focus of Earth First! has broadened to encompass a wide variety of educational activities, including taking guerrilla theatre from city streets to the National Parks. They have developed detailed plans for the reclamation and expansion of wilderness areas threatened by development, carrying their plans to the appropriate officials with the backing of national letter-writing campaigns and, when necessary, through sit-ins, office takeovers and the direct obstruction of logging and road-building operations.

Earth First! groups are not tied to any formal organizational structure, but keep in close contact through the mails and through their newspaper, which has become a major national forum for the renewal of ecological activism and thought. They have also helped publicize action campaigns to save wilderness in other parts of the world – in recent years, people have put their bodies on the line to hold back the bulldozers and chain saws in the Australian rainforest, on the last remaining wild stretch of the Danube River in Austria and on Indian lands in British Columbia. . . .

As Green ideas become more widely understood in this country, a third sphere of activity becomes increasingly attractive to Green activists, the world of electoral politics. The electoral successes of the European Greens have raised hopes that Greens in this country could directly influence local and national policies by campaigning for and winning elective offices.

Green electoral campaigns can help bring ecological ideas to a wider audience. They can attract substantial media attention and provide an opening for Greens to speak with a greater cross-section of their neighbours. Sometimes these efforts will have a tangible effect on public policies, occasionally as a result of a Green candidate being elected to office, but more often by reshaping public debate around important issues. In a time when the terms of national political debate are so influenced by the extreme right, local Green candidates can help maintain a public focus on issues of environmental protection, democracy and human liberation. When broad popular support for such causes can be demonstrated, it can have a significant impact on the positions taken by major party candidates.

Green electoral politics is not without its serious pitfalls, however. It is one thing to acquire an 'audience' for Green ideas; it is quite another to create activities that really change political institutions. Electoral involvements can complement more grass-roots efforts, but they can also undermine them by helping sustain the illusion that we can change the way things are by simply choosing the right leaders to represent us. . . .

As Green ideas spread, politicians are likely to come forward who will claim to speak for ecology and for a politics of decentralism and home rule. Such individuals will probably emerge both from within local Green organizations and from conventional political circles. Many will be sincere in their desire to be a voice for this new politics and bring genuinely transformative proposals into the mainstream arena; many will be using Green ideas primarily as a vehicle for their own political ambitions. Before diving in to support such individuals, Greens should ask whether such an effort will really enhance the cause of popular empowerment. One possible litmus test might be the potential candidate's willingness to subordinate their personal ambitions to the needs of local Green alliances that are fully democratic and open to wide participation. It is important to maintain the distinction between individual political campaigns and efforts to create a political expression for a larger ecological and social movement. . . .

In the short-term, Green electoral campaigns could help mobilize an ecological constituency that politicians would then have to pay attention to. They could help push the system to reform itself, as established institutions seek to accommodate popular movements and mainstream politicians try to catch up with their constituents' views. But until we begin to see real changes in our political institutions, all types of ecologists are easily lumped together as just another 'special interest' whose demands simply get in the way of corporate and other élite efforts to manage our society.

In the middle 1970s, a group of influential business leaders from the United States, Western Europe and Japan formed a panel called the Trilateral Commission to begin formulating economic and political strategies for the decades to come. . . .

In the United States, they concluded that a 'democratic distemper' had arisen during the 1960s, that too many new sectors of the population had come to expect a voice in public decision-making. This 'excess of democracy' had, for the Trilateralists, led to a problematic rise in government activity and a decline in its authority.

People's desire to control their own lives creates a real dilemma for those who have long been able to manage society to serve their own economic and political ends. The radical decentralist outlook of many Greens escalates this dilemma one step further: if federations of self-reliant communities begin to take meaningful steps toward withdrawing from the system, what measures will be taken to prevent the 'distemper' from spreading even further?

A major hope for Greens everywhere lies in the development of new community-based institutions and experiments in local democracy. Such efforts could begin to create a genuine counter-power to the influence of established institutions. If a few communities in a few regions can begin mapping out a more independent course for themselves, they can help others discover how to break the web of dependencies that keep people believing in the present system. As the system increasingly fails to satisfy many people's most basic needs, the search for alternatives can evolve to an entirely new level.

In the near-term, the Green movement can become an important vehicle for renewing public activity at the local level. It can articulate a sweeping critique of our present way of life and catalyse efforts to develop bioregional consciousness and an ethic of local self-reliance. Green groups in neighbouring communities can federate together to create changes in economic and social policies on a wider scale. We can begin at the grass-roots level to transform our relationships with peoples in other parts of the world. A new politics of neighbourhood and community, grounded in an ecological awareness, can offer an essential challege to the forces of destruction at work all around us, a challenge that can spread by example to all the far corners of our land.

The Parliamentary Road? (1)

The question of the role of a Green parliamentary party is evidently a crucial one. At its most radical, Green politics seeks a total restructuring of social, political and economic life, and it is a matter of historical fact that no such radical changes have ever been brought about by parliamentary parties. But does this mean that Green politics is best carried on outside parliament? In the extract below Petra Kelly, of *die Grünen*, and possibly the best-known member of the Green movement in the world, wrestles with this question and comes to the conclusion that there *is* a role for Green parliamentary parties – with provisos. She describes them as 'anti-party parties', by which she means that their role is to subvert traditional parties by opposing their ways of working and by providing a model for alternative forms of parliamentary activity. She also asserts that a Green party should remain Green and not enter into pacts with other parties – an attitude which has led her, and those who agree with her, to be called a 'fundamentalist' rather than a 'realist'. This is a debate which will last as long as the Green movement believes that there is a role for Green parties in parliament.

From Petra Kelly, *Fighting for Hope* (London: Chatto and Windus, The Hogarth Press, 1984) pp. 17–23.

We can no longer rely on the established parties, nor can we go on working solely through extra-parliamentary channels. There is a need for a new force, both in parliament and outside it. One element of this new force is represented by the anti-party party, the Greens. It has become increasingly important to vote for what one believes to be right on the basis of content, rather than wasting one's vote on lesser evils. The debates conducted in the established parties about the Greens are a shocking revelation of their inability to address themselves to new questions of survival. We demand a radical rethink of all the fundamental issues facing society on the part of the established parties, and this must be a condition of any talks with the Greens.

Within the peace movement, independently of the established parties, we voice the needs of those no longer able to express their concern for a peaceful and environment-conscious future through the established party system. However, a movement operating exclusively outside parliament, does not have as many opportunities to implement demands, say, for a new attitude to security, as it would if these demands were also put forward in parliament. Despite the great autonomy of the peace and ecology movements, it seems to me that they have no option but to relate to the political system as it is, given the nature of power in our society.

At the moment, the party system is still the main mechanism for selecting and deciding which issues figure on the political agenda. Consequently it is imperative, I believe, for many people in the ecology and peace movements to push themselves to the forefront of the party political stage. At the same time, we know that these movements can only be effective if autonomous bodies and local action groups continue to proliferate both within and outside parliament. We need more grass-roots organization: rank and file groups in the trade unions, alternative media, the peace movement and its members in the Green party.

We aim for a party system that is truly representative, with no entry restrictions. Right now, there is a very real need for an anti-party, a new kind of party, which will genuinely espouse the cause of the weaker members of society, old people, the handicapped, women, young people, the unemployed and foreign workers and their families. The aspirations of the peace and ecology movements should be represented within a political forum, in addition to their expression outside parliament.

As Greens, it is not part of our understanding of politics to find a place in the sun alongside the established parties, nor to help maintain power and privilege in concert with them. Nor will we accept any alliances or coalitions. That is wishful thinking on the part of the traditional parties, who seek to exploit the Greens to keep themselves in power. The very last thing we seek is to use Green ideas to rejuvenate any other political party. The way the Social Democrats (SPD) have courted the Greens simply demonstrates the arrogance of power and underlines their sterility of vision. The environment, peace, society and the economy now pose such a threat to survival that they can only be resolved by structural change, not by crisis management and cosmetic adjustments. The

Greens can make no compromise on the fundamental questions of the environment, peace, sexual equality and the economy.

We must make it clear that we will not just go away, nor will we abdicate our responsibility. Nuclear energy, the nuclear state, and the growing use of military force threaten our lives. We feel obliged to take public, non-violent action and to engage in civil disobedience outside and inside parliament, throwing a spotlight on the inhumanity of the system.

We do not want violence, not even against our political opponents. We have no wish to use the power of money or the state to resolve conflicts in such a way that someone must always lose. On the contrary, our anti-party party should encourage non-violent action as central to the new political culture. . . .

There can be no future for the Greens if they go in for gaining power in the same way as the established parties. The Greens are ready to work with others if the demand that parliament should speak the language of the people is finally met. So far, parliaments have acted simply as the executive body of the bureaucracy in the ministries, especially where important proposals such as airports or nuclear power stations are concerned. The Greens take a different view of parliament. We believe that parliament must represent the interests of the people, including minorities.

Parliaments have proved themselves incapable of responding to the demands of local action groups. The Greens believe that part of the work of parliament is to conduct hearings and committees of enquiry in public and to make them open to everyone. We aim to democratize parliament as much as possible putting the issues, and the costs of solving them, squarely before the public. We must set ourselves uncompromising programmatic objectives in order to stimulate debate and discussion inside and outside parliament. A place in parliament, together with the success of a non-violent opposition movement on the streets, should, we hope, put us in a position to shake people out of their apathy and quiescence.

We are, and I hope we will remain, half party and half local action group – we shall go on being an anti-party party. The learning process that takes place on the streets, on construction sites, at nuclear bases, must be carried into parliament.

All three parties currently represented in the West German parliament (*Bundestag*) have allowed their social democratic, Christian or liberal intentions to disappear into thin air. What they have in common is a hierarchical structure making spontaneous, committed action impossible, so that politically meaningful decisions are taken only at the top and party democracy exists in name only.

Where in the party hierarchy is the housewife who knows just how difficult it is to feed a family when prices keep rising? Where is the senior citizen with a chance to speak for his fellows at last? Where is the worker with the monotonous job who can question the meaning of work? The men at the top with their fat salaries and their own way of life, not to mention the token women at their sides, lost all contact with the 'man in the street' a long time ago. They simply cannot think themselves into the fears and the worries of whole sectors of society.

After years of arduous, detailed work in the committees and working groups of these parties, many of us were driven to despair because, when it finally came to a decision, the party bureaucrats had it all their own way every time. Many established politicians claim that the Greens are drop-outs. Quite the reverse – we have stepped into the system in order to change it. The real drop-outs are the career politicians who have deserted their original professions to work their way up the party career ladder. With their secure incomes behind them, they can deliver themselves of sound advice to working people on how savings can be made to pay for yesterday's American missile horror.

Thus it can be seen that whole sectors of the population are not represented in parliament, nor elected to it. Representing their interests will only be the first step. Direct democracy means that we will fight for real influence for the people ignored by government. In doing so, can we expect the established parties to meet us half-way? Can we hope for a positive desire for change on their part? Given that their very structures run counter to the principles of democracy, can their representatives change their policies?

A political party must never become an end in itself, as have the established parties of the *Bundestag*. A party is a vehicle for the expression of opinion and interest. However, it is essential for these interests and the role of the party to be under constant and critical review. All too often in the past, we have seen the ways in which ready-made ideologies have led to destruction and aggression. So, as Greens, we offer no ready-made ideology. One can neither delegate nor dictate one's own understanding of life. The stories of Martin Luther King and Mahatma Gandhi show that one is most likely to win people over through actually living by one's principles. Consequently, the function of the Green party within the peace and ecology movements is not to lead, but only to support. Parties and parliament can only ever act as support systems when it comes to transforming the lives of entire groups of people. Looked at historically, it seems to me that the ecology movement cannot expect the unions of the Social Democrats to react other than tactically to the matters that concern us. . . .

For the Greens, parliamentary work should be of benefit to our many supporters at grass-roots level; it must never be undertaken for its own sake.

The Parliamentary Road? (2)

As far as Green political strategy is concerned, the East German exile Rudolf Bahro has turned out to be one of those most implacably opposed to working through parliament. At one time he agreed with the sentiments of Petra Kelly, outlined in the previous extract, but the piece below (from a speech he gave at *die Grünen*'s Hagen Congress in June 1985) illustrates his belief in the unacceptability of the compromises that Green parties in parliament have to make. The particular point at issue here is that of animal experimentation, but the general conclusion is that 'a party is a counter-productive tool'. Bahro's alternative can be found in the extract which follows this one: the commune strategy.

From Rudolf Bahro, *Building the Green Movement* (London: GMP, 1986) pp. 210–11.

What people are trying to do here is to save a party – no matter what kind of party, and no matter for what purpose. The main thing is for it to get re-elected to parliament in 1987. It has no basic ecological position; it is not a party for the protection of life and I know now that it never will be, for it is rapidly distancing itself from that position. Yesterday, on the question of animal experiments, it clearly came down in favour of the position taken by the speaker who said, more or less: 'If even one human life can be saved, the torture of animals is permissible'. This sentence expresses the basic principle by which human beings are exterminating plants, animals and finally themselves. . . .

There is not a single issue where the Greens are taking seriously the purpose for which they ostensibly entered the political scene. You can blame it if you like on 'Realos' or 'fundamentalists' or – more narrowly – on the paedophile issue. We are in decline because the people who had placed their hopes in us realized, at least when they saw the behaviour of the North-Rhine-Westphalian Greens after the Saarland elections, that their course is not a sincere one;

they are like everybody else, only they are trying to kid both others and themselves that they are different.

The Greens have identified themselves – critically – with the industrial system and its political administration. Nowhere do they want to get out. Instead of spreading consciousness they are obscuring it all along the line. They are helping to patch up the cracks in the general consensus. The theorists of realpolitik state directly that nothing else will do but to 'rule out' extremes. . . .

It once looked as if some kind of salvation would come from us – but the applause for Petra's speech, which reminded us of this, won't bring it back. All that will be left is a normal party along with all the others. I can't carry on in it in that situation. After what happened yesterday am I still supposed to try to win serious animal protectionists on to our side? With us they will just waste both time and energy. Or cleaning up pollution. The proposal accepts that alternatives must be 'competitive' in the market. 'Mission to nowhere' *with* the chemical industry. I feel all the more sad in that some of the people involved would 'really' like things to be different.

I want above all to ask those people who genuinely regret my departure and have pleaded with me not to go, to be clear as to their motive. Do you need me so that despite your doubts you have something to hold on to? That can't depend on me. Everyone has to reach their own decision. I can't carry on as if nothing had happened, as if nothing were happening, as if the exit were still open. Michael Stamm is telling the truth. His solution is the only one left if we admit to ourselves what we really are as a party. Bankrupt.

This experience is the end of traditional political existence for me altogether. At last I have understood that a party is a counterproductive tool, that the given political space is a trap into which life energy disappears, indeed, where it is rededicated to the spiral of death. This is not a general but a quite concrete type of despair. It is directed not at the original project which is today called 'fundamental', but at the party. I've finished with it now. I wouldn't consider it right just to withdraw silently. I am not becoming unpolitical. I am not saying goodbye to the intellectual process. I want to contribute to creating a new place and a new practice. Clearly we have to take a longer run-up. We must risk some cold water if we want to assemble the necessary substance for our withdrawal from the industrial system, first of all within ourselves.

Communes

Many Green Utopias revolve around the idea of a self-reliant community, but not all Green theorists see the commune as a political means as well as a social end. Rudolf Bahro does. In the previous extract we saw him giving reasons as to why he believed the parliamentary road to sustainability to be counter-productive. Here he argues that the changes which need to be brought about are so radical that a complete change of consciousness is required. He suggests that in order to achieve this, a strategic withdrawal from the hurly-burly of traditional political activity is called for, and, in a move designed to draw parallels between our contemporary situation and that of the Dark Ages, he calls for a 'new Benedictine order' organized in a 'commune-type framework'. All this is based on the belief both that commune living makes human fulfilment more likely than any other, and because it constitutes the 'longer run-up' (referred to in the previous extract) which reaching radical goals requires.

From Rudolf Bahro, *Building the Green Movement* (London: GMP, 1986) pp. 87–91.

The decision in favour of a commune perspective assumes a considerably longer path than the 'march through the institutions', and envisages a much deeper reorganization than any which is possible via the state. Under the Damocles sword of the Bomb, and looking at the clock with its hands pointing almost to midnight, we still trust that we have time, in the end by refusing to let this be determined by mechanical clockwork. We dare to make an experiment, not ultimately for the sake of this or that particular commune – although we won't move so easily as from one shared apartment to another – but for the principle of a life beyond the currently valid norms and career paths of civilization.

Moreover, we recognize in a relatively autonomous basic unit of social life which is no longer economically expansive (self-reliance) the only chance in the long term of tearing up the roots of the East-West conflict and above all of our opposition to the Third World. With a pinch of salt one might say (and indeed with the accent much more on the cultural than on the economic-technological aspect and with regard to the seeds of human community which are still present there), that the path of reconciliation with the Third World might consist in our becoming Third World ourselves. The existing techno-bureaucratic structure here can in no way be reformed in such a way that the rest of humanity could live with it. If we allow ourselves to be guided by the fear of 'poverty', we continue to apportion naked misery to the others.

Yet however far we may be led by the insight that communes are the main way to uproot the exterminist peril, deeper seated still is our motivation by the psychological reward which we promise ourselves from the accompanying self-transformation. We build on the fact that the commune organization is anthropologically favourable, or – in comparison with other arrangements – corresponds more to human nature, among other things by avoiding both the neurotic-making family and the alienating big organization, while the inner pressure to conform can still be balanced by sufficient external contact. It is also the social form which most readily permits the control of social power. . . .

The commune is the basic social form for a new, more economical way of life (a 'domestic' way of life, as it has been called). Its purpose is not the production of means of subsistence – whether of the agrarian or industrial type, whether in the country or in the town – but the reproduction of the commune-type community. Economic efficiency is not negated, but subordinated to ecological demands and above all to the development of social relationships and the self-development and transformation of individuals. In the ideal case the commune network is socially so strong that all material and institutional infrastructure on any but the local levels remains dependent upon it, instead of the other way round as formerly.

Historical and recent experiences show that this produces a structure in which the feminine element permeates the regulation of community affairs from the bottom up; within a large organization and with the prevailing type of rationality and division of labour women's liberation is impossible. . . .

Externally, too, the function of the commune is not primarily economic. Neither are job creation, taking the burden off the welfare state, producing food, etc. its purpose from the point of view of society as a whole. But among other things it also does all that.

Since in this respect it represents a constructive alternative to the crisis of the society of labour and the danger of an escalation of violence which is unfavourable in every respect for our objectives, there is the prospect of winning public support so that we can divert aid from the formal sector towards setting up a commune-type mass movement. The fact that such means would reach us principally via the state is in itself no counter-argument, since the resources concentrated there belong to society, as whose organ we are acting – especially as most of these resources are otherwise deployed either directly or indirectly in a destructive way, in order to continue the present overall course. The achievement of conditions under which any type of deforming state control is out of the question will depend on the social power relationship. The autonomy of the commune movement is the highest priority. . . .

The real alternative which the commune poses to the industrial Goliath is not of an economic but of a cultural nature. The subordination of economics to living is only the first condition. Basically we are talking about a system of values which is new for modern Europe and also modified in comparison with medieval Christian Europe. . . .

If we take a look in history at the foundations on which new cultures were based or existing ones essentially changed, we always come up against the fact that in such times people returned to those strata of consciousness which are traditionally described as religious. In order to be at all capable of a new definition of their culture, and thus of their behaviour, they must find a practice to dismantle their previous psychological structures and be socialized anew. Psychotherapists sometimes go part of this way, but it could hardly be completed by the individual man or woman without reference to those horizons which were symbolized by people like Christ or Buddha. . . .

With such a horizon the alternative reaches back to historical experience with modernity – particularly where it calls itself 'left' – has systematically suppressed, so that it no longer even has any direct familiarity with it.

Almost one and a half thousand years ago the Benedictines gave the new western culture emerging from the collapse of Antiquity not only a very significant economic impulse, which at its peak involved up to 30 per cent of the population. Above all, they guaranteed the cultural synthesis of the new order which was current at that time, on a meditative basis – hence 'pray (first) and work' – upon which the whole social radiation of their practice was dependent. The intellectual impulse from the monasteries which is acknowledged in all historiography was essentially a spiritual one. It came into being by people getting involved in communicating so intensively with 'God' as the epitome of our transpersonal, generic essence which ultimately originates in the universe, that they found their own true selves beneath the rubble and the character armour of their socialization – the energy source of their charismatic effect.

We need a new Benedictine order. It can only flourish in a socially effective way within a commune-type framework. At the moment, those who must come together in it are still divided up into religious (and sometimes also pseudo-religious) sectarianism on the one hand and political sectarianism on the other, and one of the most important reasons might be that between these two poles the load-bearing social centre, the real context of life, is lacking. Certainly, for a preparatory phase in which the model is crystallized, separation or dissociation from the remainder of society will outweigh association with it, that is internal contact will outweigh external. (In this connection our Third World debate is to a greater degree than we think also about our own alternative to 'development'.) Without a retreat at times there will be no transformation of ourselves and no radical influence on the general consciousness. . . .

This new Benedictine movement will be different from the old in at least the following two respects, both of which concern the break with the foundations of patriarchy:

The spiritual culture will not be linked to a repressive monotheistic idea of God, which stems from oriental despotism and is designed for a hierarchical church. On this point the Judeo-Christian tradition must be broken. Happily Christ himself breaks out of this line at the deepest level of the image of him which has been handed down.

Social organization will not be linked to the separation of the sexes and sexual oppression, which corresponded to the Near Eastern and also the Hellenic origin of Christianity, a tradition which Christ likewise seems partially to have broken with.

'God' will be for both sexes simultaneously male and female, in some respects more the one, in others more the other. Community life will be based on the natural equilibrium between separation and communication of the sexes, and will give space to the uninhibited development of sensuality and sexuality. . . .

For the beginning it comes down to one thing: that there should be some initiators (men and women) who make a personal decision, begin by preparing themselves and a project and gather around them a circle of fellow strivers. When, if not now, would the time be ripe?

The Technological Fix

The Green movement is split between those who believe that
environmental problems can be solved by tinkering with the
present way of doing things, and those who argue that wholesale political and economic changes are needed to bring about
sustainability. A typical belief of the first group is that, although
the blame for many of our troubles (pollution, resource exhaustion, land erosion) can be laid upon technology, it is technology
which will get us out of the mess it has helped create. This
belief has been dubbed the 'technological fix' by its detractors.
In the following extract, Ted Trainer argues that we don't
have sufficient reason to assume that the necessary technical
breakthroughs will be made and – more importantly – that
these aren't technological problems anyway, but social and
political ones. It is this conclusion which leads us into the
realms of Green politics proper.

From Ted Trainer, *Abandon Affluence!* (London: Zed Brooks
Ltd., 1985) pp. 208–14.

Can technology solve the problems?

Over the last two decades many, if not most, people have come to
the point where they will readily agree that industrialized societies
are generating many disturbing problems. Yet it is widely believed
that advances in science and technology will permit the solution
of these problems without great inconvenience. The technical-fix
optimist is eager to point to the miracles technology has achieved
in the past. 'Just fifty years ago no one imagined uranium could be
a source of energy. Who knows what resources and procedures we
will find?'

In its most general form this argument wins by a knock-out in
the first round. For example, no one can say that a vast and cheap
form of energy will not be discovered tomorrow. The important
question, however, is *how good are the grounds for thinking that*

sufficient technical breakthroughs will occur? We are accelerating in a direction that will result in catastrophe unless many crucial things do turn up and our problem now is to decide whether it is wise to go on or whether it would be most sensible to change. Before the technical optimist can reasonably expect us to agree to proceed in the present dangerous direction, we must be given good reason to think that solutions to each and all of the serious problems ahead will be found. We must be convinced that solutions to the energy problem, to the carbon dioxide problem, and to the problem of Third World hunger, are all likely to be found, and so on through the list. The optimist must reply in quantitative detail. In the case of energy a specific question should be asked, such as, 'It seems that late next century there will be about eleven billion people. If they are all to use as much liquid fuel as people in rich nations now use world production will have to be about ten times what it is today. Where will we get 600 million barrels a day?' . . .

As time goes by the technical optimist will surely be able to present evidence of impressive progress on some of these problems; but remember that we should be convinced that it is not necessary to think about changing from pursuit of maximum affluence and growth, even in view of *the whole range* of different and difficult problems facing us. Even if there were good reasons for thinking we will soon have cheap solar cells and a cheap and durable battery making the electric car widely available, there would still be many serious energy problems, *aside from other problems* requiring solution before it would make sense to go on gearing our society to expensive lifestyles. The limits-to-growth argument is that this pursuit will run us into so many clearly identified problems and so many unknowns that it is not worth the risk. Even if some of these problems do not eventuate, many of them will, unless many crucial breakthroughs and discoveries and innovations are made. In a number of cases it is at present difficult even to imagine what those developments could possibly be. The limits-to-growth answer to the technical optimist is, 'If we go on this way all of these problems look as if they will get worse. Any one of a number of them could, on its own, result in global catastrophe. Would it not be much wiser and safer to undertake social change to values and structures that do not generate any of these problems?'. . .

What technology will have to come up with

The technical optimist should also be reminded of the Herculean tasks technology is expected to solve. If eleven billion people are to have the 1979 living standards of the developed countries, then every year technology will have to deliver nine times as much energy as the world produced in 1979. . . .

Most technical optimists object to being expected to explain how eleven billion people can be provided with our high living standards. They usually take the challenge to be how to provide for continuation of business-as-usual wherein relatively few of the world's people have high consumption rates. The technical problems in this option are difficult enough but the political and security problems are intimidating. To focus only on whether high living standards can continue to be provided for the few is to ignore the explosive political and security problems that must be generated by worsening inequality between rich and poor nations. It will take truly remarkable 'advances in technology' to keep the lid on a world where 1.5 billion rich confront 9.5 billion poor who are expected to go on decade after decade tolerating a grossly unjust share of global wealth while watching more and more of their resources flow out to the rich few. Clearly the technical optimist cannot confine the discussion to how business-as-usual might be sustained in developed countries. *It must either be explained how all people on earth are to live as affluently as we are, or why a world containing 1.5 billion very rich people and 9.5 billion very poor people from whom the rich draw most of their resources is morally tolerable and/or not likely to self-destruct in vicious international conflict.* No position between eleven billion at high living standards and only 1.5 billion at those standards makes the overall task much easier; the more inequality is assumed the easier the resource problems become, but the more acute the political, security and moral problems will be. . . .

They are not technical problems after all

The basic criticism to be made of the technical-fix position is that it erroneously assumes the problems before us to be technical, as distinct from social, problems and, therefore, that the problems can be solved without undertaking basic social change. It implies that we can go on pursuing the same values and employing the same social structures that we do now. Americans can expect to continue consuming twenty-nine barrels of oil each year because scientists

will find new sources of liquid fuel as oil supplies dwindle, land in
the Third World does not need to be redistributed in order to
solve the food problem because our agronomists will develop higher
yielding crops, we need not cut down on fossil fuel consumption
because our technologists will develop ways to extract carbon dioxide and other pollutants from the atmosphere. We can go on living
in our extremely resource-affluent and wasteful ways. We need not
radically redistribute global resources, the powerful and privileged
need not give a better deal to the poor, our basically free enterprise
economic structures need not be altered . . . because technology
will solve the problems these practices and values are creating.

The argument throughout this book is that this view is mistaken
because our main problems are not technical problems. They arise
from faulty social systems and values and they can only be solved by
change to quite different social systems and values. This argument is
perhaps best illustrated in the case of hunger where the technical-
fix view implies that what we need is to discover how to produce
more food. The Green revolution introduced techniques yielding
much greater quantities of food; yet it is quite arguable that this
whole development has had the net effect of increasing hunger. The
benefits went mainly to the richer farmers, the increased harvests
were usually of crops grown for sale in the cities or overseas and
the expansion of these croplands turned many peasants into landless
poor. This is precisely what we should expect when more effective
production techniques are introduced into societies where there are
marked inequalities and free market economies; the rich and powerful are in a much better position to seize on the new techniques and
use them to become richer and to impoverish and dispossess the
poor. Remember that there is really no need for greater food production at present because much more food is produced than is
needed to feed all adequately. Poverty and hunger are social problems; they result from faulty distributions of resources and power
between classes and they are not problems open to solution by
advances in productive technique. Is more scientific research and
development on technical gadgets likely to increase our security
from annihilation in a nuclear war? Technical advance is actually
making this problem worse day by day. Long-term security from
this threat cannot be achieved unless we abandon the social values
and systems that lead nations into conflict for scarce resources and
markets.

Green Education

Many Greens believe that changes in political and economic structures will only come about once the battle for hearts and minds has been won. This leads them to place great emphasis on the value of education (in the widest sense) as a strategy for change. In the extract below Aldous Huxley confines his description of an ecological education to schoolchildren on the mythical island of Pala, but the principles of what he says are applicable to all ages and all walks of life. Green education invites us to understand that 'living is relationship' and that 'balance, give and take, no excesses' is a rule of nature which ought to be a rule of society. As far as Huxley is concerned the omens for Green education are not good, as the island of Pala is overwhelmed by the oil-fired industrialism of neighbouring Rendang. Many others have felt that a fully Green conversion through education is unlikely while the reins of political and economic power are so firmly held by its opponents.

From Aldous Huxley, *Island* (London: Grafton Books, 1990) (first published 1962) pp. 247–9.

'Meanwhile we have got to get on with our job, which is education. Is there anything more that you'd like to hear about, Mr Farnaby?'

'Lots more,' said Will. 'For example, how early do you start your science teaching?'

'We start it at the same time as we start multiplication and division. First lessons in ecology.'

'Ecology? Isn't that a bit complicated?'

'That's precisely the reason why we begin with it. Never give children a chance of imagining that anything exists in isolation. Make it plain from the very first that all living is relationship. Show them relationships in the woods, in the fields, in the ponds and streams, in the village and the country around it. Rub it in.'

'And let me add,' said the Principal, 'that we always teach the science of relationship in conjunction with the ethics of relationship. Balance, give and take, no excesses – it's the rule in nature and, translated out of fact into morality, it *ought* to be the rule among people. As I said before, children find it very easy to understand an idea when it's presented to them in a parable about animals. We give them an up-to-date version of *Aesop's Fables*. Not the old anthropomorphic fictions, but true ecological fables with built-in, cosmic morals. And another wonderful parable for children is the story of erosion. We don't have any good examples of erosion here; so we show them photographs of what has happened in Rendang, in India and China, in Greece and the Levant, in Africa and America – all the places where greedy, stupid people have tried to take without giving, to exploit without love or understanding. Treat nature well, and nature will treat you well. Hurt or destroy nature, and nature will soon destroy you. In a Dust Bowl, "Do as you would be done by" is self-evident – much easier for a child to recognize and understand than in an eroded family or village. Psychological wounds don't show – and anyhow children know so little about their elders. And, having no standards of comparison, they tend to take even the worst situation for granted, as though it were part of the nature of things. Whereas the difference between ten acres of meadow and ten acres of gullies and blowing sand is obvious. Sand and gullies are parables. Confronted by them, it's easy for the child to see the need for conservation and then to go on from conservation to morality – easy for him to go from the Golden Rule in relation to plants and animals and the earth that supports them to the Golden Rule in relation to human beings. And here's another important point. The morality to which a child goes on from the facts of ecology and the parables of erosion is a universal ethic. There are no Chosen People in nature, no Holy Lands, no Unique Historical Revelations. Conservation-morality gives nobody an excuse for feeling superior, or claiming special privileges. "Do as you would be done by" applies to our dealings with all kinds of life in every part of the world. We shall be permitted to live on this planet only for as long as we treat all nature with compassion and intelligence. Elementary ecology leads straight to elementary Buddhism.'

Green Capitalism

Can there be a marriage between Green politics and capitalism? Elsewhere ('industrialism'*) Jonathon Porritt argues that there is nothing to choose between capitalism and socialism in that they are both ideologies of economic growth. Both are unreformable, he suggests, and need to be transcended towards a new kind of politics – Green politics. However, John Elkington and Tom Burke suggest below that a 'new breed of "green" capitalists' has emerged which is just as concerned about sustainability as the most fundamentalist Green. Their greenness is not motivated by a concern for the environment as such, but by the understanding that 'environmentally unsound activities are ultimately economically unsound'. Industrialists know that if their resource base runs out, then so will their profits. Other industrialists know that there are profits to be made from marketing environmentally-sound goods, and so the phenomenon of 'green consumerism'* has emerged.

From John Elkington with Tom Burke, *The Green Capitalists* (London: Gollancz, 1987) pp. 14–23, 250.

Most western environmentalists have been inclined to blame such problems on capitalism, which they see as little more than institutionalized greed. The scandals which have plagued Wall Street and London's City have done nothing to change their minds. Ivan Boesky, who pleaded guilty to 'insider trading' on the grand scale, had once bragged that 'greed is healthy. You can be greedy and still feel good about yourself.' Short-sighted greed, however, is an enemy both of the environment and of sustainable economic growth.

There certainly is no denying that market pressures have encouraged many businesses to 'externalize' a significant proportion of their production costs by imposing them on their workforces (with, for example, unsafe working conditions), on local communities (for example, high noise levels), on consumers (for example, defective products based on inadequate research or quality control) and on the environment (for example, pollution).

From an environmental perspective, it is fair to say, there are some fundamental flaws in today's economic rationality. The Greens, who espouse the 'politics of ecology', have challenged many key economic concepts, including the inevitability (and desirability) of exponential economic growth, the conventional definitions of 'wealth' and the methods currently used to calculate Gross National Product (GNP)*. . . .

There is no reason why private enterprise should be any more environmentally damaging than public or state enterprise. The United States may have given us Three Mile Island, but the Soviet Union topped that with Chernobyl. Early estimates put the cost of the Chernobyl disaster, which has spread radioactivity across Europe, at around £4 billion – and the figure has continued to climb. Indeed, some of today's worst examples of conventional, non-nuclear pollution are also to be found in such communist bloc countries as Poland, Czechoslovakia and the Soviet Union. The evidence suggests that once capitalists and entrepreneurs are convinced that environmental regulations are here to stay and that they will be enforced, they respond much more rapidly to the challenge than do highly bureaucratic societies. . . .

Private enterprise certainly has a critical role to play in the drive for sustainable development, but will need to ensure that it achieves environmental excellence in its investments and operations. Environmentally unsound activities are ultimately economically unsound. At the same time, even industrialists who are relatively optimistic about the environmental outlook accept that their companies have a great deal to do if their operations are to remain environmentally sustainable. . . .

The emergence of a new breed of 'green' capitalist and of what one might call 'environmental entrepreneurs' is an enormously hopeful trend. They are bringing new perspectives to bear on the future. Indeed, the time has come to identify and develop the industrial constituency for sustainable development. As Continental Group chairman Bruce Smart put it, 'the needs of future generations must rank equally with those now on earth. Yet the unborn do not vote, invest or demonstrate. Someone must speak for them.'

The Green Capitalists shows how environmentalists are moving from reaction to action, from analysis to response. In taking a more positive stance on some issues they are not replacing conflict with co-operation, but adding more constructive roles to their existing

campaigning activities. They recognize that no government, or collection of governments, can cope with the environmental agenda in
isolation. The role of the non-governmental sector, and increasingly
of the new breed of environmental entrepreneur, is likely to be an
essential ingredient in the transformation which is beginning to take
place in the economies of most major industrial nations.

The book also reveals that the world's environmentalists no longer
have a monopoly on environmental thinking. Indeed, later chapters
explore the ways in which leading companies in the oil industry, the
chemical industry, the engineering industry and the biotechnology
industry, to take just a few examples, have adapted to environmental
constraints and are beginning, in many cases, to exploit environmental opportunities.

iiiiiii

Perhaps what we are seeing is the emergence of a new age capitalism,
appropriate to a new millennium, in which the boundary between
corporate and human values is beginning to dissolve. It is now clear
from the results who won the nineteenth-century argument about
capital and labour. Socialism, as an economic theory, though not as
a moral crusade, is dead. The argument now is about what kind of
capitalism we want. In this book we have explored one dimension,
the green dimension, of the kind of capitalism we must have if there
is to be a planet worth having for our children to inherit.

Green Consumerism

When the *Green Consumer Guide* was first published in Britain in September 1988 it shot straight to the top of the bestseller lists and was reprinted fourteen times in its first year. In truth, the British came late to green consumerism (it is hard to buy aerosols which *do* have chlorofluorocarbons [CFCs] in them in Germany) but we have taken to it with a vengeance. The idea that we can have our shampoo and champagne *and* help to create a healthier environment at the same time is a potent one, speaking simultaneously as it does to our altruism and our self-interest. This has been a breath of fresh air in a movement more often associated with sacrifice than indulgence. Boycotts are out, and buying is in, and supporters of green consumerism can produce long lists of manufacturers who have tailored their products to suit increasingly environmentally-conscious populations. The extract below is taken from the *Green Consumer Guide*'s introduction where the authors describe who the green consumer is, what s/he can do, and how successful s/he can be. By no means everyone in the Green movement is persuaded by Green consumerism, however, and in the extract which follows this one the strategy of buying a better future is called into question.

From John Elkington and Julia Hailes, *The Green Consumer Guide* (London: Gollancz, 1988) pp. 1–5.

Every day of the week, whether we are shopping for simple necessities or for luxury items, for fish fingers or for fur coats, we are making choices that affect the environmental quality of the world in which we live.

Take a bite out of a hamburger, we are told, and we may be taking a bite out of the world's rainforests. Buy the wrong car and we may end up not only with a large fuel bill, but also with fewer trees and, quite possibly, less intelligent children. Spray a handful of hair gel or a mist of furniture polish from certain aerosols, and you help destroy the planet's atmosphere – increasing everybody's chances of contracting skin cancer.

Few of us can spot the links between what we do day-to-day and the environmental destruction which is happening around the world. How many fast-fooders know about what is happening to the world's tropical forests, for example? Yet cattle ranching has been one of the causes of deforestation in countries like Brazil and Costa Rica, particularly from the mid-1970s to the mid-1980s. A good deal of the meat produced went into fast-food products of one kind or another, although it is now clear that McDonald's – which has been accused of *causing* such deforestation – is innocent in this respect.

And how many of us, even if we have seen TV programmes on the newly-discovered Antarctic 'ozone hole', could say exactly what chlorofluorocarbons (CFCs) are? However, the dramatic success of the anti-CFC campaign means that millions of us *do* now know about the earth's protective ozone layer. And we are also beginning to be aware of the damage that the CFC propellants used to squirt many products through the nozzle of an aerosol, that pinnacle of convenience in twentieth-century packaging, can do to the ozone layer.

But more and more of us want to do the right thing – we simply don't know how. Clearly, if the relevant information is presented in the right way, then more and more of us will become sufficiently interested to take action through our day-to-day decisions.

Part of the solution, in fact, is in your hands. Whether you are in the supermarket, the garage, the garden centre or the travel agent's, this first edition of *The Green Consumer Guide* tells you which products to avoid and which to buy.

The *Guide* does not promote a 'hair-shirt' lifestyle. It is designed to appeal to a 'sandals-to-Saabs' spectrum of consumers. The information provided is intended to ensure that, whatever your lifestyle, you will know where to find attractive, cost-competitive products and services which are environmentally acceptable and – as far as possible – a pleasure to use.

The *Guide* does not aim to be totally comprehensive. Instead, it looks at the environment implications of a wide range of consumer decisions and pinpoints what ordinary consumers can do to cut down their contribution to priority environmental problems. Nor can we aspire to be totally up-to-date. The speed with which this whole area is moving means that new issues are constantly emerging, leading to new business initiatives and to the launch of new environment-friendly products.

The real message of the *Guide* is that the green consumer is here and is already having a tremendous impact. Remember the changes that have already taken place: the replacement of 'hard' detergents with 'soft', more biodegradable products; the gradual shift from leaded to unleaded petrol; and the growth in demand for health foods and organically-grown produce.

Many environmental organizations and some consumer groups are now working to accelerate this trend. We set out on the preparation of the *Guide* by sending a questionnaire to Britain's leading environmental organizations. We asked them whether they thought that the consumer could play a significant role in tackling the problems that most concerned them. An overwhelming 88 per cent said that the consumer could have a major impact.

When asked what consumers could do, most of the organizations mentioned product boycotts. If consumer power is to be used in support of environmental objectives, however, boycotts alone are unlikely to be sufficient. Indeed, groups like Friends of the Earth are now developing more sophisticated initiatives, like *The Good Wood Guide*, designed to help consumers switch from products made from hardwoods stripped from tropical forests to those made from wood grown in forests managed with the future very much in mind.

It is the consumer's ability to change from Brand X to Brand Y – or, even more worryingly for manufacturers and retailers, to stop buying a particular product altogether – that makes producers sit up and take notice. In Britain, three days before Friends of the Earth was to follow up its listing of 'ozone-friendly' aerosols with a listing of those brands which do contain CFCs, the eight largest aerosol manufacturers (Beecham, Carter-Wallace, Colgate-Palmolive, Cussons, Elida Gibbs, Gillette, L'Oreal and Reckitt and Colman) announced that they would phase out CFC propellants by the end of 1989. Those companies alone accounted for 65 per cent of the UK toiletries market. Boots and Schwarzkopf said they would follow suit. Several companies, including Johnson Wax and Osmond Aerosols, had helped force the industry's hand by agreeing to label their products as CFC-free.

So don't feel that your decision to buy or not to buy scarcely registers on the scale. Market researchers, and the companies they serve, sit up and take notice when thousands of people start to behave in the same way. Make sure manufacturers or retailers notice you by writing to tell them why you are avoiding their products or why you have switched to their brands. Remember, unless you ask for organic food, CFC-free aerosols or environment-friendly holiday packages, they are unlikely to be offered.

Demand green products and you help develop new market opportunities for manufacturers and retailers – encouraging them to invest in new products and services specifically aimed at the Green consumer.

Persuade one major company to change its tack and others are likely to follow. McDonald's decision to abandon the use of CFCs in fast-food cartons in the States was one of the environmental milestones of 1987. The threat that consumers might boycott *Big Macs* was surely a factor in influencing the company's decision. Competitors promptly started talking to their carton suppliers, explaining: 'We don't want to be left behind.' In 1988, McDonald's announced that they had completed the process of removing CFCs from their cartons in the UK.

One of the trends which is giving the Green consumer much greater commercial clout is the ageing of the 'Baby Boom' generation, which can also be described as the first 'environmental generation', now aged between twenty-five and forty-five. This is also the sector of society enjoying the most rapid growth in disposable income and so it is their spending power that many manufacturers are particularly concerned to capture.

Twenty years on from the heady days of the late 1960s, many baby boomers still subscribe to the idea of the 'low impact lifestyle'. Some of them may, for instance, decide to eat more raw food in a bid to save energy, or use vinegar instead of bleach as a toilet cleaner in order to cut pollution. But for many of their contemporaries shopping has become a leisure activity in itself. For these consumers the choice is between different brands of commercially produced goods, not between consumerism and non-consumerism. It would be wrong to underestimate the importance of either group. The Lifestyle movement is absolutely right when it calls on people to 'Live Simply That Others May Simply Live'. But in today's consumer-orientated society the high-spending Green consumer can pack more environmental punch than almost anyone else.

Wherever you fall on the spectrum of Green consumer life-styles, *The Green Consumer Guide* is designed to help you make informed choices and to leave manufacturers and retailers in no doubt that a growing number of their customers are now looking for products that are not going, quite literally, to cost the earth.

Don't forget how important it is to let other people know about the issues. Write to your local newspapers and to the national press.

Contact your MP. And if local issues are your target, get in touch with your local councillors and with the relevant local government department, water authority or central government department. Above all, join relevant campaigning or lobbying organizations. Your subscription counts – and your membership stands as a 'vote' for the agenda promoted by the organization – or organizations – you are backing. Wherever possible, buy goods through the catalogues offered by such organizations. . . .

Key issues for the green consumer

In general, the Green consumer avoids products which are likely to:

1. Endanger the health of the consumer or of others.
2. Cause significant damage to the environment during manufacture, use or disposal.
3. Consume a disproportionate amount of energy during manufacture, use or disposal.
4. Cause unnecessary waste, either because of over-packaging or because of an unduly short useful life.
5. Use materials derived from threatened species or from threatened environments.
6. Involve the unnecessary use – or cruelty to – animals, whether this be for toxicity testing or for other purposes.
7. Adversely affect other countries, particularly in the Third World.

Against Green Consumerism

Some members of the Green movement see green consumerism as at best grubbily materialistic and at worst a nonsense which will do more to deflect us from sustainable living than encourage us to achieve it. A year after *The Green Consumer Guide** appeared, Friends of the Earth (Great Britain) saw fit to devote the first of a series of discussion papers to questioning green consumerism. In the extract below Sandy Irvine, of the British Green Party, points out the benefits of green consumerism and then attacks it in the name of the social, economic and ecological limits to growth*. The bottom line of this attack is that 'genuinely green consumerism . . . would focus on reducing rather than simply changing personal levels of consumption'. In other words, the point is not so much to choose the CFC-free aerosol or to buy the car which will take lead-free petrol, but to ask yourself whether you need the aerosol or the car at all. Green consumers talk of electric cars as being non-polluting, but what of the resources consumed in making them, and the pollution generated in production? In this sense, attitudes to green consumerism have come to be a way of distinguishing green reformists from Green radicals.

From Sandy Irvine, *Beyond Green Consumerism* (London: Friends of the Earth, 1989) pp. 7–8, 15–22.

The benefits of green consumerism

Green consumers have realized that in many instances it is possible to change what they consume to the benefit of the environment and of themselves. There is no better illustration of this than most of the foodstuffs that fill the supermarket shelves. Their production harms the environment; their consumption harms our health; the cost of the subsidies that underwrite 'industrial' agriculture harms our pockets. Many farmers are heavily in debt, at the same time as farm technology has destroyed the jobs on which thriving rural communities depend. Intensive livestock production is also intensely harmful to the well-being of farm animals, and the countryside has become uninhabitable for many species. This food system is also deeply implicated in the exploitation of the 'Third World'. . . .

They [green consumers] can also help reduce world poverty. Products from firms such as Equal Exchange are not only additive-free, but are also brought under fair terms of trade. They can help governments such as that of Nicaragua which, whatever their specific failings, have made unparalleled efforts to promote education and health care as well as more fairly share out land ownership.

Green consumerism puts pressure on government to act. It becomes harder for them to hide behind excuses that there is no demand for change. It bolsters the work of the organized lobbies and pressure groups as well as the greener elements in the major parties. It also rewards those producers and retailers who are making genuine efforts to switch to less wasteful and less polluting alternatives whilst encouraging others to follow suit. . . .

Most important of all, Green consumerism is enabling individuals to act in their own right to help save the world. They do not have to sit back and wait for someone else to take action on their behalf. One individual choosing one brand rather than another may not seem very significant. Yet much environmental destruction is not the product of big projects: it is the consequence of the demand created out of all those little decisions made by each and every one of us every time we go to the shops. For many people, changing what they buy is a practical and realistic first step. They can make a positive contribution, no matter how small, to safeguarding the future.

᠃᠃᠃᠃᠃᠃᠃

Social and economic limits to green consumerism

Consumerism has created a society in which many people undoubtedly enjoy more physical comforts and ease than their ancestors. But the debit side includes both environmental and social costs.

A constant flood of 'new' or 'improved' goods holds out the promise of more satisfactions, whilst at the same time promoting actual dissatisfaction with what we already possess. . . .

More insidiously, consumerism also makes people less able or willing to trust their own skills and judgment. Consumerism's assault on self-reliance has been most clearly spotlighted in recent

scares about contamination of jars of baby food. TV studio discussion programmes were full of anxious parents wanting to know
how they were going to feed their children, something humanity
has been doing successfully for rather a long time before the rise of
the baby food industry!

In a number of ways, the 'trappings' of material affluence can
turn into traps. A vicious circle is created in which people have to
work long hours to afford the cars, the deep freezers, and the other
devices that allow them . . . to work long hours! Sometimes the
leisure the labour-saving gadgets bring is illusory.

Consumer choice and the freedom of the individual

Central to traditional consumerisms is the overwhelming emphasis
on freedom of choice. It has opposed the restrictive practices of
monopolies and other constraints on consumer power. It fights for
the liberty to buy brand X, rather than brand Y. A recent *Which?*
report on 1992 and the creation of the single European market posed
as the key question, 'will it mean cheaper goods and more choice
for the consumer?'

There can be no real freedom of choice without proper freedom
of information. To be a perfect Green consumer under present
conditions, a shopper would have to be free to spend all day if
necessary going from one store to another, comparing prices and
labels, consulting copies of *The Green Consumer Guide**, books on
who owns whom and what is the maker's track record on human
rights and other issues. The shopper would have to know from
where products have originally come, what has gone into them, how
long they will last etc. Given the sheer volume and rapid changing
of products on the market (many of whose specifications are compre-
hensible only to the expert and which often contain chemical compounds whose combined effects are quite unknown), an individual
consumer's judgment is bound to be inadequate.

Freedom of choice is also invoked to justify 'the voluntary
approach' often identified by both government and private enterprise as being preferable to regulation. The concept of the voluntary
approach assumes that individuals and organizations have a 'right'
to abuse the 'common' property of soil, water and air on which we
all depend. Today's 'freedom of choice' often boils down to a refusal
to make the choices that really matters. As will be seen in the next
chapter, further erosion of our environmental 'life-support systems'
will curtail peoples' 'freedom of choice' far more dramatically than

exercising proper restraint today. The simple truth of the matter is that saving the environment is going to place limits on what is available in the shops. It will mean people saying 'no' to certain lifestyles, to certain goods and services, to certain institutions if they are incompatible with what might best be called 'a conserver society'.

At stake, therefore, in contrast to the traditional goals of consumerism, are certain limitations on the freedom to choose in what are, after all, comparatively trivial areas for the sake of choosing a safe and sustainable way of life for future generations and other species. For our greater well-being we already accept all kinds of restrictions on the right of the individual to do whatever he or she feels like: highway codes, fire regulations, crimes against person and property. There can be no greater crime against posterity than to permit the present slide to environmental disaster to continue.

Equity

There are also fundamental questions concerning equal rights and opportunities that a truly Green consumer must face. There is a very real danger, for example, that Green consumerism could become something for the well-to-do, while the poorer sections of society have to make do with inferior produce.

Defenders of the free market system claim that a person's willingness to pay is the best way to find out who wants what. This kind of bidding, however, can only take place between people who have the wherewithal to do the bidding! Those with more money, therefore, can command that foodstuffs are grown to feed their pets, not starving human beings. Furthermore, those yet to be born can hardly turn up to make a bid. So if people alive today are prepared to pay lots of money to drive petrol-guzzling cars, there will necessarily be less oil left over for future generations. The market cannot cope with absolute scarcities such as individuals who lack purchasing power or resources that will run out.

At present, even if the 'greenest' product is correctly identified and is readily available, its price may be beyond many consumers' means. Many people cannot afford the price of organic produce or of putting a catalytic converter on their car, assuming they own one. Important energy conservation projects, such as insulating your house, still demand a lot of upfront investment even if the cost is paid back over time.

The kind of lifestyle envisaged in *The Green Consumer Guide* would obviously eliminate a great deal of waste and pollution. Nevertheless, if we assume that the Green consumer is going to own all the things that the *Guide* reviews, from 'green' dishwashers to anti-perspirants, it is clear that the majority of the world's population will have to do without, and the challenge of global poverty will not be met. . . .

The ecological limits to Green consumerism

As we have seen, Green consumerism is only tackling one part of the equation that determines the level of impact we humans make on our environment – technology. The consequences of the technologies we choose have to be multiplied by two other factors. First there is the sheer number of consumers; then there is the amount each member of population consumes. Take the example of clothing. Part of the impact of the 'technology' of a shirt is what kind of materials are used, how they are grown, whether they are made to last etc. It also depends upon how many shirts a person has in the wardrobe, and of course how many 'shirt wearers', there are altogether.

In the next twenty years, there will be nearly two billion more people putting pressure on an already depleted planet. Furthermore, rising human numbers are being accompanied by rising expectations of goods and services as the luxuries of yesterday become the 'necessities' of today. . . .

Limit one: earth

The finite size of the earth limits not only the amount of energy and raw materials available for economic activity, but also the capacity to absorb the waste and pollution inevitably generated by production and consumption. There is, for example, a limit to the amount of fertile soil or sites that are suitable for hydro-electricity. Many American towns are running out of space for landfall sites for their wastes. The skies cannot endlessly absorb air pollution.

Limit two: entropy

Contrary to those who view pollution simply as a sign of bad resource management, its roots lie in the laws of energy and matter. Their transformation by the human economy inevitably generates by-products which return as pollutants to the environmental 'sink' of air, soil and sea.

Basic physical laws tell us that all energy usage is, of course, a one way process. You cannot relight a fire from yesterday's ashes nor can a car run on exhaust fumes. This 'entropy' law also applies to matter as much as energy.

We sometimes call it wear and tear, at every stage in the usage of raw material some of it is lost for ever. Recovering the rest and restoring it to a reusable form takes more energy and creates more pollution.

Limit three: ecology

The significance of all those processes studied by ecologists can be understood by simply looking up into the sky on a clear night. There we can see the dead moon on which humans can only survive inside spacesuits. Down here on earth, life flourishes thanks to the health and integrity of all those self-sustaining, self-regulating and self-repairing ecological processes and life-support systems. Without them, human and non-human species alike have no future. Contrary to the popular but totally mistaken claim that 'ecology and the economy are interdependent', the reality is that our human-constructed economy is totally dependent upon the economy of nature, the 'real wealth of nations'. . . .

We are losing all those 'ecoservices' as we put more land under the plough; graze bigger herds of animals; introduce exotic plants and animals; plant monocultural tree farms; drown land beneath river dams and tidal barrages; mine and quarry; drain marshlands and fill in estuaries; channelize waterways; and most of all, pave the earth with tarmac and concrete for buildings, roads and airports. . . .

Green consumerism is a great step forward and has great potential. Yet it contains certain dangers. It must not be allowed to reinforce complacency by suggesting that all we need to do to make a comparatively small number of changes and then all will be well. Nor should it divert attention from the need to change the institutional and regulatory framework of society by a one-sided focus on the individual. As we've seen, its biggest failing is to be found in the idea that environmental problems are due to the kind of produce we are consuming.

The truth of the matter is that humanity as a whole is going to have to consume not just better but less. The solution to pollution is simply to generate less pollution in the first place. The only way to halt and reverse environmental degradation is less building over open spaces and less intensive land usage.

Genuinely Green consumerism, therefore, would focus on reducing rather than simply changing personal levels of consumption. This would work against society's economic structures and many other social institutions which are based on the more is better mentality. It would also make central the notion of equity between social groups, between countries, between generations and between species. It would pay attention not just to our material needs but also to the spiritual side of our being.

Hopefully, however, Green consumerism will stimulate an increasing number of people to examine critically both their own lifestyles and society as a whole. A truly Green consumer would be asking first and foremost 'do I really need all these things?' It would involve a change to thinking in terms of what is the minimum necessary to satisfy essential human needs, rather than novelty, fashion, status and all the other hooks of materialism.

Moreover, one question often leads to another. When people start questioning how, for example, the food they eat is produced, they are more likely to begin to examine the reality behind all kinds of other products. Books such as Richard North's *The Real Cost* show how products ranging from a pair of fashionable jeans to high-tech silicon chips combine to create pressures that are costing the earth. Although everyone has to start somewhere, starting points are most useful when they lead forward. There are encouraging signs that this is now happening.

Earth First!

In 1980 a radical environmental group called Earth First! (always with the '!') was founded by a group of activists in the United States of America concerned that timid campaigning was doing too little, too late to save the planet. From the outset, Earth First! recommended direct action (or what they call 'monkeywrenching', after their techniques for disabling bulldozers and other heavy machinery) as a strategy for opposing industrialism and preserving wilderness. Their activities have drawn criticism from both inside and outside the Green movement, and they are variously accused of valuing animals and trees above human beings, of endangering human life, and of getting the rest of the environmental movement a bad name. *Ecodefense*, from which these passages are taken, is a handbook for monkeywrenchers and gives advice on a range of activities from spiking roads and trees to the best sorts of camouflage. The first two extracts deal with the principles of monkeywrenching and its political effectiveness (and are by Dave Foreman and the pseudonymous T. O. Hellenbach respectively). Dave Foreman is the editor and publisher of *Earth First! The Radical Environmental Journal*, and he describes himself as a 'river runner, backpacker, birdwatcher, fly-fisherman and bowhunter'. The third extract is from Edward Abbey's novel *The Monkey Wrench Gang* which continues to inspire the tactic of ecological sabotage.

From Dave Foreman and Bill Haywood (eds.), *Ecodefense:A Field Guide to Monkeywrenching* (second edition) (Tucson: Ned Ludd Books, 1989) pp. 14–17, 21–3.

From Edward Abbey, *The Monkey Wrench Gang* (Utah; Dream Garden Press, 1990) pp. 76, 78, 80–81.

Many of the projects that will destroy roadless areas are economically marginal. It is costly for the Forest Service, BLM [Bureau of Land Management], timber companies, oil companies, mining companies and others to scratch out the 'resources' in these last wild areas. It is expensive to maintain the necessary infrastructure of roads for the exploitation of wild lands. The cost of repairs, the hassle, the delay, the down-time may just be too much for the bureaucrats and exploiters to accept if there is a widely-dispersed, unorganized, *strategic* movement of resistance across the land.

It is time for women and men, individually and in small groups, to act heroically and admittedly illegally in defence of the wild, to put a monkeywrench into the gears of the machine destroying natural diversity. This strategic monkeywrenching can be safe, it can be easy, it can be fun, and – most importantly – it can be effective in stopping timber cutting, road building, overgrazing, oil and gas exploration, mining, dam building, powerline construction, off-road-vehicle use, trapping, ski area development and other forms of destruction of the wilderness, as well as cancerous suburban sprawl.

But it must be strategic, it must be thoughtful, it must be deliberate in order to succeed. Such a campaign of resistance would follow these principles:

Monkeywrenching is non-violent

Monkeywrenching is non-violent resistance to the destruction of natural diversity and wilderness. It is not directed toward harming human beings or other forms of life. It is aimed at inanimate machines and tools. Care is always taken to minimize any possible threat to other people (and to the monkeywrenchers themselves).

Monkeywrenching is not organized

There can be no central direction or organization to monkeywrenching. Any type of network would invite infiltration, *agents provocateurs* and repression. It is truly individual action. Because of this, communication among monkeywrenchers is difficult and dangerous. Anonymous discussion through this book and its future editions, and through the Dear Ned Ludd section of the *Earth First! Journal*, seems to be the safest avenue of communication to refine techniques, security procedures and strategy. . . .

Monkeywrenching is targeted

Ecodefenders pick their targets. Mindless, erratic vandalism is counterproductive. Monkeywrenchers know that they do not stop a specific logging sale by destroying any piece of logging equipment which they come across. They make sure it belongs to the proper culprit. They ask themselves what is the most vulnerable point of a wilderness-destroying project and strike there. Senseless vandalism leads to loss of popular sympathy. . . .

Monkeywrenching is diverse

All kinds of people in all kinds of situations can be monkeywrenchers. Some pick a large area of wild country, declare it wilderness in their own minds, and resist any intrusion. Others specialize against logging or ORVs [off-road vehicles] in a variety of areas. Certain monkeywrenchers may target a specific project, such as a giant powerline, construction of a road, or an oil operation. Some operate in their backyards, others lie low at home and plan their ecotage a thousand miles away. Some are loners, others operate in small groups. . . .

Monkeywrenching is not revolutionary

It does *not* aim to overthrow any social, political or economic system. It is merely non-violent self-defence of the wild. It is aimed at keeping industrial 'civilization' out of natural areas and causing its retreat from areas that should be wild. It is not major industrial sabotage. Explosives, firearms and other dangerous tools are usually avoided. They invite greater scrutiny from law enforcement agencies, repression and loss of public support. (The Direct Action group in Canada is a good example of what monkeywrenching is *not*). Even Republicans monkeywrench. . . .

Monkeywrenching is deliberate and ethical

Monkeywrenching is not something to do cavalierly. Monkeywrenchers are very conscious of the gravity of what they do. They are deliberate about taking such a serious step. They are thoughtful. Monkeywrenchers – although non-violent – are warriors. They are exposing themselves to possible arrest or injury. It is not a casual or flippant affair. They keep a pure heart and mind about it. They remember that they are engaged in the most moral of all actions: protecting life, defending the earth.

A movement based on these principles could protect millions of acres of wilderness more stringently than any congressional act, could insure the propagation of the grizzly and other threatened life forms better than an army of game wardens, and could lead to the retreat of industrial civilization from large areas of forest, mountain, desert, plain, seashore, swamp, tundra and woodland that are better suited to the maintenance of natural diversity than to the production of raw materials for overconsumptive technological human society.

If loggers know that a timber sale is spiked, they won't bid on the timber. If a Forest Supervisor knows that a road will be continually destroyed, he won't try to build it. If seismographers know that they will be constantly harassed in an area, they go elsewhere. If ORVers know that they'll get flat tyres miles from nowhere, they won't drive in such areas.

John Muir said that if it ever came to a war between the races, he would side with the bears. That day has arrived. . . .

⁂

Most businesses, both large and small, operate to produce a relatively small margin of profit, frequently a single digit percentage of overall gross sales. This small net profit is vulnerable to outside tampering, such as a successful consumer boycott which reduces sales. A determined campaign of monkeywrenching affects the other end, by increasing operating costs to the point that they cut into profits. The random act of sabotage accomplishes little, but when cautiously repeated, striking weak points again and again, an exploitative corporation is forced to expand their security efforts and related expenses. Repairs of damages, such as abrasives in lubricating oils, result in several costs, including down-time. Since many businesses run on tight budgets or borrowed money, loss of production, even on a temporary basis, becomes costly. Interest payments on borrowed funds increase, payrolls for idled workers must be met, and buyers of finished products become impatient with missed deadlines. Since reputation, as much as other factors, influences credit, imagine the chilling effect on banks, finance companies, equipment manufacturers (who often extend credit to buyers), and insurance companies (who finance anything these days) when they realize that a few operators, working in critical wild lands, are more susceptible to delays in repayment.

Production scheduling is so critical to financial planning that most businesses have various contingencies to minimize the impact of mechanical failure, inclement weather and other factors. They may anticipate losing an average of two weeks to weather when logging in a certain season. Or there may be plans to rent extra equipment in the event of serious breakdowns. Repeated hits by ecoteurs exhaust the contingencies and cut into the eventual profit.

Some ecotage damage is repaired by funds from insurance companies. If the damage is recurrent, the insurer will increase the deductible, thereby forcing higher out-of-pocket expenses upon the operator. The insurer will also often increase premiums, insist on higher security expenditures and may even cancel coverage. Also, of course, the operator's standing with his insurance company is of critical importance to his lenders. . . .

Ultimately, the entire industry and its financial backers must be made aware that operations in *de facto* wilderness areas face higher risks and higher costs. Press coverage of monkeywrenching can drive this point home and alert the public in a manner that hurts the corporate image. The charge that monkeywrenching alienates public opinion stems from an incomplete understanding of propaganda and history. Scientific studies of propaganda and the press show that the vast majority of the public remembers the news only in vaguest outline. Details rapidly fade from memory. Basic concepts like 'opposition to logging' are all that are retained. History informs us that direct action engenders as much support as opposition. The American Revolution saw as many colonists enter the Tory ranks as enlisted in the Continental Army. During the Second World War, as many Frenchmen joined Nazi forces as participated in the famous French Underground. The majority of the public floats non-commitally between conflicting forces.

Finally, the actions of monkeywrenchers invariably enhance the status and bargaining position of more 'reasonable' opponents. Industry considers mainline environmentalists to be radical until they get a taste of real radical activism. Suddenly the soft-sell of the Sierra Club and other white-shirt-and-tie eco-bureaucrats becomes much more attractive and worthy of serious negotiation. These moderate environmentalists must condemn monkeywrenching so as to preserve their own image, but they should take full advantage of the credence it lends to their approach.

As for other types of activism, picketing and sit-ins quickly lose their newsworthiness. Boycotts can't touch primary industries because they lack a consumer market. Even letter-writing campaigns

and lobbyists are losing ground as the high cost of television advertising places election financing in the hands of well-heeled industrial
and labour union PACs (Political Action Committees set up to
undermine campaign 'reform' laws).

In these desperate times, it is difficult to be both close to earth
and optimistic about her future. The hope that remains is found in
the minds who care, and the hearts of those few who dare to act.

⠿⠿⠿

Down in the centre of the wash below the ridge the scrapers, the
earthmovers and the dump trucks with eighty-ton beds unloaded
their loads, building up the fill as the machines beyond were deepen-
ing the cut. Cut and fill, cut and fill, all afternoon the work went
on. The object in mind was a modern high-speed highway for the
convenience of the trucking industry, with grades no greater than
eight percent. That was the immediate object. The ideal lay still
farther on. The engineer's dream is a model of perfect sphericity,
the planet Earth with all irregularities removed, highways merely
painted on a surface smooth as glass. Of course the engineers still
have a long way to go but they are patient tireless little fellows;
they keep hustling on, like termites in a termitorium. It's steady
work, and their only natural enemies, they believe, are mechanical
breakdown or 'down time' for the equipment, and labour troubles,
and bad weather, and sometimes faulty preparation by the geologists
and surveyors.

The one enemy the contractor would not and did not think of
was the band of four idealists stretched out on their stomachs on a
rock under the desert sky. . . .

Now the stillness was complete. The watchers on the rim, eating
their suppers from tin plates, heard the croon of a mourning dove
far down the wash. They heard the hoot of an owl, the cries of little
birds retiring to sleep in the dusty cottonwoods. The great golden
light of the setting sun streamed across the sky, glowing upon the
clouds and the mountains. Almost all the country within their view
was roadless, uninhabited, a wilderness, They meant to keep it that
way. They sure meant to try. *Keep it like it was.*

The sun went down.

Tactics, materials, tools, gear. . . .

'The anthill,' said Doc, 'is sign, symbol and symptom of what
we are about out here, stumbling through the gloaming like so many
stumblebums. I mean it is the model in microcosm of what we must

find a way to oppose and halt. The anthill, like the Fullerian foam fungus, is the mark of social disease. Anthills abound where over-grazing prevails. The plastic dome follows the plague of runaway industrialism, prefigures technological tyranny and reveals the true quality of our lives, which sinks in inverse ratio to the growth of the Gross National Product. End of mini-lecture by Dr. Sarvis.'

'Good,' Bonnie said.

'Amen,' said Smith.

The evening gave way to night, a dense violet solution of starlight and darkness mixed with energy, each rock and shrub and tree and scarp outlined by an aura of silent radiation. Smith led the conspirators along the contour of the terrain until they came to the brink of something, an edge, a verge, beyond which stood nothing tangible. This was not the rim of the monocline, however, but the edge of the big man-made cut *through* the monocline. Below in the gloom those with sufficient night vision could see the broad new roadway and the dark forms of machines, two hundred feet down.

Smith and friends proceeded along this new drop-off until they reached a point where it was possible to scramble down to the crushed rock and heavy dust of the roadbed. Looking northeast, toward Blanding, they saw this pale raw freeway leading straight across the desert, through the scrub forest and out of sight in the darkness. No lights were visible, only the faint glow of the town fifteen miles away. In the opposite direction the roadbed curved down between the walls of the cut, sinking out of view toward the wash. They walked into the cut.

The first thing they encountered, on the shoulder of the roadbed, were survey stakes. Hayduke pulled them up and tossed them into the brush.

'Always pull up survey stakes,' he said. 'Anywhere you find them. Always. That's the first goddamned general order in the monkey wrench business. Always pull up survey stakes.'

They walked deeper into the cut to where it was possible, looking down and west, to make out though dimly the bottom of Comb Wash, the fill area, the scattered earth-moving equipment. Here they stopped for further consultation.

'We want our first lookout here,' Hayduke said.

'Doc or Bonnie?'

'I want to wreck something,' Bonnie said. 'I don't want to sit here in the dark making owl noises.'

'I'll stay here,' Doc said.

Once more they rehearsed signals. All in order. Doc made himself comfortable on the operator's seat of a giant compactor machine. He toyed with the controls. 'Stiff,' he said, 'but it's transportation.'

'Why don't we start with this fucker right here?' Hayduke said, meaning Doc's machine. 'Just for the practice.'

Why not? Packs were opened, tools and flashlights brought out. While Doc stood watch above them his three comrades entertained themselves cutting up the wiring, fuel lines, control link rods and hydraulic hoses of the machine, a beautiful new 27-ton tandem-drummed yellow Hyster C-450A, Caterpillar 330 HP diesel engine, sheepsfoot rollers, manufacturer's suggested retail price only $29,500 FOB Saginaw, Michigan. One of the best. A dreamboat.

They worked happily. Hard hats clinked and clanked against the steel. Lines and rods snapped apart with the rich *spang!* and solid *clunk!* of metal severed under tension. Doc lit another stogie. Smith wiped a drop of oil from his eyelid. The sharp smell of hydraulic fluid floated on the air, mixing uneasily with the aroma of Doc's smoke. Running oil pattered on the dust. There was another sound, far away, as of a motor. They paused. Doc stared into the dark. Nothing. The noise faded.

'All's clear,' he said. 'Carry on, lads.'

When everything was cut which they could reach and cut, Hayduke pulled the dipstick from the engine block – to check the oil? not exactly – and poured a handful of fine sand into the crankcase. Too slow. He unscrewed the oil-filler cap, took chisel and hammer and punched a hole through the oil strainer and poured in more sand. Smith removed the fuel-tank cap and emptied four quart bottles of sweet Karo syrup into the fuel tank. Injected into the cylinders, that sugar would form a solid coat of carbon on cylinder walls and piston rings. The engine should seize up like a block of iron, when they got it running. If they could get it running.

What else? Abbzug, Smith and Hayduke stood back a little and stared at the quiet hulk of the machine. All were impressed by what they had done. The murder of a machine. Deicide.

GREEN PHILOSOPHY

Animal Rights

Members of the Green movement spend much of their time
arguing for the rights of the non-human natural world, demanding that it be brought within the boundaries of the ethical
community – i.e. that it be allowed the same sort of moral
treatment as we allow for human beings. So they argue that
trees, plants, even stones, and, of course, animals, are entitled
to respectful treatment. Tom Regan's *The Case for Animal
Rights* has come to be seen as a classic of close philosophical
argumentation in favour of granting (some) animals moral
rights, and four extracts from it are reproduced below. These
extracts are not designed to represent Regan's argument, but
rather to show how a philosophical strategy which might successfully defend the rights-claims of one part of the non-human
community will not necessarily do for *all* parts of it. Those
who seek an ethic for the environment (Leopold*, Naess*) will,
for example, want to go much further in extending the ethical
community than Regan manages to do ('normal mammalian
animals aged one or more'). In this sense, Regan's individualist
rights-based strategy is important to the intellectual archae-
ology of the Green movement for its limitations as well as its
successes.

From Tom Regan, *The Case for Animal Rights* (London and
New York: Routledge, 1988) pp. 78, 81, 327, 328.

A variety of reasons make it reasonable to view mammalian animals
as individuals who, like us, have beliefs and desires. Common sense
and ordinary language support this, as does evolutionary theory;
their behaviour is consistent with this view; and the question of the
relative mental sophistication and powers of these animals is only
confusedly tied to asking whether they have immaterial immortal
souls. These reasons taken together (the cumulative argument) provide the basis for a burden-of-proof argument; unless or until we
are shown that there are better reasons for denying that these ani-

mals have beliefs and desires we are rationally entitled to believe
that they do. . . .

Perception, memory, desire, belief, self-consciousness, intention, a
sense of the future – these are among the leading attributes of the
mental life of normal mammalian animals aged one or more. Add
to this list the not unimportant categories of emotion (e.g., fear and
hatred) and sentience, understood as the capacity to experience
pleasure and pain, and we begin to approach a fair rendering of the
mental life of these animals. To deny a mental life of this complexity
to these creatures in favour of, for example, a stimulus-response
theory of their behaviour, while affirming a complex mental life to
human beings is, let us agree, a *theoretical* possibility. But one wants
arguments to support viewing humans and animals so differently,
arguments that meet the burden of proof issued by the cumulative
argument. This chapter examines major arguments that explicitly
address the question of animal beliefs and desires. Though not all
the options could be examined, and while it was freely conceded
that not all the controversies discussed along the way were settled
with philosophical finality, enough was considered and argued, it is
to be hoped, to show that these major arguments fail to meet the
burden of proof. To continue, in the face of the failure of these
arguments, to apply a stimulus-response theory to animals but to
favour the application of the belief-desire theory to humans, or
worse still, to disparage those who subscribe to this latter understanding of animals and their behaviour as 'anthropomorphizers', is
to bespeak a prejudice rather than to unmask one. To cling to and
perpetuate a vision of the world that concedes a 'primitive' mental
life to animals or – for there are closet Cartesians in our midst – to
deny *any* mental life to them is as far removed from having an
accurate conception of what these animals are like as the lion in
Stefen Lochner's painting is from representing a real lion. . . .

The principal conclusion reached in the present chapter is that all
moral agents and patients have certain basic moral rights. To say
that these individuals possess basic (or unacquired) moral rights
means that (1) they possess certain rights independently of anyone's
voluntary acts, either their own or those of others, and independently of the position they happen to occupy in any given institutional arrangement; (2) these rights are universal – that is, they
are possessed by all relevantly similar individuals, independently of
those considerations mentioned in (1); and (3) all who possess these
rights possess them equally. Basic moral rights thus differ *both* from

acquired moral rights (e.g., the right of the promise against the promiser) because one acquires these rights as a result of someone's voluntary acts or one's place in an institutional arrangement *and* from legal rights (e.g., the right to vote) since legal rights, unlike basic moral rights, are not equal or universal. . . .

Moral rights, whether basic or acquired, were analysed as valid claims. . . . To make a claim is to affirm that certain treatment is owed or is due, either to oneself or to another (or others). A claim is valid if and only if (a) it is a valid claim-against assignable individuals and (b) it is a valid claim-to treatment owed by these individuals, the validity of any claim-to resting ultimately on the validity of principles of direct duty. Because the primary concern of the present chapter was the question of basic moral rights, major emphasis was placed on validating rights of this kind.

The principal basic moral right possessed by all moral agents and patients is the right to respectful treatment. . . .

Thus has the case for animal rights been offered. If it is sound, then, like us, animals have certain basic moral rights, including in particular the fundamental right to be treated with respect that, as possessors of inherent value, they are due as a matter of strict justice. Like us therefore – assuming the soundness of the arguments that have gone before – they must never be treated as mere receptacles of intrinsic values (e.g., pleasure, or preference-satisfaction), and any harm that is done to them must be consistent with the recognition of their equal inherent value and their equal *prima facie* right not to be harmed.

A Land Ethic

The American naturalist, forester and game manager Aldo
Leopold is often referred to in Green literature as the first
person to articulate an ethic for the environment. The central
point in the first extract is that such an ethic – which Leopold
calls a 'land ethic' – should extend beyond animals, and even
plants, to include the non-living environment as well. This is
the position that has inspired the likes of Arne Naess* and
others in the deep ecology* movement, and Leopold's *A Sand
County Almanac* provides a constant source of reference and
inspiration for them. The second extract contains early inti-
mations of themes now common in the Green movement: the
damaging separation of human beings from the land, the tendency to judge the value of the environment solely in economic
terms, and the recognition of the necessity for intellectual as
well as emotional defences of the environmentalist position.
The extract also contains Leopold's general environmental rule
of thumb: 'A thing is right when it tends to preserve the
integrity, stability, and beauty of the biotic community. It is
wrong when it tends otherwise.' This early formulation raises
questions which have dogged supporters of the environmental
ethic ever since: does it unduly privilege the community over
the individual?, and, does it imply that the human being is of
the same value as other members of the planetary community,
and is this acceptable?

From Aldo Leopold, *A Sand County Almanac* (1949) (Oxford:
Oxford University Press, 1968) pp. 201–4, 223–5.

There is as yet no ethic dealing with man's relation to land and to
the animals and plants which grow upon it. Land, like Odysseus'
slave-girls, is still property. The land-relation is still strictly economic, entailing privileges but not obligations.

The extension of ethics to this third element in human environment is, if I read the evidence correctly, an evolutionary possibility

and an ecological necessity. It is the third step in a sequence. The first two[1] have already been taken. Individual thinkers since the days of Ezekiel and Isaiah have asserted that the despoliation of land is not only inexpedient but wrong. Society, however, has not yet affirmed their belief. I regard the present conservation movement as the embryo of such an affirmation.

An ethic may be regarded as a mode of guidance for meeting ecological situations so new or intricate, or involving such deferred reactions, that the path of social expediency is not discernible to the average individual. Animal instincts are modes of guidance for the individual in meeting such situations. Ethics are possibly a kind of community instinct in-the-making. . . .

All ethics so far evolved rest upon a single premise: that the individual is a member of a community of interdependent parts. His instincts prompt him to compete for his place in that community, but his ethics prompt him also to co-operate (perhaps in order that there may be a place to compete for).

The land ethic simply enlarges the boundaries of the community to include soils, waters, plants, and animals, or collectively: the land.

This sounds simple: do we not already sing our love for obligation to the land of the free and the home of the brave? Yes, but just what and whom do we love? Certainly not the soil, which we are sending helter-skelter downriver. Certainly not the waters, which we assume have no function except to turn turbines, float barges, and carry off sewage. Certainly not the plants, of which we exterminate whole communities without batting an eye. Certainly not the animals, of which we have already extirpated many of the largest and most beautiful species. A land ethic of course cannot prevent the alteration, management, and use of these 'resources' but it does affirm their right to continued existence, and, at least in spots, their continued existence in a natural state.

In short, a land ethic changes the role of *Homo sapiens* from conqueror of the land-community to plain member and citizen of it. It implies respect for his fellow-members, and also respect for the community as such.

In human history, we have learned (I hope) that the conqueror role is eventually self-defeating. Why? Because it is implicit in such a role that the conqueror knows, *ex cathedra*, just what makes the

---

[1] That is, ethics dealing with the relationships between individuals, and between individuals and society as a whole.

community clock tick, and just what and who is valuable, and what and who is worthless, in community life. It always turns out that he knows neither, and this is why his conquests eventually defeat themselves. . . .

It is inconceivable to me that an ethical relation to land can exist without love, respect, and admiration for land, and a high regard for its value. By value, I of course mean something far broader than mere economic value; I mean value in the philosophical sense.

Perhaps the most serious obstacle impeding the evolution of a land ethic is the fact that our educational and economic system is headed away from, rather than toward, an intense consciousness of land. Your true modern is separated from the land by many middlemen, and by innumerable physical gadgets. He has no vital relation to it; to him it is the space between cities on which crops grow. Turn him loose for a day on the land, and if the spot does not happen to be a golf links or a 'scenic' area, he is bored stiff. If crops could be raised by hydroponics instead of farming, it would suit him very well. Synthetic substitutes for wood, leather, wool, and other natural land products suit him better than the originals. In short, land is something he has 'outgrown'.

Almost equally serious as an obstacle to a land ethic is the attitude of the farmer for whom the land is still an adversary, or a taskmaster that keeps him in slavery. Theoretically, the mechanization of farming ought to cut the farmer's chains, but whether it really does is debatable.

One of the requisites for an ecological comprehension of land is an understanding of ecology, and this is by no means co-extensive with 'education'; in fact, much higher education seems deliberately to avoid ecological concepts. An understanding of ecology does not necessarily originate in courses bearing ecological labels; it is quite as likely to be labelled geography, botany, agronomy, history, or economics. This is as it should be, but whatever the label, ecological training is scarce.

The case for a land ethic would appear hopeless but for the minority which is in obvious revolt against these 'modern' trends.

The 'key-log' which must be moved to release the evolutionary process for an ethic is simply this: quit thinking about decent land-use as solely an economic problem. Examine each question in terms of what is ethically and esthetically right, as well as what is economically expedient. A thing is right when it tends to preserve the integrity, stability, and beauty of the biotic community. It is wrong when it tends otherwise.

It of course goes without saying that economic feasibility limits the tether of what can or cannot be done for land. It always has and it always will. The fallacy the economic determinists have tied around our collective neck, and which we now need to cast off, is the belief that economics determines *all* land-use. This is simply not true. An innumerable host of actions and attitudes, comprising perhaps the bulk of all land relations, is determined by the land-users' tastes and predilections, rather than by his purse. The bulk of all land relations hinges on investments of time, forethought, skill, and faith rather than on investments of cash. As a land-user thinketh, so is he.

I have purposely presented the land ethic as a product of social evolution because nothing so important as an ethic is ever 'written'. Only the most superficial student of history supposes that Moses 'wrote' the Decalogue; it evolved in the minds of a thinking community, and Moses wrote a tentative summary of it for a 'seminar'. I say tentative because evolution never stops.

The evolution of a land ethic is an intellectual as well as emotional process. Conservation is paved with good intentions which prove to be futile, or even dangerous, because they are devoid of critical understanding either of the land, or of economic land-use. I think it is a truism that as the ethical frontier advances from the individual to the community, its intellectual content increases.

The mechanism of operation is the same for any ethic: social approbation for right actions: social disapproval for wrong actions.

By and large, our present problem is one of attitudes and implements. We are remodelling the Alhambra with a steamshovel, and we are proud of our yardage. We shall hardly relinquish the shovel, which after all has many good points, but we are in need of gentler and more objective criteria for its successful use.

Deep Ecology

Arguments for the preservation of the non-human natural world (the subject of 'environmental ethics') have taken many forms. Very roughly they can be divided into two groups: those that argue for its preservation for human-centred reasons, and those that argue that the non-human natural world has a right to exist irrespective of how useful it might be for us. Members of the Green movement can be found on both sides of this divide. The distinction corresponds (again roughly) to that between 'shallow' and 'deep' ecology, which was first developed by the Norwegian philosopher Arne Naess in a speech in Bucharest in 1972, and which has come to be the focus of probably the most important debate in Green philosophy. The text reproduced below is a version of that speech, and the mountain of words that has been written on deep ecology since then can justifiably be regarded as a lengthy footnote to it. Some of the difficulties to which deep ecology has given rise are: the principle of 'biospherical egalitarianism' (how much 'killing, exploitation, and suppression' is allowed, and how do we decide?); how legitimate is it to apply ecological principles to human society – for example, how much diversity in 'human ways of life' should be tolerated (is cannibalism allowed?); and can a successful political movement be based on ways of thinking which seem alien to the modern, industrial way of life?

From Arne Naess, 'The Shallow and the Deep, Long-Range Ecology Movement. A Summary', *Inquiry*, 16, 1973 pp. 95–9.

Ecologically responsible policies are concerned only in part with pollution and resource depletion. There are deeper concerns which touch upon principles of diversity, complexity, autonomy, decentralization, symbiosis, egalitarianism, and classlessness.

The emergence of ecologists from their former relative obscurity marks a turning-point in our scientific communities. But their message is twisted and misused. A shallow, but presently rather powerful movement, and a deep, but less influential movement, compete for our attention. I shall make an effort to characterize the two:

1. The shallow ecology movement

Fight against pollution and resource depletion. Central objective: the health and affluence of people in the developed countries.

2. The deep ecology movement

(1) Rejection of the man-in-environment image in favour of the relational, total-field image

Organisms as knots in the biospherical net or field of intrinsic relations. An intrinsic relation between two things *A* and *B* is such that the relation belongs to the definitions or basic constitutions of *A* and *B*, so that without the relation, *A* and *B* are no longer the same things. The total-field model dissolves not only the man-in-environment concept, but every compact thing-in-milieu concept – except when talking at a superficial or preliminary level of communication.

(2) Biospherical egalitarianism – in principle

The 'in principle' clause is inserted because any realistic praxis necessitates some killing, exploitation, and suppression. The ecological field-worker acquires a deep-seated respect, or even veneration, for ways and forms of life. He reaches an understanding from within, a kind of understanding that others reserve for fellow men and for a narrow section of ways and forms of life. To the ecological field-worker, *the equal right to live and blossom* is an intuitively clear and obvious value axiom. Its restriction to humans is an anthropocentrism with detrimental effects upon the life quality of humans themselves. This quality depends in part upon the deep pleasure and satisfaction we receive from close partnership with other forms of life. The attempt to ignore our dependence and to establish a master-slave role has contributed to the alienation of man from himself.

Ecological egalitarianism implies the reinterpretation of the future-research variable, 'level of crowding', so that *general* mammalian crowding and loss of life-quality is taken seriously, not only human crowding. (Research on the high requirements of free space of certain mammals has, incidentally, suggested that theorists of human urbanism have largely underestimated human life-space requirements. Behavioural crowding symptoms [neurosis, aggressiveness, loss of traditions . . .] are largely the same among mammals.)

(3) Principles of diversity and of symbiosis

Diversity enhances the potentialities of survival, the chances of new modes of life, the richness of forms. And the so-called struggle of life, and survival of the fittest, should be interpreted in the sense of ability to co-exist and co-operate in complex relationships, rather than ability to kill, exploit and suppress. 'Live and let live' is a more powerful ecological principle than 'Either you or me'.

The latter tends to reduce the multiplicity of kinds of forms of life, and also to create destruction within the communities of the same species. Ecologically-inspired attitudes therefore favour diversity of human ways of life, of cultures, of occupations, of economies. They support the fight against economic and cultural, as much as military, invasion and domination, and they are opposed to the annihilation of seals and whales as much as to that of human tribes or cultures.

(4) Anti-class posture

Diversity of human ways of life is in part due to (intended or unintended) exploitation and suppression on the part of certain groups. The exploiter lives differently from the exploited, but both are adversely affected in their potentialities of self-realization. The principle of diversity does not cover differences due merely to certain attitudes or behaviours forcibly blocked or restrained. The principles of ecological egalitarianism and of symbiosis support the same anti-class posture. The ecological attitude favours the extension of all three principles to any group conflicts, including those of today between developing and developed nations. The three principles also favour extreme caution towards any overall plans for the future, except those consistent with wide and widening classless diversity.

(5) Fight against pollution and resource depletion

In this fight ecologists have found powerful supporters, but sometimes to the detriment of their total stand. This happens when
attention is focused on pollution and resource depletion rather than
on the other points, or when projects are implemented which reduce
pollution but increase evils of the other kinds. Thus, if prices of
life necessities increase because of the installation of anti-pollution
devices, class differences increase too. An ethics of responsibility
implies that ecologists do not serve the shallow, but the deep ecological movement. That is, not only point (5), but all seven points must
be considered together.

Ecologists are irreplaceable informants in any society, whatever
their political colour. If well organized, they have the power to
reject jobs in which they submit themselves to institutions or to
planners with limited ecological perspectives. As it is now, ecologists
sometimes serve masters who deliberately ignore the wider perspectives.

(6) Complexity, not complication

The theory of ecosystems contains an important distinction between
what is complicated without any Gestalt or unifying principles – we
may think of finding our way through a chaotic city – and what is
complex. A multiplicity of more or less lawful, interacting factors
may operate together to form a unity, a system. We make a shoe
or use a map or integrate a variety of activities into a workaday
pattern. Organisms, ways of life, and interactions in the biosphere
in general, exhibit complexity of such an astoundingly high level as
to colour the general outlook of ecologists. Such complexity makes
thinking in terms of vast systems inevitable. It also makes for a keen,
steady perception of the profound *human ignorance* of biospherical
relationships and therefore of the effect of disturbances.

Applied to humans, the complexity-not-complication principle
favours division of labour, *not fragmentation of labour*. It favours
integrated actions in which the whole person is active, not mere
reactions. It favours complex economies, an integrated variety of
means of living. (Combinations of industrial and agricultural
activity, of intellectual and manual work, of specialized and non-
specialized occupations, of urban and non-urban activity, of work
in city and recreation in nature with recreation in city and work in
nature.)

It favours soft technique and 'soft future-research', less prognosis, more clarification of possibilities. More sensitivity towards continuity and live traditions, and – most importantly, towards our state of ignorance.

The implementation of ecologically responsible policies requires in this century an exponential growth of technical skill and invention – but in new directions, directions which today are not consistently and liberally supported by the research policy organs of our nation-states.

(7) *Local autonomy and decentralization*

The vulnerability of a form of life is roughly proportional to the weight of influences from afar, from outside the local region in which that form has obtained an ecological equilibrium. This lends support to our efforts to strengthen local self-government and material and mental self-sufficiency. But these efforts presuppose an impetus towards decentralization. Pollution problems, including those of thermal pollution and recirculation of materials, also lead us in this direction, because increased local autonomy, if we are able to keep other factors constant, reduces energy consumption.

Summing up, then, it should, first of all, be borne in mind that the norms and tendencies of the 'deep ecology' movement are not derived from ecology by logic or induction. Ecological knowledge and the lifestyle of the ecological field-worker have *suggested, inspired, and fortified* the perspectives of the deep ecology movement. Many of the formulations in the above seven-point survey are rather vague generalizations, only tenable if made more precise in certain directions. But all over the world the inspiration from ecology has shown remarkable convergencies. The survey does not pretend to be more than one of the possible condensed codifications of these convergencies.

Secondly, it should be fully appreciated that the significant tenets of the 'deep ecology' movement are clearly and forcefully *normative*. They express a value priority system only in part based on results (or lack of results, cf. point [6]) of scientific research. Today, ecologists try to influence policy-making bodies largely through threats, through predictions concerning pollutants and resource depletion, knowing that policy-makers accept at least certain minimum *norms* concerning health and just distribution. But it is clear that there is a vast number of people in all countries, and even a considerable number of people in power, who accept as valid the wider norms and values characteristic of the 'deep ecology' movement. There are political potentials in this movement which should not be overlooked and which have little to do with pollution and resource depletion. In plotting possible futures, the norms should be freely used and elaborated.

Thirdly, in so far as ecology movements deserve our attention, they are *ecophilosphical* rather than ecological. Ecology is a *limited* science which makes *use* of scientific methods. Philosophy is the most general forum of debate on fundamentals, descriptive as well as prescriptive, and political philosophy is one of its subsections. By an *ecosophy* I mean a philosophy of ecological harmony or equilibrium. A philosophy as a kind of *sofia* wisdom, is openly normative, it contains *both* norms, rules, postulates, value priority announcements *and* hypotheses concerning the state of affairs in our universe. Wisdom is policy wisdom, prescription, not only scientific description and prediction.

The details of an ecosophy will show many variations due to significant differences concerning not only 'facts' of pollution, resources, population, etc., but also value priorities. Today, however, the seven points listed provide one unified framework for ecosophical systems.

Touch the Earth

The earth-based spirituality of North American Indians has long been a source of inspiration for Greens who argue for a more responsible attitude towards the environment. Based as it is on the belief that the fate of humanity is inextricably bound up with the fate of the natural world, it demands a humility towards nature which is conspicuously lacking in our modern dealings with it. In the first extract below, an old holy Wintu Indian woman, of California, contrasts White with Indian treatment of the land; and in the second, Chief Luther Standing Bear, of the Lakota (or Dakota) tribe speaks of the 'life-giving' force of the earth and the Indian's kinship with it. Some forms of 'deep ecology' (see previous extract) argue for the same closeness between humanity and nature as Indians experience, and James Lovelock's 'Gaia hypothesis' (see p. 264) can be read as a modern version of the Wintu woman's certainty that the earth is alive.

From T. C. McLuhan (ed.), *Touch the Earth* (London: Abacus, 1973) p. 6 and p. 15.

The White people never cared for land or deer or bear. When we Indians kill meat, we eat it all up. When we dig roots we make little holes. When we build houses, we make little holes. When we burn grass for grasshoppers, we don't ruin things. We shake down acorns and pinenuts. We don't chop down the trees. We only use dead wood. But the White people plough up the ground, pull down the trees, kill everything. The tree says, 'Don't. I am sore. Don't hurt me.' But they chop it down and cut it up. The spirit of the land hates them. They blast out trees and stir it up to its depths. They saw up the trees. That hurts them. The Indians never hurt anything, but the White people destroy all. They blast rocks and scatter them on the ground. The rock says, 'Don't. You are hurting me.' But the White people pay no attention. When the Indians use rocks, they take little round ones for their cooking. . . . How can the spirit of the earth like the White man? . . . Everywhere the White man has touched it, it is sore.

The Lakota was a true naturist – a lover of nature. He loved the earth and all things of the earth, the attachment growing with age. The old people came literally to love the soil and they sat or reclined on the ground with a feeling of being close to a mothering power. It was good for the skin to touch the earth and the old people liked to remove their moccasins and walk with bare feet on the sacred earth. Their tepees were built upon the earth and their altars were made of earth. The birds that flew in the air came to rest upon the earth and it was the final abiding place of all things that lived and grew. The soil was soothing, strengthening, cleansing and healing.

That is why the old Indian still sits upon the earth instead of propping himself up and away from its life-giving forces. For him, to sit or lie upon the ground is to be able to think more deeply and to feel more keenly; he can see more clearly into the mysteries of life and closer in kinship to other lives about him. . . .

Kinship with all creatures of the earth, sky and water was a real and active principle. For the animal and bird world there existed a brotherly feeling that kept the Lakota safe among them and so close did some of the Lakotas come to their feathered and furred friends that in true brotherhood they spoke a common tongue.

The old Lakota was wise. He knew that man's heart away from nature becomes hard; he knew that lack of respect for growing, living things soon led to lack of respect for humans too. So he kept his youth close to its softening influence.

Future Generations

Green politics demands that we extend our moral thinking in a number of novel directions – towards the rights of animals* and wilderness, for example. Another dimension which emerges is that of the future: how far do we have a moral obligation towards future generations to ensure that they inherit a planet fit to live on? The extract below from the Australian philosophers Richard and Val Routley is designed to show that we have an intuitive sense of such an obligation, but that our practice runs counter to it. The Routleys here consider the particular issue of nuclear waste, but Greens could in principle extend the argument to any of the practices associated with modern industrialism which threaten to leave future generations with a dirtier and more depleted planet.

From Richard and Val Routley, 'Nuclear Energy and Obligations to the Future', *Inquiry*, 21, 1978, pp. 133–5.

The bus example

Suppose we consider a bus, a bus which we hope is to make a very long journey. This bus, a Third World bus, carries both passengers and freight. The bus sets down and picks up many different passengers in the course of its long journey and the drivers change many times, but because of the way the bus line is managed and the poor service on the route it is nearly always full to overcrowded, with passengers hanging off the back, and as in Afghanistan, passengers riding on the roof, and chickens and goats in the freight compartment.

Early in the bus's journey someone consigns on it, to a far distant destination, a package containing a highly toxic and explosive gas. This is packaged in a very thin container, which as the consigner well knows is unlikely to contain the gas for the full distance for which it is consigned, and certainly will not do so if the bus should encounter any trouble, for example, if there is a breakdown and the interior of the bus becomes very hot, if the bus should strike a very large bump or pothole of the sort commonly found on some of the bad roads it has to traverse, or if some passenger should interfere deliberately or inadvertently with the cargo or perhaps try to steal some of the freight, as also frequently happens. *All* of these things, let us suppose, have happened on some of the bus's previous journeys. If the container should break the resulting disaster would probably kill at least some of the people and animals on the bus, while others could be maimed or contract serious diseases.

There does not seem much doubt about what most of us would say about the morality of the consigner's actions, and there is certainly no doubt about what the passengers would say. The consigner's action in putting the safety of the occupants of the bus at risk is appalling. What could excuse such an action, what sort of circumstances might justify it, and what sort of case could the consigner reasonably put up? The consigner might say that it is by no means certain that the gas will escape; he himself is an optimist and therefore feels that such unfavourable possible outcomes should be ignored. In any case the bus might have an accident and the passengers be killed long before the container gets a chance to leak; or the passengers might change to another bus and leave the lethal parcel behind.

He might say that it is the responsibility of the passengers and the driver to ensure that the journey is a smooth one, and that if they fail to do so, the results are not his fault. He might say that the journey is such a long one that many of the passengers may have become mere mindless vegetables or degenerate wretches about whose fate no decent person need concern himself, or that they might not care about losing their lives or health or possessions anyway by that time.

Most of these excuses will seem little more than a bad joke, and certainly would not usually be reckoned any sort of justification. The main argument the consigner of the lethal parcel employs, however, is that his own pressing needs justify his actions. He has no option but to consign his potentially lethal parcel, he says, since the firm he owns, and which has produced the material as a by-product, is in bad financial straits and cannot afford to produce a better container or to stop the production of the gas. If the firm goes out of business, the consigner says, his wife will leave him, and he will lose his family happiness, the comfortable way of life to which he has become accustomed and sees now as a necessity; his employees will lose their jobs and have to look for others;

not only will the firm's customers be inconvenienced but he, the consigner, will have to break some business contracts; the inhabitants of the local village through loss of spending and cancellation of the multiplier effect will suffer financial hardship, and, worst of all, the tiny flow of droplets that the poor of the village might receive (theoretically at any rate) as a result of the trickling down of these good things would dry up entirely. In short, some basic and some perhaps uncomfortable changes will be needed in the village.

Even if the consigner's story were accepted at face value – and it would be wise to look critically at his story – only someone whose moral sensibilities had been paralysed by the disease of galloping economism could see such a set of considerations, based on 'needs', comfort, and the goal of local prosperity, as justifying the consigner's action.

One is not generally entitled thus simply to *transfer* the risks and costs arising from one's own life on to other uninvolved parties, to get oneself out of a hole of one's own making by creating harm or risk of harm to someone else who has had no share in creating the situation. To create serious risks and costs, especially risks of life or health for such others, simply to avoid having to make some changes to a comfortable lifestyle, or even for a somewhat better reason, is usually thought deserving of moral condemnation, and sometimes considered a crime; for example, the action of a company in creating risks to the lives or health of its workers or customers to prevent itself from going bankrupt. What the consigner says may be an explanation of his behaviour, but it is not a justification.

The problem raised by nuclear waste disposal is by no means a perfect analogy to the bus case, since, for example, the passengers on the nuclear bus cannot get off the bus or easily throw out the lethal package. In many crucial moral respects, however, the nuclear waste storage problem as it affects future people, the passengers in the bus we are considering, resembles the consignment of the faultily packaged lethal gas. Not only are rather similar moral principles involved, but a rather similar set of arguments to the lamentable excuses the consigner presents have been seriously put up to justify nuclear development, the difference being that in the nuclear case these arguments have been widely accepted.

Green Conservatism

Green thinkers like to define their political position as 'beyond left and right'. There are various tests to which we can put this claim, and while it emerges that Green politics might differ from, say, both conservatism and socialism in its opposition to what Greens call 'industrialism'* (i.e. that people's needs are best satisfied by increasing economic growth), it also borrows from those traditions from which it wants to distance itself. In one important way, not often noticed, Green politics agrees with a basic principle of traditional conservatism: that the fundamental ignorance of human beings in the face of the enormous complexity of the world which surrounds us should be a basis for our thinking twice before intervening in it. Arne Naess expresses this quite clearly in the following passage, and suggests that the burden of persuasion should be shifted onto those who would encroach on the environment rather than those who want to preserve it. Promoting this shift is basically what Green politics is all about.

From Arne Naess, *Ecology, Community and Lifestyle* (Cambridge: Cambridge University Press, 1989), pp. 26–7.

The ecological movement relies upon the results of research in ecology and more recently in conservation biology. But to the great amazement of many, the scientific conclusions are often statements of ignorance: 'We do not know what long-range consequences the proposed interference in the ecosystem will beget, so we cannot make any hard and fast conclusions.' Only rarely can scientists predict with any certainty the effect of a new chemical on even a single small ecosystem.

The so-called ecological doomsday prophecies are statements about catastrophical states of affairs which cannot be precluded *if* certain new policies are *not* put into effect very soon. We know little or nothing about the extent to which such new policies will come into being. The fact that the human population is on a catastrophic course does not lead to the conclusion that catastrophe will occur. The situation is critical because we do not know *whether* the course will be promptly and radically changed.

Politicians and others now attentive to the words of environmental scientists are thunderstruck that science itself is proclaiming so much ignorance! It is a strange feeling to have new, politically brazen policies recommended on the basis of ignorance. But we do not know the consequences! Should we proceed with the project or not? The burden of proof rests with those who are encroaching upon the environment.

Why does the burden of proof rest with the encroachers? The ecosystems in which we intervene are generally in a particular state of balance which there are grounds to assume to be of more service to mankind than states of disturbance and their resultant unpredictable and far-reaching changes. In general, it is not possible to regain the original state after an intervention has wrought serious, undesired consequences. And intervention, ordinarily with a short-sighted gain for some minor part of mankind in view, has a tendency to be detrimental for most or all forms of life.

The study of ecosystems makes us conscious of our ignorance. Faced with experts who, after calling attention to a critical situation, emphasize their lack of knowledge and suggest research programmes which may diminish this lack of knowledge, the most natural response for the politicians is to propose that the matter be put on the table or postponed until more information is available. For example, a proposal which would counter the possible death of forests is postponed in order to gather more information on what makes the trees die. It appears that public and private officials who heed ecological expertise must become accustomed to a new normal procedure: the recommendation and instigation of bold, radical conservation steps justified by the statements of our lack of knowledge.

Holism

Not many Greens will be happy to know that the inventor of the term which underpins much of their philosophical world-view was the Boer general, scourge of Mahatma Gandhi and Prime Minister of South Africa, The Right Honourable Jan C. Smuts. During one of the short periods when he was out of political office, Smuts decided to set down his thoughts on the nature of the relationships he had observed in both human and non-human realms, and the result was *Holism and Evolution*. The science of ecology is itself holistic, based on the idea that 'the whole and the parts . . . reciprocally influence and determine each other', and it is easy to see from Smuts's description why holism is so useful to Greens both in their attack on mechanistic science (Capra*) and in their attempt to heal the wounds between human beings and the natural world.

From General The Right Honourable Jan C. Smuts, *Holism and Evolution* (London: Macmillan, 1926) pp. 86, 103–4, 108–9.

The idea of wholes and wholeness should therefore not be confined to the biological domain; it covers both inorganic substances and the highest manifestations of the human spirit. Taking a plant or an animal as a type of a whole, we notice the fundamental holistic characters as a unity of parts which is so close and intense as to be more than the sum of its parts; which not only gives a particular conformation or structure to the parts, but so relates and determines them in their synthesis that their functions are altered; the synthesis affects and determines the parts, so that they function towards the 'whole'; and the whole and the parts therefore reciprocally influence and determine each other, and appear more or less to merge their individual characters: the whole is in the parts and the parts are in the whole, and this synthesis of whole and parts is reflected in the holistic character of the functions of the parts as well as of the whole. . . .

The whole is not a mere mechanical system. It consists indeed of parts, but it is more than the sum of its parts, which a purely mechanical system necessarily is. The essence of a mechanical system is the absence of all inwardness, of all inner tendencies and relations and activities of the system or its parts. All action in a mechanical system is external, being either the external action of the mechanical body on some other body, or the external action of the latter on the former. And similarly when the parts of the body or system are considered, the only action of which they are capable is their external action on each other or on the body generally. There is no inwardness of action or function either on the part of the body or its parts. Such is a mechanical body, and only such bodies have been assumed to exist on the mechanistic hypothesis. A whole, which is *more* than the sum of its parts, has something internal, some inwardness of structure and function, some specific inner relations, some internality of character or nature, which constitutes that *more*. And it is for us in this inquiry to try to elucidate what that *more* is. The point to grasp at this stage is that, while the mechanical theory assumes only external action as alone capable of mathematical treatment, and banishes all inner action, relation or function, the theory of the whole, on the contrary, is based on the assumption that in addition to external action between bodies, there is also an additional interior element or action of bodies which are wholes, and that this element or action is of a specific ascertainable character.

Wholes are therefore composites which have an internal structure, function or character which clearly differentiates them from mere mechanical additions or constructions, such as science assumes on the mechanical hypothesis. And this internal element which transforms a mere mechanical addition or sum into a whole shows a progressive development in nature. Wholes are dynamic, organic, evolutionary, creative. The mere idea of creativeness should be enough to negative the purely mechanical conception of the universe.

It is very important to recognize that the whole is not something additional to the parts; it *is* the parts in a definite structural arrangement and with mutual activities that constitute the whole. The structure and the activities differ in character according to the stage of development of the whole; but the whole is just this specific structure of parts with their appropriate activities and functions. . . .

The fundamental concept of holism will bring us nearer to that unitary or monistic conception of the universe which is the immanent ideal of all scientific and philosophic explanation. At the same time it will enable us to bridge the chasms and to resolve the antinomies which divide the concepts of matter, life and mind *inter se*. Their absolute separateness as concepts is overcome, and their actual overlapping (in the way we have seen) is explained, by viewing them as phases of the development of a more fundamental activity in the universe. The concept of holism, so to say, dissolves the heterogeneous concepts of matter, life and mind, and then recrystallizes them out as polymorphous forms of itself. The monism which results is not static or barren, as monism necessarily is in the philosophy of Absolutism, but progressive, creative and pluralistic in accordance with the demands of scientific theory. We shall thus be prepared to find more of life in matter, and more of mind in life, because the hard-and-fast demarcations between them have fallen away. While accepting these terms (matter, life and mind) as generally and roughly marking off the main divisions of reality, we shall not be tempted to force their application too far, and we shall be prepared for such limits to their extensions as science may show to be necessary.

Women and Nature

Feminists and others in the Green movement have long been pointing out that women and nature have common cause. Historically, but particularly since the scientific revolution, women and nature have been seen as inferior to men and culture, respectively. Women and nature are said to possess similar qualities, and these qualities are held to be less worthy than those possessed by men and by culture. The Green movement has called into question the notion of a dumb, subordinate nature and, likewise, some feminists have sought to celebrate, rather than denigrate, the relationship of women to nature. On the one hand this has led, for Greens, to the notion of the 'feminine principle', which is tender and nurturing, and by which they claim we ought to live; and, on the other, for feminists, to 'ecofeminism'.* Carolyn Merchant is an American professor of philosophy and her book *The Death of Nature* is central to this debate. In the three extracts below she illustrates the common interests of the women's and ecology movements, the connected subordination of nature to culture and of women to men, and how when the earth is seen as a living mother a miner can be accused of matricide.

From Carolyn Merchant, *The Death of Nature* (New York: Harper and Row, 1990) pp. ixx–xxi, 143–4, 32–3.

Women and nature have an age-old association – an affiliation that has persisted throughout culture, language, and history. Their ancient interconnections have been dramatized by the simultaneity of two recent social movements – women's liberation, symbolized in its controversial infancy by Betty Friedan's *Feminine Mystique* (1963), and the ecology movement, which built up during the 1960s and finally captured national attention on Earth Day, 1970. Common to both is an egalitarian perspective. Women are struggling to free themselves from cultural and economic contraints that have kept them subordinate to men in American society. Environmentalists, warning us of the irreversible consequences of continuing environmental exploitation, are developing an ecological ethic emphasizing the interconnectedness between people and nature. Juxtaposing the goals of the two movements can suggest new values and social structures, based not on the domination of women and nature as resources but on the full expression of both male and female talent and on the maintenance of environmental integrity.

New social concerns generate new intellectual and historical problems. Conversely, new interpretations of the past provide perspectives on the present and hence the power to change it. Today's feminist and ecological consciousness can be used to examine the historical interconnections between women and nature that developed as the modern scientific and economic world took form in the sixteenth and seventeenth centuries – a transformation that shaped and pervades today's mainstream values and perceptions.

Feminist history in the broadest sense requires that we look at history with egalitarian eyes, seeing it anew from the viewpoint not only of women but also of social and racial groups and the natural environment, previously ignored as the underlying resources on which western culture and its progress have been built. To write history from a feminist perspective is to turn it upside down – to see social structure from the bottom up and to flip-flop mainstream values. An egalitarian perspective accords both women and men their place in history and delineates their ideas and roles. The impact of sexual differences and sex-linked language on cultural ideology and the use of male, female, and androgynous imagery will have important places in the new history.

The ancient identity of nature as a nurturing mother links women's history with the history of the environment and ecological change. The female earth was central to the organic cosmology that was undermined by the scientific revolution and the rise of a market-oriented culture in early modern Europe. The ecology movement has reawakened interest in the values and concepts associated historically with the premodern organic world. The ecological model and its associated ethics make possible a fresh and critical interpretation of the rise of modern science in the crucial period when our cosmos ceased to be viewed as an organism and became instead a machine.

Both the women's movement and the ecology movement are sharply critical of the costs of competition, aggression, and domination arising from the market economy's *modus operandi* in nature and society. Ecology has been a subversive science in its criticism of the consequences of uncontrolled growth associated with capitalism, technology, and progress – concepts that over the last two hundred years have been treated with reverence in western culture. The vision of the ecology movement has been to restore the balance of nature disrupted by industrialization and overpopulation. It has emphasized the need to live within the cycles of nature, as opposed to the exploitative, linear mentality of forward progress. It focuses on the costs of progress, the limits to growth, the deficiencies of technological decision-making, and the urgency of the conservation and recycling of nature resources. Similarly, the women's movement has exposed the costs for all human beings of competition in the marketplace, the loss of meaningful productive economic roles for women in early capitalist society, and the view of both women and nature as psychological and recreational resources for the harried entrepreneur-husband. . . .

Women's place in the order of nature. At the root of the identification of women and animality with a lower form of human life lies the distinction between nature and culture fundamental to humanistic disciplines such as history, literature, and anthropology, which accept that distinction as an unquestioned assumption. Nature-culture dualism is a key factor in western civilization's advance at the expense of nature. As the unifying bonds of the old hierarchical cosmos were severed, European culture increasingly set itself above and apart from all that was symbolized by nature. Similarly, in America the nature-culture dichotomy was basic to the tension between civilization and the frontier in westward expansion and helped to justify the continuing exploitation of nature's resources. Much of American literature is founded on the underlying assumption of the superiority of culture to nature. If nature and women, Indians and blacks are to be liberated from the strictures of this ideology, a radical critique of the very categories *nature* and *culture*, as organizing concepts in all disciplines, must be undertaken.

Anthropologists have pointed out that nature and women are both perceived to be on a lower level than culture, which has been associated symbolically and historically with men. Because women's physiological functions of reproduction, nurture, and child rearing are viewed as closer to nature, their social role is lower on the cultural scale than that of the male. Women are devalued by their tasks and roles, by their exclusion from community functions whence power is derived, and through symbolism.

In early modern Europe, the assumption of a nature-culture

dichotomy was used as a justification for keeping women in their place in the established hierarchical order of nature, where they were placed below the men of their status group. The reaction against the disorder in nature symbolized by women was directed not only at lower-class witches, but at the queens and noblewomen who during the Protestant Reformation seemed to be overturning the order of nature. . . .

An allegorical tale, reputedly sent to Paul Schneevogel, a professor at Leipzig about 1490–5, expressed opposition to mining encroachments into the farmlands of Lichtenstat in Saxony, Germany, an area where the new mining activities were developing rapidly. Reminiscent of Alain of Lille's *Natura* and her torn gown and illustrative of the force of the ancient strictures against mining is the following allegorical vision of an old hermit of Lichtenstat. Mother Earth, dressed in a tattered green robe and seated on the right hand of Jupiter, is represented in a court case by 'glib-tongued Mercury' who charges a miner with matricide. Testimony is presented by several of nature's deities:

Bacchus complained that his vines were uprooted and fed to the flames and his most sacred places desecrated. Ceres stated that her fields were devastated; Pluto that the blows of the miners resound like thunder through the depths of the earth, so that he could hardly reside in his own kingdom; the Naiad, that the subterranean waters were diverted and her fountains dried up; Charon that the volume of the underground waters had been so diminished that he was unable to float his boat on Acheron and carry the souls across to Pluto's realm, and the Fauns protested that the charcoal burners had destroyed whole forests to obtain fuel to smelt the miner's ores.

In his defence, the miner argued that the earth was not a real mother, but a wicked stepmother who hides and conceals the metals in her inner parts instead of making them available for human use.

The final judgment, handed down by Fortune, stated that if men deign 'to mine and dig in mountains, to tend the fields, to engage in trade, to injure the earth, to throw away knowledge, to disturb Pluto and finally to search for veins of metal in the sources of rivers, their bodies ought to be swallowed up by the earth, suffocated by its vapours . . . intoxicated by wine . . . afflicted by hunger and remain ignorant of what is best. These and many other dangers are proper of men. Farewell.'

Humbling the Human

As we have seen, it is important to many Greens that we seek to preserve the environment for reasons other than that human beings depend upon it for their welfare. Various strategies are used to persuade us of the environment's independent right to exist, and one of them is to induce in us a sense of awe at the extraordinary complexity of ecological relationships. Such is the intended effect of the following extract from Rachel Carson's *Silent Spring*. It is often a by-product of these ideas that we are forced to recognize that human beings are dependent for their existence on creatures to which we normally don't give a second thought. In Carson's piece this role is played by soil bacteria. While all this might result in 'merely' human-providential reasons for care for the environment, the humility it hopes to encourage can have the effect of displacing the human being from the centre of attention long enough to allow the environment – in its own right – to enter through the back door for ethical consideration.

From Rachel Carson, *Silent Spring* (Harmondsworth: Penguin, 1965) pp. 61–3.

The thin layer of soil that forms a patchy covering over the continents controls our own existence and that of every other animal of the land. Without soil, land plants as we know them could not grow, and without plants no animals could survive. . . .

There are few studies more fascinating, and at the same time more neglected, than those of the teeming populations that exist in the dark realms of the soil. We know too little of the threads that bind the soil organisms to each other and to their world, and to the world above.

Perhaps the most essential organisms in the soil are the smallest – the invisible hosts of bacteria and of threadlike fungi. Statistics of their abundance take us at once into astronomical figures. A teaspoonful of top soil may contain billions of bacteria. In spite of their minute size, the total weight of this host of bacteria in the top foot of a single acre of fertile soil may be as much as a thousand pounds. Ray fungi, growing in long threadlike filaments, are somewhat less numerous than the bacteria, yet because they are larger their total weight in a given amount of soil may be about the same. With small green cells called algae, these make up the microscopic plant life of the soil.

Bacteria, fungi, and algae are the principal agents of decay, reducing plant and animal residue to their component materials. The vast cyclic movements of chemical elements such as carbon and nitrogen through soil and air and living tissue could not proceed without these microplants. Without the nitrogen-fixing bacteria, for example, plants would starve for want of nitrogen, though surrounded by a sea of nitrogen-containing air. Other organisms form carbon dioxide, which, as carbonic acid, aids in dissolving rock. Still other soil microbes perform various oxidations and reductions by which minerals such as iron, manganese, and sulphur are transformed and made available to plants.

Also present in prodigious numbers are microscopic mites and primitive wingless insects called springtails. Despite their small size they play an important part in breaking down the residues of plants, aiding in the slow conversion of the litter of the forest floor to soil. The specialization of some of these minute creatures for their task is almost incredible. Several species of mites, for example, can begin life only with the fallen needles of a spruce tree. Sheltered here, they digest out the inner tissues of the needle. When the mites have completed their development only the outer layer of cells remains. The truly staggering task of dealing with the tremendous amount of plant material in the annual leaf fall belongs to some of the small insects of the soil and the forest floor. They macerate and digest the leaves, and aid in mixing the decomposed matter with the surface soil.

Besides all this horde of minute but ceaselessly toiling creatures there are of course many larger forms, for soil life runs the gamut from bacteria to mammals. Some are permanent residents of the dark subsurface layers; some hibernate or spend definite parts of their life cycles in underground chambers; some freely come and go between their burrows and the upper world. In general the effect of all this habitation of the soil is to aerate and improve both its drainage and the penetration of water throughout the layers of plant growth.

The Gaia Hypothesis

In the early 1960s the British scientist and inventor James Lovelock was part of a team working for NASA (National Aeronautics and Space Administration) on ways of detecting life on the planet Mars. He concluded that the best way of doing this was not by sending expensive experiments to the planet's surface, but by pointing an infra red telescope at Mars and studying the atmosphere's chemical composition. If life existed, he reasoned, the atmosphere on Mars would be recognizably different from that of a dead planet. His research led him from Mars back to earth and, via the observation that the earth's atmosphere is a 'highly improbable' mixture of gases, to the Gaia hypothesis which is outlined in the passages below. The 'improbable mixture,' he writes, is 'manipulated on a day-to-day basis . . . and the manipulator is life itself.' Lovelock's Gaia hypothesis was quickly taken up by the Green movement as evidence of the puny nature of the human being compared with the planetary-sized organism of which we are but a small part, and as an illustration of the complexity of life processes, with which we meddle at our peril. Gaia's self-defence mechanisms are such that if a part of her – e.g. us and our polluting way of life – threatens the integrity of the whole, then the offender may be dealt with appropriately.

From James Lovelock, *Gaia: A new look at life on Earth* (Oxford: Oxford University Press, 1979), pp 152, vii, 9–11, 19–20, 25–6.

Gaia Hypothesis

This postulates that the physical and chemical condition of the surface of the earth, of the atmosphere, and of the oceans has been and is actively made fit and comfortable by the presence of life itself. This is in contrast to the conventional wisdom which held that life adapted to the planetary conditions as it and they evolved their separate ways. . . .

⠿⠿⠿

The concept of Mother Earth or, as the Greeks called her long ago, Gaia, has been widely held throughout history and has been the basis of a belief which still coexists with the great religions. As a result of the accumulation of evidence about the natural environment and the growth of the science of ecology, there have recently been speculations that the biosphere may be more than just the complete range of all living things within their natural habitat of soil, sea, and air. Ancient belief and modern knowledge have fused emotionally in the awe with which astronauts with their own eyes and we by indirect vision have seen the earth revealed in all its shining beauty against the deep darkness of space. Yet this feeling, however strong, does not prove that Mother Earth lives. Like a religious belief, it is scientifically untestable and therefore incapable in its own context of further rationalization.

Journeys into space did more than present the earth in a new perspective. They also sent back information about its atmosphere and its surface which provided a new insight into the interactions between the living and the inorganic parts of the planet. From this has arisen the hypothesis, the model, in which the earth's living matter, air, oceans, and land surface form a complex system which can be seen as a single organism and which has the capacity to keep our planet a fit place for life. . . .

⠿⠿⠿

Working in a new intellectual environment, I was able to forget Mars and to concentrate on the earth and the nature of its atmosphere. The result of this more single-minded approach was the development of the hypothesis that the entire range of living matter on earth, from whales to viruses, and from oaks to algae, could be regarded as constituting a single living entity, capable of manipulating the earth's atmosphere to suit its overall needs and endowed with faculties and power far beyond those of its constituent parts.

It is a long way from a plausible life-detection experiment to the hypothesis that the earth's atmosphere is actively maintained and regulated by life on the surface, that is, by the biosphere. Much of this book deals with more recent evidence in supporting this view.

In 1967 the reasons for making the hypothetical stride were briefly these:

1. Life first appeared on the earth about 3,500 million years ago. From that time until now, the presence of fossils shows that the earth's climate has changed very little. Yet the output of heat from the sun, the surface properties of the earth, and the composition of the atmosphere have almost certainly varied greatly over the same period.

2. The chemical composition of the atmosphere bears no relation to the expectations of steady-state chemical equilibrium. The presence of methane, nitrous oxide, and even nitrogen in our present oxidizing atmosphere represents violation of the rules of chemistry to be measured in tens of orders of magnitude. Disequilibria on this scale suggest that the atmosphere is not merely a biological product, but more probably a biological construction: not living, but like a cat's fur, a bird's feathers, or the paper of a wasp's nest, an extension of a living system designed to maintain a chosen environment. Thus the atmospheric concentration of gases such as oxygen and ammonia is found to be kept at an optimum value from which even small departures could have disastrous consequences for life.

3. The climate and the chemical properties of the earth now and throughout history seem always to have been optimal for life. For this to have happened by chance is as unlikely as to survive unscathed a drive blindfold through rush-hour traffic.

By now a planet-sized entity, albeit hypothetical, had been born, with properties which could not be predicted from the sum of its parts. It needed a name. Fortunately the author William Golding was a fellow-villager. Without hesitation he recommended that this creature be called Gaia, after the Greek Earth goddess also known as Ge, from which root the sciences of geography and geology derive their names. . . .

We have since defined Gaia as a complex entity involving the earth's biosphere, atmosphere, oceans, and soil; the totality constituting a feedback or cybernetic system which seeks an optimal physical and chemical environment for life on this planet. The maintenance of relatively constant conditions by active control may be conveniently described by the term 'homoeostasis'. . . .

⠿⠿⠿

The history of the earth's climate is one of the more compelling arguments in favour of Gaia's existence. We know from the record of the sedimentary rocks that for the past three and a half aeons the climate has never been, even for a short period, wholly unfavourable for life. Because of the unbroken record of life, we also know that the oceans can never have either frozen or boiled. Indeed, subtle evidence from the ratio of the different forms of oxygen atoms laid down in the rocks over the course of time strongly suggests that the climate has always been much as it is now, except during the glacial periods or near the beginning of life when it was somewhat warmer. The glacial cold spells – Ice Ages, as they are called, often with exaggeration – affected only those parts of the earth outside latitudes 45° North and 45° South. We are inclined to overlook the fact that 70 per cent of the earth's surface lies between these latitudes. The so-called Ice Age only affected the plant and animal life which had colonized the remaining 30 per cent, which is often partially frozen even between glacial periods, as it is now.

We may at first think that there is nothing particularly odd about this picture of a stable climate over the past three and a half aeons. The earth had no doubt long since settled down in orbit around that great and constant radiator, the sun, so why should we expect anything different? Yet it is odd, and for this reason. Our sun, being a typical star, has evolved according to a standard and well-established pattern. A consequence of this is that during the three and a half aeons of life's existence on the earth, the sun's output of energy will have increased by at least 30 per cent. Thirty per cent less heat from the sun would imply a mean temperature for the earth well below the freezing point of water. If the earth's climate were determined solely by the output from the sun, our planet would have been in a frozen state during the first one and a half aeons of life's existence. We know from the record of the rocks and from the persistence of life itself that no such adverse conditions existed.

If the earth were simply a solid inanimate object, its surface temperature would follow the variations in solar output. No amount of insulating clothing will indefinitely protect a stone statue from winter cold or summer heat. Yet somehow, through three and half aeons, the surface temperature has remained constant and favourable for life, much as our body temperatures remain constant whether it is summer or winter and whether we find ourselves in a polar or tropical environment. . . .

If we are prepared to consider the biosphere as being able, like most living things, to adapt the environment to its needs, there are many ways in which these early critical climatic problems might have been solved. Most creatures can adapt their colouring for purpose of camouflage, warning, or display. As ammonia was depleted or as the continents drifted to unfavourable positions which raised the albedo, it may have been possible for the biosphere to have kept itself and the earth warm simply by darkening. Awramik and Golubic of Boston University have observed that on salt marshes, where the albedo is normally high, lighter-coloured carpets of micro-organisms have turned black, as the seasons change. Could these black mats, produced by a life form with a long ancestry, be living reminders of an ancient method of conserving warmth?

Conversely, if over-heating were the cause of trouble, a marine biosphere would be able to control evaporation by producing a monomolecular layer with insulating properties to cover the surface of the waters. If evaporation from the warmer regions of the oceans were hindered by this means, it would prevent the excessive accumulation of water vapour in the atmosphere and the conditions of runaway heating by infrared absorption.

These are examples of devices by which a biosphere might actively keep the environment comfortable. Investigations of simpler systems such as a beehive or a man suggest that temperature control would probably operate through the combined application of many different techniques rather than through any single one. The true history of these very remote periods will never be known. We can only speculate on the basis of probability and in the near-certainty that life did persist and enjoyed an equable climate.

POSTSCRIPT

From the Golden Age to the Age of Gold

In the beginning was the Golden Age, when men of their own accord, without threat of punishment, without laws, maintained good faith and did what was right. There were no penalties to be afraid of, no bronze tablets were erected, carrying threats of legal action, no crowd of wrong-doers, anxious for mercy, trembled before the face of their judge: indeed, there were no judges, men lived securely without them. Never yet had any pine tree, cut down from its home on the mountains, been launched on ocean's waves, to visit foreign lands: men knew only their own shores. Their cities were not yet surrounded by sheer moats, they had no straight brass trumpets, no coiling brass horns, no helmets and no swords. The peoples of the world, untroubled by any fears, enjoyed a leisurely and peaceful existence, and had no use for soldiers. The earth itself, without compulsion, untouched by the hoe, unfurrowed by any share, produced all things spontaneously, and men were content with foods that grew without cultivation. They gathered arbute berries and mountain strawberries, wild cherries and blackberries that cling to thorny bramble bushes: or acorns, fallen from Jupiter's spreading oak. It was a season of everlasting spring, when peaceful zephyrs, with their warm breath, caressed the flowers that sprang up without having been planted. In time the earth, though untilled, produced corn too, and fields that never lay fallow whitened with heavy ears of grain. Then there flowed rivers of milk and rivers of nectar, and golden honey dripped from the green holm-oak.

When Saturn was consigned to the darkness of Tartarus, and the world passed under the rule of Jove, the age of silver replaced that of gold, inferior to it, but superior to the age of tawny bronze. Jupiter shortened the springtime which had prevailed of old, and instituted, a cycle of four seasons in the year, winter, summer, changeable autumn, and a brief spring. Then, for the first time, the air became parched and arid, and glowed with white heat, then hanging icicles formed under the chilling blasts of the wind. It was in those days that men first sought covered dwelling places: they made their homes in caves and thick shrubberies, or bound branches together with bark. Then corn, the gift of Ceres, first began to be sown in long furrows, and straining bullocks groaned beneath the yoke.

After that came the third age, the age of bronze, when men were of a fiercer character, more ready to turn to cruel warfare, but still free from any taint of wickedness.

Last of all arose the age of hard iron: immediately, in this period which took its name from a baser ore, all manner of crime broke out; modesty, truth, and loyalty fled. Treachery and wickedness took their place, deceit and violence and criminal greed. Now sailors spread their canvas to the winds, though they had as yet but little knowledge of these, and trees which had once clothed the high mountains were fashioned into ships, and tossed upon the ocean waves, far removed from their own element. The land, which had previously been common to all, like the sunlight and the breezes, was now divided up far and wide by boundaries, set by cautious surveyors. Nor was it only corn and their due nourishment that men demanded of the rich earth: they explored its very bowels, and dug out the wealth which it had hidden away, close to the Stygian shades; and this wealth was a further incitement to wickedness. By this time iron had been discovered, to the hurt of mankind, and gold, more hurtful still than iron. War made its appearance, using both those metals in its conflict, and shaking clashing weapons in bloodstained hands. Men lived on what they could plunder: friend was not safe from friend, nor father-in-law from son-in-law, and even between brothers affection was rare. Husbands waited eagerly for the death of their wives, and wives for that of their husbands. Ruthless stepmothers mixed brews of deadly aconite, and sons pried into their father's horoscopes, impatient for them to die. All proper affection lay vanquished and, last of the immortals, the maiden Justice left the blood-soaked earth.

From Publius Ovid, *Metamorphoses* [Book I] (Harmondsworth: Penguin, 1968) pp. 31–3.

Acknowledgments

I would like to thank: all those who so helpfully read and commented on the Introduction to this anthology; the library staff at Keele University for their invaluable help in locating awkward texts; Alex Stitt for his early support; and my editor, Sally Lane, for her indispensable advice and enthusiasm.

Source acknowledgments

The Green Critique

'Ecology' from *Oxford English Dictionary* (Oxford: Oxford University Press, 1989)

'The limits to growth' from *The Limits to Growth: a report for the Club of Rome's project on the predicament of mankind*, by Donella H. Meadows, Dennis L. Meadows, Jørgen Randers, William W. Behrens, III. A Potomac Associates book published by Universe Books, N.Y., 1972. Graphics by Potomac Associates.

'The science of ecology' by D. F. Owen, from *What is Ecology?* (Oxford: Oxford University Press, 2nd ed. 1980) © D. F. Owen 1980, by permission of Oxford University Press

'Silent Spring' by Rachel Carson, from *Silent Spring* (London: Hamish Hamilton, 1965), reprinted with the kind permission of the Estate of Rachel Carson and Frances Collin, Trustee, Copyright © 1962 by Rachel L. Carson

'The problem of production' by E. F. Schumacher, from *Small is Beautiful* (London: Random Century Limited, 1974)

'Industrialism' by Jonathon Porritt, from *Seeing Green: the politics of ecology explained* (Oxford: Blackwell, 1984)

'The Tragedy of the Commons' from *Managing the Commons* by Garrett Hardin and John Baden. Copyright © 1977 by W. H. Freeman and Company. Reprinted with permission

'The Turning Point' by Fritjof Capra, from *The Turning Point* (London: Fontana, 1983)

'The Arrogance of Humanism' from *The Arrogance of Humanism*

by David Ehrenfeld. Copyright © 1978, 1981, by Oxford
University Press, Inc. Reprinted by permission
'Problems with the enlightenment' by Vandana Shiva, from
Staying Alive (London: Zed Books, 1988)
'The real and surrogate worlds' by Edward Goldsmith, from
The Great U-Turn (Bideford: Green Books, 1988)
'Population explosion' by Sandy Irvine and Alec Ponton, from
A Green Manifesto (London: Macdonald, 1988)
'Social ecology' by Murray Bookchin, from *Toward an Ecological
Society* (Montreal: Black Rose Books, 1980), reprinted with the
kind permission of Black Rose Books, Montreal, Quebec,
Canada
'Third world poverty' by Ted Trainer, from *Abandon Affluence!*
(London: Zed Books, 1985)

The Green Society

'Decentralization' by The Ecologist, from *A Blueprint for Survival*
(London: Penguin) © *The Ecologist* 1972
'Bioregionalism' by Kirkpatrick Sale, from *The Schumacher
Lectures Vol 2* (London: Random Century Limited, 1974)
'Abandon affluence!' by Ted Trainer, from *Abandon Affluence!*
(London: Zed Books, 1985)
'Green Defence' from *The Green Alternative* by Brian Tokar ©
1987; R. and E. Miles, by permission
'A possible utopia' by André Gorz, reprinted from *Ecology as
Politics*, by André Gorz, with permission from the publisher,
South End Press, 116 Saint Botolph Street, Boston, MA 02115,
U.S.A.
'Ecofeminism' by Judith Plant, from 'Women and Nature'
(Oxford: *Green Line*)
'The spiritual dimension' by Walter and Dorothy Schwarz, from
Breaking Through (Bideford: Green Books, 1987)
'Frugality and freedom' by William Ophuls, from 'The Politics of
the Sustainable Society' in *The Sustainable Society* D. Pirages
ed. (New York: Praeger Publishers, 1977), reprinted with
permission
'Small or appropriate' by E. F. Schumacher, from *Small is
Beautiful* (London: Random Century Limited, 1974)
'Organic farming' by Lady Eve Balfour, from 'Towards a
Sustainable Agriculture: the Living Soil', reprinted by kind
permission of the Soil Association

'Soft energy paths' by Amory B. Lovins, from *Soft Energy Paths:
Towards a durable peace* (London: Penguin, 1977)
'Intermediate technology' by E. F. Schumacher, from *Small is
Beautiful* (London: Random Century Limited, 1974)
'Sustainable development' by Czech Conroy and Miles Litvinoff,
from *The Greening of Aid* (London: Earthscan, 1988)
'Ecosocialism' by Martin Ryle, from *Ecology and Socialism*
(London: Random Century, 1988)

Green Economics

'The steady-state economy' by Herman Daly, from 'The Steady-
State Economy: What, Why and How?' in *The Sustainable
Society*, D. Pirages ed. (New York: Praeger Publishers, 1977),
reprinted with permission
'The basic income scheme' from *The Living Economy* Paul Ekins
ed. (London: Routledge, 1986)
'Buddhist economics' by E. F. Schumacher, from *Small is
Beautiful* (London: Random Century Limited, 1984)
'The problems with GNP' from *The Living Economy* Paul Ekins
ed. (London: Routledge)
'Local money' by Guy Dauncey, from *After the Crash: the emergence
of the rainbow economy* (London: Green Print, 1988)
'Valuing the environment' by David Pearce, Ail Markandya,
Edward B. Barbier, from *Blueprint for a Green Economy*
(London: Earthscan, 1989), reprinted with the kind permission
of the Controller of Her Majesty's Stationery Office
'Depletion quotas vs. pollution taxes' by Herman Daly, from
'The Steady-State Economy: What, Why and How?' in *The
Sustainable Society* D. Pirages ed. (New York: Praeger
Publishers, 1977), reprinted with permission

Green Political Strategies

'Changing to green' from *The Green Alternative* by Brian Tokar ©
1987; R. and E. Miles, by permission
'The parliamentary road? (1)' by Petra Kelly, from *Fighting for
Hope* (London: Chatto and Windus, The Hogarth Press, 1984),
reprinted with the kind permission of Lamuv Verlag GmbH
'The parliamentary road? (2)' by Rudolf Bahro, from *Building the
Green Movement* (London: Heretic Books, 1986)
'Communes' by Rudolf Bahro, from *Building the Green Movement*
(London: Heretic Books, 1986)

'The technological fix' by Ted Trainer, from *Abandon Affluence!* (London: Zed Books, 1985)

'Green education' by Aldous Huxley, from *Island* (London: Grafton Books, 1990), reprinted with the kind permission of Mrs Laura Huxley and Chatto and Windus Ltd., publishers

'Green capitalism' by John Elkington with Tom Burke, from *The Green Capitalists* (London: Victor Gollancz, 1987)

'Green consumerism' by John Elkington and Julia Hailes, from *The Green Consumer Guide* (London: Victor Gollancz Limited, 1988). Used by permission of Viking Penguin USA; McClelland and Stewart, Toronto; and Penguin Books Australia Ltd

'Against green consumerism' by Sandy Irvine, from *Beyond Green Consumerism* (London: Friends of the Earth, 1987)

'Earth First!' by Dave Foreman and T. O. Hellenbach, from *Ecodefense: a field guild to monkeywrenching* (Tucson: Ned Ludd Books, 1989)

'The Monkey Wrench Gang' from *The Monkey Wrench Gang* by Edward Abbey, reprinted by permission of Don Congdon Associates, Inc. Copyright © 1975 by Edward Abbey

Green Philosophy

'Animal rights' by Tom Regan, from *The Case for Animal Rights* (London: Routledge, 1988)

'A Land Ethic' by Aldo Leopold, from *A Sand County Almanac: and Sketches here and there.* Copyright 1949, 1977 by Oxford University Press, Inc. Reprinted by permission. Special commemorative edition.

'Deep ecology' by Arne Naess, from 'The Shallow and the Deep', *Inquiry*, Vol. 16, 1973

'Touch the Earth' by Wintu Indian woman and Chief Luther Standing Bear, from *Touch the Earth* (London: Abacus, 1973)

'Future generations' by Richard and Val Routley, from 'Nuclear Energy and Obligations to the Future', *Inquiry*, Vol. 21, 1978

'Green conservatism' by Arne Naess, from *Ecology, Community and Lifestyle* (Cambridge: Cambridge University Press, 1989)

'Holism' by Jan Smuts, from *Holism and Evolution* (London: Macmillan, 1926)

'Women and nature' by Carolyn Merchant, from *The Death of Nature* (New York: Harper and Row, 1990). © 1980 by Carolyn Merchant. Reprinted by permission of Harper and Row Publishers, Inc., and the Gower Publishing Group

Carolyn Merchant. Reprinted by permission of Harper and Row Publishers, Inc., and the Gower Publishing Group

'Humbling the Human' by Rachel Carson, from *Silent Spring* (London: Hamish Hamilton, 1965), reprinted with the kind permission of the Estate of Rachel Carson

'The Gaia hypothesis' by James Lovelock, from *Gaia: a new look at life on earth* (Oxford: Oxford University Press) © James Lovelock 1979, by permission of Oxford University Press

'From the golden age to the age of gold' by Publius Ovid, from *The Metamorphoses of Ovid* (London: Penguin, 1968), © Mary M. Innes, 1955

Index

Figures in *italics* after an entry indicate an entire extract on or by that entry.